SHTF Survival Stories

SHTF Survival Stories

SELCO BEGOVIC

LUTHER PUBLISHING

SHTF Survival Stories Copyright © by Luther Publishing. All Rights Reserved.

Contents

Foreword ix

Part I. Part One

The Truth About How Things Change When the SHTF 3

Survival's First Lesson: Staying Out of Trouble 11

The Five Things That Will Shock You the Most About the SHTF 16

The Return of Natural Selection 24

The First Trades After the Collapse 30

Where to Start for Prepper Newbies 38

Dealing with Differences 47

New Generations 51

An Average Day 59

Gun Control? No, Thanks 62

The Cost of Violence 66

The True Nature of Survival 73

Raiders 78

USA: Looking in the Balkan Mirror? 82

Myth Busting: Knife Attacks 91

The Sweetest Treat I Have Ever Had	97
The Temptation of Being Evil	102
The Orlando Nightclub Attack: Some Thoughts	106
Plans without Preps	112
Post-Disaster Violence	119
The Human Side of Authorities	129
When More Chaos Helps for Survival	136
Dogs in Violent Survival Situations	142
Deciding What to Do	147
The Different Faces of Fear	153
On a "Good Day"....	158
Heat	162
A Lesson in Survival and Dying	167
In at The Deep End...	170
Old Guys...	178
How We Celebrated During the SHTF	185
Skills and Training	189
Under Pressure	196
Survival Situation – Action Wins	204
An 'Ordinary Day'	207
You Get What You Give – But Different	222
Some Thoughts on 'Reality' TV	227
Some Thoughts on Food...	234
Under The Bridge...	241
A Way Out of Town	245

'Lone Wolf' Life Expectancy	256
If I was in America, I would…	262
The 4 Types of Real Survivalists	267
Reality Check: What You May Be Doing Wrong and How It Will Get You Killed	291

Part II. Part Two

Introduction	301
Una's Story	303
Elzi: The Gang Member's Story	311
Ed's Story	316
Sasa's Story	332
Nerko's Story	346
The Intersection	362
Survival with a Guitar	383
Laura's Story	386
Baron's Story	397
Goran's Story - Part 1	402
Goran's Story - Part 2	422
Goran's Story - Part 3	443
About the Author	473

Foreword

There are many books out there on all the different aspects of preparedness and survival that can provide you with information, checklists, and theoretical solutions to potential problems. But no matter how much you read or how well-researched the books you choose are, there's only so much you can take away from these tomes.

That's why I've spent the past two years traveling, taking courses, and meeting experts in their fields.

I really hit the motherlode when I went to Croatia and took a course with Selco Begovic and Toby Cowern back in 2019. Out of all the things I have learned, these guys provided a dose of reality that can only be obtained from those who have lived extraordinary lives.

Nearly everyone in the survival world knows of Selco. He *survived* a year in a city under siege with no supplies, no utilities, and the constant threat of death in a thousand different ways. His business partner, Toby, is the perfect complement to Selco's grim reality. Toby is a former member of the elite infantry British Royal Marines and current member of 119 Infantry regiment which serves above the Arctic Circle, a risk management specialist, and a wilderness survival instructor who specializes in extremely cold environments.

The two are a formidable team. Selco is able to tell the

stories that will chill your soul, and Toby is able to pull the lessons out of Selco's stories that can help you to stay alive.

Out of the many courses I have taken and places I have traveled, I've learned a great deal. But nobody has taught me more than these two gentlemen. And now, if you're willing to let go of your romantic, pre-conceived notions of survival, you can learn from them too.

This book is a collection of stories written by Selco. It's really a collection of memories from the darkest days of the Balkan War, where each moment could have been his last. You'll find notes from Toby and me throughout the book which will provide you with additional points to consider.

Selco's first language is not English. These stories have only been lightly edited for clarity. They're much more powerful when shared in Selco's own words.

I have to warn you – this isn't a cheerful and uplifting guide to survival. There's no misplaced optimism.

There's only Selco, the darkness he faced, and the grim reality of a SHTF scenario most of us can't even fathom. But if you can grasp it all before it happens, you'll be much further ahead than those who are frozen in shock.

Part One of this book is assorted stories and memories of Selco himself. In Part Two, he shares the stories of other survivors. The value you will get from reading this book cannot be overstated.

Are you ready?

Daisy Luther

Jan. 23, 2020

PART I
PART ONE

The Truth About How Things Change When the SHTF

I wrote my first survival article-comment back in 2000, and I still remember why I wrote it, what pushed me to sit down and write it so people who read/discuss survival over the internet for years could read my opinion.

I was checking the survival forums to learn something about wilderness survival because I found I was missing lot of knowledge there, and then I stumbled upon a discussion about what real SHTF looks like and will look like in the future.

And there I realized how the whole survival movement foundation is messed up or built on the wrong perception.

It is like digging through a whole bunch of other people's good skills and opinions (together with wrong ones of course) but completely misplaced and misguided.

After writing that first article years ago, I am still writing and trying to point out my view of things, and my way is learned through the experience of 4 years of civil war in a destroyed society.

I still do not know a lot of things. I do not know how to operate 20 different weapons, I am not an ex-special forces member, I do not know how to survive in a prolonged period in the wilderness, and I am still learning a lot of things from different kinds of people, on the internet and forums and in physical courses too.

But I know how I survived SHTF and what a real SHTF looks like.

And the real problem is that it definitely does not look like the majority of preppers imagine it.

Over time, a lot of my articles are telling the story about the same thing on different ways, and it might look like I am telling the same story over and over, but again, I am writing from real experience and there are good reasons why I point out the same things often.

So please allow me to address again some common misconceptions about SHTF.

Changing From "Before to Now"

The biggest problem about SHTF misconception is that people have problems to imagine something that they are not experienced in, so if you have not experienced the collapse of society you will build your opinion about it based on many things: other people experiences, books, movies, documentaries...

When you add to this a whole survival industry of selling things for doomsday, you are going to end up forming your opinion about how life in a collapse will look like based on some weird things, and as a result, your prepping and expectations may be completely wrong.

For example, you have been bombarded with information from the internet that if you buy some product, you'll be not only safe when SHTF but also, you'll thrive and you are gonna have something like best time of your life in the middle of a collapse.

Now when you multiply this with many numbers (products) you end up buying peace of mind for yourself built on the fact that someone wants to earn money from your fears.

And it is not the biggest problem. The *real* problem is waking up one morning in the collapse realizing that you have the whole bunch of things that simply do not work for your situation.

I like to use an example that I read a long time ago, about transportation in the city when SHTF. One guy offer idea of using a skateboard in urban SHTF as transport and a lot of other folks commented that is a good idea.

On first look, it is a great idea. There's no fuel, no cars or buses, so a skateboard, as a transport means, looks good.

The only problem here is that probably the man who mentioned it never experienced a real urban SHTF so he cannot know what a useless idea it is.

To put it really concisely:

When the SHTF, city services will collapse, street is pretty soon simply full of everything, there are other people in the city too, because services are gone there are not enough resources and because of that other people will simply almost always mean possible danger, so point is to avoid people, or to be quiet when moving, so…

You need to stop to think in terms of normal times. You need to change your priorities when the SHTF. It is a different time.

For example, moving faster (or most comfortably) stops being a priority. The new priority is to move safer (or quieter). You need to stop thinking about having the coolest things. The new priority is to have things that will work best for your situation.

Value of the Things

Again, it is about thinking in new terms, in the terms of SHTF, and those terms are completely different than in normal times.

I have a kind of survival philosophy where my goal is to be ready to survive with the least things as possible, and it is like everything else based on my experienced SHTF.

What does that mean?

By developing and learning skills and techniques I am trying to be less depended on physical things.

In reality that does not mean that when SHTF I will immediately bug out to the wilderness with a knife only. No, of course not. I too have preps and things, stashes and plans, weapons, meds etc.

It means when the time comes, I am READY to leave all of that, EVERYTHING – all my possessions, and move away in a split second if that means I will save my life.

Are you ready for that?

Are you gonna be able to leave all your preps that you were buying for years, all your fancy weapons, stashes of cans, etc., and run with what you have on you?

Or are you gonna die in a "blaze of glory" defending physical things?

Survival is about resilience, to move on and on, to overcome difficult situations and come back again.

Do not get attached to physical things, no matter how expensive they are, or how fancy they are, or even if people promised that you'll "survive and thrive" if you own these things when the SHTF.

Life is precious. Things are just things.

The problem here is that survival movement today is built on the way that preppers are taught to believe that they cannot survive if they do not own a particular survival product. So as a result there are gonna be bunch of preppers getting shot because they are defending physical things that someone told them they really need to have when SHTF.

I was refugee more than once. I still remember the moment when all my possessions were an old Browning pistol with three rounds, a T-shirt, boots (with wet socks inside) and pants that could stand on their own because of how dirty they were...

I had lost all my other physical possessions, everything was torched or taken away. If I stayed my life would be taken away too, in a very painful way.

I ran, and survived, and fought again for survival.

And you know what? I bought all those things again.

Things can be obtained again. Life cannot.

Sometimes you just have to move on and forget the physical things that are dear to you.

Faith

This is one of the topics that I'm most reluctant to discuss because I find it really personal, but it is there, it is important, so some things need to be considered.

And I'll be short here, because it is personal for me, and every one of you should think about it for yourself.

Yes, there were times when I simply had to reach deep in myself and connect to something higher, to find some sense, to have faith in order to not lose my mind or kill myself because everything was falling apart around me.

So, faith is important, or spirituality, or some kind of moral values – call it as you like.

You need to have something.

But the problem here is that people often think if they are good folks by nature, everybody else is good by default (until proven otherwise).

Through my experience, I adopt the opinion that everybody is bad until proven different (even if I am a good guy)

Or let me put it like this, in really bad times, when everything is going to sh*t, you'll see more bad folks than good folks.

Be prepared for that…

Survival Notes from Toby:

A quote from our good friend. "Most of the time, martial artists talking about violence sound just like first graders talking about sex." – Rory Miller, Meditations on Violence.

This observation correlates incredibly well with the Preppersphere as well. There are a lot of well-meaning but misinformed folks trying to share their 'knowledge', all the way through to serious scams and fraudsters tapping into a very lucrative market. Many, MANY of the things Selco and I are forced to watch and read in our research is as painful as it is infuriating.

At the very foundations of Preparedness, we most constantly question the source and credibility of the information we are working with and relying on... *AND how that translates into your individual plans and intentions.*

Survival's First Lesson: Staying Out of Trouble

Looking for goods and usable items during the war often meant I got myself in some weird situations and scenarios. I knew lots of guys who risked their lives just to get to some destroyed places because they knew they could find some items that meant a lot for them personally. But actually, those items were useless given the situation around us at that time.

But people often act like fools and if you find yourself in a survival situation it is the perfect time to lose your life if you act like a fool.

Like a friend who lost his eye just because he went to his house and searched through a closet full of audio tapes in order to collect some of his favorite punk band titles. Not to mention that electricity in that time was something like faint memory, and he could not do anything with those tapes.

Anyway, a booby trap exploded. Luckily, he survived but he lost one of his eyes.

When you have young people or in general inexperienced

people and fighting around you, it is the perfect combination for foolish actions

Dangerous situations cause bad decisions

There is something about dangerous and new situations that make you want to do stupid things. Young folks do that mostly, but it can happen to anyone. It happened to me too.

Good old "stay out of the trouble" advice is one of the best survival lessons one can learn.

Whenever I read on survival forum threads about gangs and how during SHTF people should get organized and simply defeat them, I remember how young and enthusiastic I was about that too. But luckily, the enthusiasm went away quickly and I survived.

The problem here is holding onto old concepts and not accepting change. One day, you have law and order. You can call someone when you see trouble because it is not right. The next day suddenly there is no one to call and you might feel you have to jump in to make things right.

You may find it cowardly that man wants to stay put when bad things happen around him, but in reality, in most of the situations you cannot do anything without a huge organization that helps you and a big personal risk.

Getting into trouble can ruin the rest of your life.

My relative was outside the country when the war started. He was working for an electrical company in the Middle

East. The contract was good, and he had a monthly salary there equal to 6 months salaries here at that time.

At the first news about fighting and war, he returned to the country to join the army and fight. Blockades and battles had already started and his trip back to his town took a lot of time and troubles.

He was 26 years old back then and he told me that when he entered the country at a small city where he and a few other guys wanted to join the fighting forces, he saw that war is not like in books and movies for the first time.

A military unit that welcomed them asked who they are and what they wanted. They said that they wanted to join the fighting forces. He said he expected some kind of questions about their military experience or similar but instead of that the small unit commander asked them: "Do you want some women? "

They stared at him like idiots so he explained: "We have some enemy women in prison close by here, so go there if you want first. "

My relative was raised by his grandmother. He was a nice kid, no cursing, not too much drinking. He said to me that the shock was so big that he could not open his mouth to even say, "No, man!"

He told me that later he found out that fighting includes doing lots of things in order to win the fight and stay alive. He went through lots of fighting, earned the reputation of being a tough guy, and one day when they got caught up in ambush and he was one of the few who survived.

A machine gun from a close distance destroyed his legs and belly. He was removed from the country for rehabilitation. His legs are still there, but only for "pictures ".

He is glued to a wheelchair forever. He has no kids, no wife either.

He lives today in a small apartment that looks at the big chimney of a factory that has been closed for years. The elevator is usually not working, and nobody cares to lift him up and down.

Nobody visits him too much. He is no hero. He fought for something that is now considered a "wrong and not needed war," as they say.

Now and then I visit him in his city and that apartment, and every time I conclude two things:

First how lucky I am even with all my issues and traumas from the war compared to him. Second is that every time when I left him in his misery and bitterness, I am expecting to see in few days in news something like "old war veteran in wheelchair went crazy and start to shoot from AK47 at people in street from his apartment at 6th floor. "

I asked him once why he returned to the country at the beginning of the war while at the same time thousands fled? I expected to hear something patriotic or similar, but he said: "Man, at that time it was something so exciting and new! "

Stay out of the trouble.

So just listen to this first and most important survival lesson: Stay out of the trouble.

Life is very real and it is easy to forget how brutal real life can be. With real life, I mean life without our civilized society or just life without all support and help we take for granted. I hope I will never have to use everything I trained for or any lesson I share with you here ever again.

The Five Things That Will Shock You the Most About the SHTF

I run one course where I take a small group of students to the city where I survived the war and take them around and physically show them the realities of what we faced.

Here are the top five surprises the students had about what the SHTF is really like. This is not a picture book but a few photos are necessary here.

- **1) How 'Close' the fighting will be.**

This picture, taken very close to my house, was one of the 'front lines' for some time.

One side was in houses on the left of the alley, another side (the enemy) was in the right-side houses. This seems INCREDIBLY close (and it is) but then realize, there were times when the 'dividing lines' were even closer than this.

When you put that into perspective, then you can start to think about the new reality because there is nothing very static and sure when SHTF. One day the house next to you can be completely safe. Another day there might be someone inside who wants to harm you. Simply, you'll never be sure how safe and secure your surroundings are.

It is the most dangerous aspect of urban SHTF because you'll have a lot of people in a relatively small area and you'll have a higher demand for very limited resources because the system is gone.

Now when you add to that calculation the fact that a lot of houses are going to be being destroyed, you get to the point that you never know anything for sure, where is someone and what intention they have.

That is especially important if you planning to survive urban SHTF alone (lone wolf theory) so you can get a feeling how hard that's going to be.

2. **The "enemy" will look, sound, and speak like you.**

They may even have been your long-time friends who are now on the 'opposite' side. Fighting here was divided by all sorts of reasons: race, religion, affiliation, heritage, politics, and often a big mix of all these things. "Sides" were always changing as well.

That's just the "enemy." when it comes to survival you will fight to get what you need or protect what you have from whoever...

Having thoughts that some foreign forces will invade your country, forces that will look, act, speak completely different then you and people from your surroundings are mostly just fantasies, especially when we talk about the USA.

That may be the case, but you're going to have a lot of local fighting and surviving before that.

Strong systems are going to have a bigger and longer fall. There are way too many people and weapons in the US for some foreign force to choose to invade and pacify the country... it is impossible.

What *is* possible is to push some country into chaos, in order to turn on themselves, suffer hunger, prolonged collapse and similar, and maybe *then* to invade.

In the end, it all comes to you and the people who want to harm you. The fact that the people want to harm you were people who you use to know does not make it easier.

Do not expect Martians or Russians. Expect people who look, act, and talk like you. People who want to survive just like you.

Again, we come to the point that you will be forced to

fight against your neighbors and fellow countrymen for resources

3. **How busy an average day is.**

Fighting for survival is an all-day, everyday task. You are constantly hunting, scavenging, gathering, finding information, looking and checking things. All while you are the most stressed you have ever been and under constant threat. All while being hungry and thirsty.

There is no day off. There is no break. This is the big difference between a soldier and civilian in war. A soldier has a job to do, and all his other needs are taken care of. He can just focus on his one job. In a civil war, you (and your group) need to cover all the tasks, all the time...

If you served in Army, you had clear orders, topics, outside of that you did not need to think about too many things.

You had "backup" or "rear." Your job was to do tasks, and someone else takes care of all the other things in order for you to finish your tasks successfully.

In SHTF you are the first unit, rear and back up. If you f*ck up and break your leg, there is no medical evacuation. If you did not find food or any other resources, there is no service who will do that for you.

It is a hard time, and the day is full of acquiring things and finishing jobs.

Shooting at someone may look like a fun idea today, or

romantic in some way. It is maybe more romantic than to think about how to manage your waste, or take a bath or lower your kid's fever in the middle of SHTF.

You are everything when the SHTF because the system is out.

4. **The level of the threat.**

In SHTF almost everything is a threat to you.

Yes, it's easy to understand threats like sniper, gangs, angry neighbors etc., but the lack of food, complete lack of hygiene, level of contamination, risk of illness and injury, the dangers of being found, being informed on, being tricked, getting captured, and many, many, more make up a larger amount of threats than most ever consider.

Just imagine every supply you take for granted (fuel, electricity, water, stores, emergency services, etc.) being taken away and you not knowing when it will ever come back.

Then imagine the worst person you have ever known; someone you would not trust to help you in any situation. Now imagine everyone around you is like that person.

Then imagine everything you climb on, through or over can hurt you, and that everything you touch has the potential to make you ill...

Did you get all that? If you do, you are maybe about 40% of the way to imagining the reality...

The level of threat is going to be a BIG shock to you in the beginning. If you survive that shock, it is good because then you get yourself into the mode of real survival.

No matter how well you are prepared, you *will* go through that shock. With good preparation and the correct mentality, you can minimize that shock and make it shorter, and that is the point of preparing.

5. **The reality of defending and keeping your assets**

I know. All the points mentioned don't bother you that much, as you have a nice house, lots of supplies, and you are ready to fight.

But how is your plan working once your house or apartment looks like this...?

And the inside looks like this...?

And anyone who is fit must go out a lot to find things for everyday survival. How will you protect all your stuff? Who is going to protect all your things?

What happens when one day a group so big comes to ask you how you're doing so well, and what you have there? What happens when protecting your stuff from them is a clear death sentence?

Having the right mindset about the difference between defending something and getting killed, and adapting yourself in order to survive without it, makes sense here.

You have to adopt the fact that maybe you'll be forced to survive only with your skills. You do not know, and you cannot be sure.

Understand, in SHTF, every house in the city is going to

look like this, or even worse – not be there at all. In my city, there are many houses you see like this. You see them because they are made of stone or concrete.

You don't see the wood buildings because they all burned down.

Survival Notes from Toby:

The fighting will be close, with people you know, over everything that can be considered a resource, constantly...

Even the most basic of injuries received can suffer horrific complications and lead to loss of life and limb.

Surviving each day is an exhaustive grind of acquiring the most basic things...

This is just the 'highlights' of a true SHTF situation.

The Return of Natural Selection

How do you imagine a real survivalist?

Is it a man hidden inside an underground bunker with enough food for 10 years, completely cut off from the outside world? Or is it the guy with crazy haircut driving a bike on methane, in a full leather outfit with communication skills not more than screams and some strange gurgling noises, armed with swords from fantasy games and maybe a chainsaw on the back?

Both examples are something like strange fantasies or for some even wishes ("I want to be like that") that I have seen on more than one survival forum or TV show.

There is also a picture of the big savior, the guy who will do only good stuff, save other folks when SHTF, and survive everything. There is a strange opinion in some people that having a stance like "I'll do only that when SHTF," either only good or only bad in terms of pillaging and robbing, will keep them safe.

If you look at how things work in nature, you know, the natural way does not mean a happy ending.

Lots of regular people in today's society see us preppers and survivalists as weirdos in camouflage suits, conspiracy nuts, and similar. Most of them are right.

Lots of "survivalists" also help in building that image of the preparedness community. It is hard for some people to just shut up and prep. What they *should* do is to keep a low profile. But some people make survival so much a part of who they are that they want to show off. Their choice.

The point is that there are a lot of definitions of survivalists out there, and people think each one of them is "written in stone." I think survival is more about how you are as a person and not what you expect. Once disaster strikes, you will see tough guys helpless and regular guys become strong forces. True human nature shows up.

Several days after the shooting started, I arranged with a friend that he would pick me up with a car so we could go and finish a job. We went to a relative's apartment to look for useful stuff, but everything was looted already. At that time vehicles could still drive, but shootings were everywhere and checkpoints, too. So, violence within the group of people who were caught up in the city was on top of shooting and shelling from an enemy army.

At this point in time, nobody knew who shot who or why, or what groups where standing at the checkpoints, but people had already gotten killed.

When he came to pick me up, I noticed that the rear lights on his car were smashed, broken. And inside the car, he had some kind of steel plates with hooks and wooden bars that you could kind of attach to the inside of the door.

He explained to me that he smashed the rear lights when he concluded that people were getting killed when snipers and machine gunners spotted them after they hit the brake in the middle of the night during driving. Our lights were not turned during the night time drive.

That trip with him was the closest thing to the apocalyptic Mad Max version of driving. It was still possible to drive through the street, but it was full of junk, debris, and bodies here and there. He used the headlights occasionally when he really needed to see something, but only for second or two. Other than that, he was driving in the dark.

On our way back, he changed the position of some steel plates inside the car because he expected different directions of possible incoming bullets.

We survived that drive. That dude was not an ex-special forces member, or a guy that you imagine, some strong tough dude. He was a simple family guy, he worked as a postman before everything. He had no experience with violence, gunfire, or anything similar. The worst that happened before was dogs barking at him while he delivered mail.

You may say, "Oh, that is nothing too smart. It is common sense to not use brake lights and put something between you and flying bullets." And yes, you are right it *is* common sense. But the point is that you need to know WHEN you need to start to use common sense.

A great number of people got killed because they "waited to see what was gonna happen." Other folks started to use common sense early and survived (at least more of them, because no matter what we do there is always factor X that you are simply at the wrong place at wrong time).

Those who can switch fast and let ideas of normal life go increase their chances of survival a lot. Many "fantasy" survivalists will wake up to a big surprise that things are not like they thought. It is true you should understand and know what to expect. But even more important is to quickly change your way of life and how you think about security. **Flexible thinkers survive because they have many options to do things and react if they have to.**

Another time, shelling caught us on the inside of one of the apartment buildings, a group of some 5-6 of us. The whole floor collapsed around us and on us.

A few seconds later we got on our feet and found out that one of us was half buried under the rubble. The other ones got only minor wounds and scratches. We started to dig to uncover the buried guy, and after that we realized that he was almost shredded from his thighs down, and his feet were under the piece of concrete wall.

After one try to lift him, we realized that there was no way to do it.

His legs were in such bad shape that while I was trying to do some kind of bleeding control, I realized that actually, I do not have clue what leg is left and what is right. It was simply all messed up and mixed from thighs down. Under the knees, I could see that all was a mixture of white and red, pressed and mixed. And he was screaming big time.

The shelling started again, with a pretty big chance for all of us to be buried under the walls. I would be a liar if I said that I did not want to leave that dude there stranded and just get the hell out of there, but somehow, I still stupidly was trying to stop bleeding with straps from a shirt.

Then, luckily, one of the guys stepped out and pushed me out of the way. Then with a rifle bayonet he simply cut off the almost amputated feet from a stranded guy who luckily passed out. Then he took him on his back and said, "OK, let's go." After we left the place, it collapsed from shelling. And strangely, the stranded guy survived everything.

If that dude had not cut his feet off, we probably all would have been killed or would have just left that man to die there.

Luckily one of us had the common sense to do what had to be done in a very quick and efficient way, and he did not even have any medical knowledge.

There are many more stories of how people got killed in very stupid ways and stories about how people who have common sense survived, but you get my point.

A real survivalist is a man or woman who knows what to do in a certain moment and is able to do it. Everything else is just talking and wishful thinking. If you want to increase your chances to survive, learn to take action quickly. Your knowledge and your skills help you to make the right decision and execute action better.

Survival Notes from Daisy:

Throughout Selco's work there's one very common theme: adaptability is the greatest survival skill. The people who were able to quickly adapt to the new rules were the people who were most likely to survive. To be able to react quickly and sensibly, we will need to overcome a lifetime of programming about "how things are." When the SHTF, the rules change and only those who accept that will survive.

The First Trades After the Collapse

The items for trade during my SHTF very often changed value, and some of them became unavailable for some period of time, just to suddenly show up again much more expensive.

Yes, the situation in the city dictated that, but also people, the black-market lords, made this happen.

The whole situation was always changing where and if you would be able to find what you were looking for.

There were many new things in the city.

Some of the items that were circulating in the city were completely new to everyone. One of the reasons was that all sorts of stuff from humanitarian aid was coming to the city through different channels and from all different parts of the world.

Some of those things became popular fast, and others remained completely strange for us, but all had some kind of value.

Of course, practical things like MREs were very good to have. Some other things like Turkish army crackers (salt cookies, or so-called "Turks") were strange for us. The taste was awkward, that's why they had a lower value, but we were starving, so of course everyone would eat it and trade it.

In one period there were big amounts of some French cigarettes in the city. We called it "black tobacco."

It was very, very strong tobacco, packaged in nice small boxes, and you did not need too much of this tobacco, even if you were a very passionate smoker. Simply way too strong.

Some smart guy smuggled this into the city and it is a perfect example of a successful product besides weapons and ammunition for trading.

A strange new kind of rice (it was much too soft), canned meat without any declaration of meat type or expiration date (we called it "sick horse.") We ate it and used grease leftovers for lamps. Sometimes there were also big metal sealed boxes with dry cookies inside – some of the boxes had expiration dates that said it was expired like 20 years ago. We called those "Vietnam war cookies" and we ate them and traded them as well.

Of course, it was always a good few days when we had some sort of food. In many other periods (most of the time) we ate much, much worse things. Often soup with anything we could find that could provide some energy.

One of the items at the beginning of everything that was very interesting for me was powdered eggs.

As I can remember, we did not see that before. I mean,

we heard it from the stories of the old guys who survived WW2 that they used it a lot in the years after that war (and they call it Truman's eggs) because it was coming in the area as a part of humanitarian aid since everything was destroyed and folks were starving at that time, too.

Those eggs were interesting for me because we loved eggs, and obviously, it became impossible to have real eggs. Food in urban survival is just a very bad version of food in wilderness survival, like rats and pigeons and some people probably also ate dogs and cats. That was in the later months after we were surrounded without any way out and lost all basics like power and drinking water.

The first trade

One day we heard that powdered eggs could be bought from some guys who had lots of stuff taken from a humanitarian aid convoy.

Violence and shootings were already happening everywhere in the city, but it was a period when we still believed it was temporary. There were three of us who went there to visit these guys. One of us had a pistol, but that was not much help because none of us yet realized how dangerous everything had become.

It was a time when the police force still existed but on the other hand some "police gangs" started to operate and you could not say who is who, and what would happen when you ran into them.

We had German money for buying the eggs – at that

moment you could still buy something with foreign money – but you could not expect any fixed price and price of everything was completely based on what happened in the negotiation.

The guys were in an apartment on the second floor in an apartment building that was maybe already half empty.

The man who opened the door for us took us to the living room of the apartment after we told him that we want to buy some goods from him. There were 4 more guys sitting next to a table there. Actually, one of them was sleeping with his head on the table.

One was trying to make some kind of sandwich with dry meat using a big old bayonet. The room stank as someone died there.

All of them looked pretty rough and ready for anything. Three of us with one pistol probably looked like easy prey for them.

The man who opened the door asked who sent us. We said the name and he said, "Who is that? I do not know him."

The silence was awkward. I felt like something was crawling over my back at that moment, especially when I noticed rifles standing next to the chairs where those guys were sitting. On the carpet under the table, there was a big stain that looked suspiciously like blood.

The man started to laugh and said, "OK, I am kidding, I know him. Just tell me, what do you need? "

The fear that crawled over my back started to disappear slowly, but still, we were like sitting ducks there.

We said what we wanted and he asked how much money we wanted to spend on powdered eggs.

My cousin stupidly took his money from a pocket and said how much money we had.

The guy said, "Give me that!"

For a few seconds there was nothing, but when the other guys from the table started to stare at us, my cousin gave him the money. From one of the rooms, we heard that someone shouted, "Oh, you motherf*cker!" And then we heard the sounds of someone being beaten.

The man started to slowly count the money, looking at us with a smile. After he put money in his pocket he said: "Ok, you can have one box of powder for this money. "

The three of us knew that we were ripped off, but I just said: "OK, it is a deal, we need to go now."

We took the box and left the apartment.

In the outside hallway, we noticed one more guy who was standing there as a guard for the apartment. When we were entering the apartment, we hadn't even noticed him.

We came home safely that time.

The feeling that we were scammed there was gone very soon because we realized that the guys could have killed us very easily if they wanted to.

Luckily at that moment they maybe did not feel like it, or what was most probable, the whole situation in the city had not the reached level yet where they felt they could do that easily and openly.

Everyone still thought the absence of rules and law was temporary.

That changed soon.

People started to kill each other as a part of trade scams. Later they often killed just out of curiosity what another guy might still hide in his pockets that he did not show.

The one of us who had a gun on his belt during the trade said, "Oh man, I completely forgot that I had a weapon with me there because how those guys looked."

Then we realized it was lucky too that he did not pull the gun there in the middle of everything because we would have ended up dead for sure.

Do you see a pattern there?

Yes, in post-collapse so many things can go wrong and often did.

I remember that trade very well because we were scared,

but much more important was afterward when we all realized that feelings of "kindness" but also "fear" went away. That day we realized we were living in a new world with new rules and acting like we did in civilized times or showing weakness could have brutal consequences.

We started to change and learn. We started to look and act like those guys during our trades, and whenever we found someone who was even harder and better at trading, we also did what they did to us. We were lucky or maybe smart enough that we learned the new rules very fast. There was little room for error.

Either you learn fast or you end up dead.

That was one of my first trades after the collapse. I traded many times later, and I often used a similar setup of intimidation like those guys there.

But there, I learned for the first time a few simple rules about trading.

- Never go to close) places where you do not know who or what to expect. How many, how well armed they are, and similar stuff.
- Never have all your goods (or money) for trade with you.
- Have a plan of what to do in case of surprises.
- Never accept offers so easily because it can be seen as weakness, and weakness sometimes calls for a problem.

There were many more.

And one more rule that we learned and you should never forget… never go and risk your life because of pure "luxury items" like those powdered eggs were for us at that moment.

Where to Start for Prepper Newbies

There is never a 'bad' time to start preparing (unless it's after SHTF), but it seems that now is a perfect time to become a prepper and survivalist. I'm seeing and hearing from a lot of folks, that for various reasons, are now interested in preparing.

I see numerous reasons for that, I do not think we really need to go into them.

Several times I had questions like, "What do you suggest to a man/woman who wants to become prepper?"

So, it is about time to make some discussion about what prepper newbie needs to understand about preparing for SHTF.

Why?

We all know our own reasons why. For someone, it is because of a coming economic collapse. For somebody else it is about the evil government. For others, it might simply be because a bad weather event is a strong possibility.

I like to think you are becoming a prepper because you want to take control of your life and actions. Remember, **you do not want to be scared – you want to be aware**.

You do not want to be dependent (more or less) on the system because you understand (I hope!!!) that the system is a complicated thing and can be disrupted or totally stopped, very easily, because of many different reasons.

You are becoming a prepper because you now see and understand how fragile all of it is.

The 7 Pillars of Preparedness

There are seven pillars of preparedness. You should focus on all of them to some degree.

1. Fire
2. Water
3. Shelter
4. Food
5. Signaling/Communication
6. Medical/Hygiene
7. Personal Safety

Remember these are not in any order. Your priorities and use will very much depend on what is happening.

Knowledge and Skills

Arm yourself with knowledge and skills. Go into every pillar of survival and start from the basics. Personally, I like the approach where you should cover all of the basic but pick up something where you are gonna be really good, become a 'master' of that skill or subject, if you will.

That means you should have knowledge ranging from

water (finding, purifying, storing), communications (you really have to know to use map and compass and different types of signals), but also pick up one of the pillars that you like most (that means pillar where you can really be good) and go in depth.

There is no man who knows everything, and also being really good in some fields gives you the possibility of a good skill to trade when the SHTF.

Do not go "Hollywood-style" in your knowledge and skills and work too much on one pillar and completely forget the others because you think it is "not important".

For example, in my time, it was perfection to find an overnight urban shelter because good thing was to find the ruined building and hide in there in order to spend the night safely.

Now that skill was to find perfect leverage in finding a building that is destroyed enough (and looks dangerous) but still good enough for you (so it would not collapse completely on you while you are sleeping), a building that gives you enough chances so you can set up some traps without too much effort, start a fire (not visible from the outside) , a building with extra exit in case of danger, etc.

Sometimes having set up a visible trap outside of your shelter can give potential intruders a sign that there are more 'not visible' traps there and that there is no value in going inside.

In some cases, it was wise to use a noise trap first, or simply alarm etc.... It is a game.

What I mean to say here is that the "shelter" pillar is not only about having a sleeping bag or putting plywood on your windows.

The "water" pillar, for example, includes knowledge about alternate sources of water in your surroundings, or simply how big is a water heater in your neighbor's home? (Because maybe it will be abandoned). How many of you will really try to collect moisture from the grass and how much time do you need for that? How much water you can get from that?

Your Setup

The most basic thing is to understand where and how you're gonna survive when SHTF, and for what SHTF scenario you are preparing.

It is the foundation from where you are going to build everything else. Everything you are going to wrap around these seven pillars of survival.

Words: BOB, BOL, bug in, bug out... are just that: words. You need to build your own setup that works for YOU.

You may have perfect Bug Out Location (BOL) 200 miles from your home, but that can mean one month of traveling by foot when SHTF.

In that 1 month, I assure you-that you will be forced to

use the whole range of knowledge from every one of the survival pillars.

Everything from the wrong kind of footwear, not enough socks, or gangs of psychopaths may be your problem then.

Do not end up dead because you exchanged basic knowledge for your opinion that you'll be able to easily drive 200 miles to your BOL when SHTF.

Remember, your well-prepared plan does not mean you do not to know how to drive a stolen manual drive car or how to purify dirty water on your way there.

Your decisions and plans

You may already have decided strongly to bug out because you are living in a big city, close to the mall, close to the bad neighborhood… and you have the perfect BOL.

Guess what?

You may not have a chance to go there. Maybe sometime in the middle of the night you will wake up and figure that the opportunity is gone, and you simply have to stay.

And only then do you realize that you did not even calculate the possibility that you may not go to your BOL when SHTF.

And then, there are you, your plan is gone, and all that you have is your knowledge and skills.

It is up to you the knowledge and skills you're going to have.

It gives me chills when I read how many preppers are taking for granted that they will have time and opportunity to reach their BOL.

Nothing is for granted and you never know. Very often you'll have to adapt.

Maybe a dirty bomb situation will find you in your office, in your suite, armed with a pencil only, and you will have to build your survival plan from that point...

Again, I got chills when I read people putting all that they have in one place, stating that they will defend it to the last.

Be flexible.

Adapt.

Knowledge and skills are something that you'll always have with you. The plan is something that will change all the time – for sure.

Thinking outside of the box

In this region there is a regular scam that happens often. You're driving and suddenly you see a man and woman standing next to what looks like a broken-down car. There are few kids in the back of the car.

The man is waving to you, wo you stop to ask what's going

on. It is daytime, kids and women are there, nothing suspicious on the first look.

The man says he is not from around here. His car is broken and he needs money for towing service, but he is without cash, his house is far blah blah blah.

He asks money from you, and in return he will give you his gold ring because his kids are hungry, his wife is crying etc.

He will give you $600 worth ring for a $100 for example, and he will give you card with a phone number so after few days you can call him and return him his ring for your money when he gets to his bank cards or whatever.

His hand is full of rings, cars are honking around you, the kids are crying, and the man keeps going, "please, please."

You said yes (sometimes because you feel sorry for them, sometimes because you want something worth $600 for $100), the man is taking off his gold ring, you feel it is heavy, you see there is a gold mark on it (like an official stamp to show it's real), and that's it.

You just lost $100.

The phone number is fake, a few hours later you find out it is the type of heavy metal material, gold plated ring with a false stamp on it. And you ask yourself how it is possible that you make fool of yourself in such a ridiculous way.

The answer is simple actually: you were blinded by greed or blinded by your good soul and rushed and outside influenced by kids crying, cars honking, the man is desperate, he is in trouble, his wife is angry at him etc. etc.

It is similar when SHTF. You can do a lot, survive a lot of weird situations, or simply get shot or mugged because outside influences are going to be huge. Confusion, lack of information, false information, uncertainty, the bombardment of new things, the constant need to adapt.

You need to stay focused and learn to adapt.

And yes, one more thing, this short ring scam story can be used in your favor when SHTF.

I have gold plated rings with false stamps as a part of my preparations for SHTF.

If you find yourself at a checkpoint, it is good to give the man your gold "engagement ring" to let you go, like we discussed many times. It is even better to give him a fake gold ring. In the confusion almost no one will see the difference.

Conclusion

Simply, focus on building credible knowledge and skills, and develop an adaptive mindset. Yes, buy some equipment and resources but this should not be the main focus of your preparing.

Even for you who are well prepared, it is good to take a step back and see what you are actually prepared for. How well do you know the scenario, and how much do you train with your equipment?

I've said before some strategies I see as very common cause me great concern. Make sure you are planning and preparing for the realities of bad situations, NOT the Hollywood (or your own) fantasy...

Survival Notes from Toby

Building knowledge and skills means you should be budgeting as much, if not more, for training, as you are for buying "supplies." Selco's key phrase here is 'credible knowledge', based in context. The Preppersphere is now full of folks selling 'knowledge', but buyer beware. Take your time, do your research and try and progress your knowledge and understanding in a meaningful manner.

Dealing with Differences

One very overlooked aspect of preparing, in my opinion, is being ready and willing to adapt to different social circumstances.

We are living in a world where there is a big mix of nationalities, customs, religions, social rituals, etc. So clearly, it makes sense to know your surroundings in order to adapt or blend in, or at least to know stuff to make your life easier when things go bad.

Forget right now about hating something or someone here. It is about knowledge that you can use in hard times. General hate is a wrong attitude, and can dangerously cripple your judgment.

Let's use a couple of examples to make it clearer here what it is all about:

Scenario 1

You are living in a peaceful neighborhood, but after a couple of days of political instabilities in your region, there are riots outside and you see a bunch of folks carrying signs about some political candidate or party, or whatever that you do not like. Actually, you hate them. But they are rioting, going through your street, smashing windows, setting things on fire, etc.

You are outside and you want to shoot them. You are angry. You attack them and after 5 minutes you are dead.

End of your survival story.

All your plans about bugging out to the BOL and everything is gone. *You* are gone right at the beginning of the SHTF.

The real solution would be to hide or if not possible to join them for an hour or two of yelling on the street, rioting, and similar. When the mob has gone through your street, then you can bug out.

Scenario 2

The sh*t has hit the fan. It's been some time and you have resorted to trading. You are in the middle of a trade. The trade is going well with the guys. They are dangerous bastards but you made a good deal with them.

After the successful deal, they offer you whiskey or whatever drink, but you offend them by refusing it because you are principled and have been clearly anti-alcohol for years. Things go bad, and the deal is off. Or even worse, you are dead.

Is it so hard to take one shot of alcohol if customs or expectations say it needs to be like that?

Scenario 3

You are bugging out. Your BOL is 400 miles away from your home, and your way there leads through another state or even country, and at some vehicle checkpoint you clearly show yourself as 'different' by wearing wrong baseball hat or T-shirt, or a small flag on your car mirror (you get the idea) or showing different political opinion. Simply some other difference than the people who stopped you.

And then you are in trouble. At the very least your bribe through that checkpoint is going to be much higher. At the worst, you can have even bigger problems.

Conclusion

The sad truth is when the SHTF first ones who are going to be in danger are people who are different from the majority at that moment and particular place.

It can be race, religion, political opinion. But it can also be much smaller and more trivial things.

I saw people being beaten when SHTF just because they had long hair.

A book could be written about this topic alone, and examples are different for different regions in the world, but the concept is completely the same everywhere. DO NOT attract attention by being different.

DO NOT say, "I will do things only this way!"

Adapt and do what the situation asks from you. Do not attract attention in the wrong time and place.

It makes perfect sense to know the customs of people

around you, political opinions, social rituals, etc. It is good to know languages or at least accents. It pays to know, for example, what will attract attention to you on your way to the BOL. Maybe it is a simple sticker on your car.

Does that "Vote for (insert name here)" sticker still make sense on your bumper?

Stay "grey" and blend in. But remember that being grey is not just about how you dress. It is how you move AND interact with people

Learn about people that you will have to deal with when SHTF. This does not mean that you need to 'love' or 'hate' them. You may not even like them. BUT know what will help you or hurt you when dealing with them.

Knowledge is (again) the key to survival.

Survival Notes from Toby:

In tough times expect 'tribal identities' and standards to become even stronger than they already are. Knowing therefore, AND using, correct courtesies and avoiding things that can cause offence will be very much needed in any and all interactions.

Along with a strengthening of identity, will be an increase in punishment for 'failing to observe the rules', what may cause just an eye roll or head shake today, can be easily something that attracts a significant beating or worse in and around disaster-stricken areas.

New Generations

These are observations from my surroundings here, but I also see and hear this type of thing happening in many places. The clearest example right now is the 'protestors' taking to the streets after the recent US election…

"Our generation is better-prepared for a zombie apocalypse than an hour without electricity."

I know that every generation looks at the youngsters that come after them as being weaker and softer than themselves. A 90-year-old man with lots of real-life experience may look at me like I am some kind of wimp, because my childhood was spent with pinball, video games on a Commodore computer, and Rambo movies on the VCR, while he maybe was growing up without electricity, without TV, playing with sticks, etc.

I may find myself in a similar loop because I was in the middle of the war searching for shelter and food when I was a young man, while young men today find themselves in the middle of reasons for living in rare and beautiful places 'avoiding' wireless connections and searching for the best selfie shot.

Here in my region over the last few months, the elections were completed. I believe, when a confrontation between parties and candidates gets more heated, the terminology and stories get less logical but harder and more provoking. (And this is almost the same everywhere, I feel.)

Suddenly there is more talk about how a candidate looks, or about their sex life or similar, instead of a discussion about their political agenda, solutions for the destroyed economy, or how to stop young folks from emigrating from this crazy region.

Here that means that hate and anger are being used in political campaigns from all sides, which brings old war stories back and stories about the new war.

And of course, there are a whole bunch of young folks who do not have clue about what war looks like, but they like the "drums call to war," stories about patriotism, sacrifices for the "tribe." In short, there are a lot of young folks who see possible war as something romantic, something high and noble.

There was a lot of same young folks just before my SHTF time. Clueless folks who do not know too much about violence and what that brings.

I was one of them.

I lost all those illusions from my youth pretty fast when people start to die around me, so words like noble, honor, death, life, and friendship got new meaning.

Or maybe it's that you discover their *real* meaning.

The point of all of the above is that today when the SHTF, it is going to be quite different than 25 years ago, because things have changed, even here where time goes kind of slower.

Let's check few things about young folks today, with the possibility that I may sound like "grumpy old man" which I am not. At least I am not that old.

How things worked, or differences between generations 70 years before

My grandparents grew up in a home without electricity, in rural settings. They owned cattle, sheep, and chickens. They grew all their food, and they grew their own tobacco.

A trip to the doctor was not so often a thing, for a few reasons: they were healthier, they did not seek medical attention for every nonsense, they had their own herbal medicines, and yes, the physician was pretty far away and a pretty luxurious item.

They had weapons because weapons were part of their everyday life. They hunted.

When WW2 started, my ancestor was in the resistance movement "in the woods".

His stories years later were like fairy stories to me. Stories about endless walking and fighting through the encirclements of German forces. Stories about bayonet fighting because of no ammo.

Freezing in the deep snow in the woods because they could not start a fire, and how they cut off black frozen fingers with knives, how the enemy did not take prisoners...

He suffered PTSD until the day he died; he became a heavy drinker. He survived WW2 but I think he kept the most interesting and horrifying stories about survival to himself.

He kept hidden in the ground a German machine gun for 40 years after the War ended, and had an illegal German Luger pistol on him until he died, even though that was highly punishable by the system in that time.

He did not hate Germans, but also did not want to watch German movies or hear the German language anymore.

30 years before

When I was a kid, maybe 7-8 years old, my father started to take me to fish. Nothing big, just simple small fish-catching. We did not even (in our home) either need that fish or like it too much to eat, but on Sundays, we would catch a few fishes, clean them, cook them, and eat them.

My father was not even a passionate fisherman. It was more like simple hanging-out time with him. He did not know too much about fishing, and I did not learn too much about fishing methods, types of hooks, baits, knots, etc.

But what I learned is that there are fish there, it is easy, more or less, to catch them in a very simple way. They can be cleaned, cooked and eaten.

Some of the procedures may not look nice for a kid, but it was kind of learning how things work in nature and life. There is fish there, and you can catch it, kill it, and eat it.

And that's it.

Nothing too deep in it.

Through my growing up, I learned how to make bread, the basics of cooking, fixing things and similar. I also learned small first aid things, and the school system was organized in a way that in primary school we had classes about "civil defense" or basics of defense from the invading force (the socialistic system was organized on a way that in case of invasion on the country doctrine of "total war" was supposed to be implemented, so every civilian would become fighter, or similar).

Obligatory army basics were for every grown-up male, usually lasting around one year. You were a soldier for one year, or a "grunt," and in the military reserves for the rest of your life.

As a result of growing up in that way, I had at least some kind of clue of what was going on when the SHTF. I mean, I knew some things. Still, I found myself completely overwhelmed with everything that was happening around me: killing, suffering, shootings, violence…

Today

When I sit at the local coffee shop these days, I can see this new generation around me. The generation that is the loudest and main candidate actually when it comes to being sheep, or cattle, or cannon fodder, if you like.

The main preoccupation is to have a cool type of beard, or to be in the "niche." Everyone seems to be in an animal rights movement, not because they care about animals, but because it is popular.

The main task of the year is to know what kind of underwear is on their favorite star from the local reality show, which, by the way, you do not know is it, man or woman, because it is cool like that, it brings 'mystery'.

For about the last 20 years, serving of mandatory military service stopped, both because of costs and probably as a way to try to add pacifism to our society. To have your own personal weapon is a task that will take you about a year of endless paperwork and checking from the state. The system, in short, does not want you to own a weapon.

This young generation is screwed when SHTF and we are too, along with them.

The great majority of them do not have a clue what hunting is. If you take them fishing, they may feel like they are finding and killing Nemo. Making a sandwich is probably the most complicated food-preparing procedure they know and so on and so on.

They may think that things like electricity and city services work by some kind of miracle from the thin air, as opposed to a complicated, technical system which is very fragile.

Their knowledge about possible SHTFs and collapses are learned not from real life stories or experiences, but from the Walking Dead TV shows.

If a zombie apocalypse happened tomorrow, they would be crushed just with the absence of a wireless connection.

What is it all about?

We are been taught – or we think – that progress is endless. That the world is going into the direction where violence, diseases, wars, are going to be a matter of history and left to the Dark Ages.

At first glance, it makes perfect sense that my grandfather knew what kind of tree bark to eat while he was starving in the freezing cold in WW2, and later had an illegal weapon for 'just in case' until the day he died. On the other end of the story we have young folks who are completely incapable of surviving anything without the help of the system.

New ages are coming, the age of science and great achievements in every field. Blah blah blah.

We are actually living in a bubble that is overinflated, and being poked more and more with things like terrorism, economic depression, big migrations, new Cold War, new types of diseases, etc.

One day pretty soon that bubble is going to burst and then this new generation will have two choices: either to die in huge numbers, or to look for resources in a way that looks the easiest to them, and that is actually by taking the resources from another.

And that is actually the real zombie apocalypse.

The real zombie apocalypse is this large number of desperate folks who will swarm to and demand the resources of anyone that has the things they need. One of the big problems with urban survival is the 'presence of people.' It is very important that folks study the types of people they are going to come across in any challenging times ahead.

Survival Notes from Toby:

Technology increasingly changes and has impact on society in faster and deeper ways. While there are many MANY things we can learn from history, these technology impacts can be considered a 'known unknown' in terms of effect and outcome in a bad situation. Those that find they have no 'hard skills' to fall back on will have a short, intense period in which to learn, or face dire consequences. It certainly does complicate the overall picture, as you will have far more people, competing over far less resources, than previous generations…

An Average Day

Actually, it is more correct to say an average night, because if we had some business to do outside the house, we did it during the night.

Night time was when we did things like trade, collecting wood, waiting for MREs, etc.

During the day we usually slept or doing the things inside our house and yard.

We waited for every rain to collect rain water from roofs into barrels, to try to filter it through gauze and boil it. Then we used that water for everything. The other solution was to go to a close-by river and take water, but mostly it was dangerous. At the beginning there were some effort from authority to supply streets with water in tankers, but soon that fell apart like everything else.

So, another precious item became a water container, some plastic canister, to carry water. We did not have any water filters or water purifying tablets, so I guess lot of diseases occurred as a result of dirty water.

Connected with carrying things like water canisters or firewood people started do make all kinds of carts. The most basic was a cart made from a plastic crate (originally used to transport bottles, beer for example). Onto that crate people attached small wheels from rollers, or toys, and that was it. Nothing fancy. Funny actually.

The hardest thing to collect was firewood for cooking and heating during cold days. Very soon the city lost all trees, so we started to use every kind of wood. I burned almost all my furniture and my books. We started with trips through ruins to collect wood like door and window frames, furniture, wooden floors, parquetry.

During cold days it was a constant problem to keep the fire going. Just to mention, all of my windows were broken. We just plugged the holes with anything, and when you add ruined roof, holes, broken windows, then you get the picture how cold it was.

You know in some of the movies of SHTF you'll see a guy who is operating from his perfect house while the world outside is falling apart. Well, everything, is falling apart, including your house, especially if you don't have the knowledge to fix things in your house, or you don't have tools. Advice: learn how things work in your house and learn how to fix things, and especially – have tools for that.

When the SHTF, there is nobody to call when your door lock is blown up, or to fix your roof tile.

I spent a few nights trying to make some system with tarps and drain pipes to collect water, but I just did not have any experience with that. Same was with almost every aspect of life. Skills, it all comes to your skills how to make something.

We were not prepared for that situation, so I guess when system failed to provide us with goods like food, water, medicine and any other kind of support, we just used skills to make them or acquire them.

It is the same today, I think, in the case of SHTF, even if we are prepared very well, sooner or later we are going to exhaust our supplies, and then we gonna use our skills to make new versions of them

I think a good example is to have a big supply of food, but still know how to work in a small garden. It was great fortune if somebody knew how to fix things, guns, locks, shoes, people…

Survival Notes from Daisy:

I think one of the things that people underestimate the most is the sheer amount of work that survival takes. When you have to provide all services and supplies for yourself and your family, it's non-stop. When I attended Selco's course in Croatia, it was activity, morning through night. We live currently in a world in which we can order food to be delivered to our door. Our work lives are often sedentary. We relax by doing more sedentary stuff, like watching television or playing around on the computer. The constant effort required to survive a SHTF scenario will be a huge wake-up call.

Gun Control? No, Thanks

Talking about weapons is popular in prepper and survivalist community and it is perfectly logical because it is really important. But outside the community, there are discussions about if it is it even OK to *have* weapons. Now if you are standing up for your right to own weapons and defend yourself, you often are seen as a person who likes violence or is a bad person in general.

I still remember the moment when I had my own personal revelation about weapons and owning weapons, and I will remember that moment until I die.

The moment I knew I would always have a weapon.

I found myself on the street, and at the end of the street, half a kilometer from me, three guys in olive-colored uniforms were beating two other guys. And then one of the guys in uniform simply raised his rifle and shot one of the guys they were just beating.

They continued to kick the other guy, then two uniformed guys took the beaten guy by the hands in order to make him hold still, and other guys shot him in the head.

Now the distance was too far, but I am still quite positive they shot him in the head, because I saw how his head exploded, splashing back onto the wall. I think two guys held him by his hands in order to give the opportunity to the third guy to shoot in the head without mistakes.

I stood still watching all that, and then my reflexes probably jumped in automatically. I panicked and started to run. The guys saw me and fired a couple of shots at me, but I continued to run.

I remember that during this time when I was running, I was looking around for something to defend myself if they caught me, something... a stick, a rock, whatever. All kinds of rubble was around me but I continued to run with one thought that was echoing in my head "F*ck! If they catch me, I can only pull my belt from my pants and try to beat them with that. F*ck!"

I kept running for maybe the next 10 minutes, through destroyed buildings. I even kicked some guy who suddenly stood in front of me out of nowhere. He was probably scared just like me.

I survived that. Those three guys most probably did not follow me at all, but the adrenaline pumping through my body simply did not let me stop until I came home and was safe more or less. And there, at my home, I had only one thought loud and clear in my head: "I need a weapon."

I saw violence before that, but the event showed me that weapons are good, weapons are necessary. Weapons save lives and take lives, but it depends on the person who uses it.

Before this, I did not like weapons.

I had some kind of opinion about weapons before that event, just like most of the guys, that weapons kill people, that violence is bad.

I believed that there were good guys with weapons like police or similar and there are bad guys with weapon like criminals. I believed there was some kind of control between them (leverage) and there was the whole bunch of other common folks who trust in that leverage and control.

Yeah, there are common folks with weapons too, but they still have faith in that balance, and weapons for these guys was nothing more than a hobby, or some kind of internal thing that they felt strong when having a weapon around.

But after that event, everything changed.

From that moment all words like law, police, criminals, system, and everything else disappeared for me.

After this event – and this sounds stupid – I fell in love with weapons. In the months that followed weapons were some of the most important tools for survival. It became very natural to handle a weapon and to have it all the time with me.

I mean *all the time*.

Now you may say that during the war it is natural to have a weapon, and it is nothing big. You may think that wars happen somewhere inland where savages live, and that you have system there where you live. You may believe there are good guys with weapons and bad guys with weapons, and you are in the middle. Maybe you think that all that you need is to obey and then the system is going to protect you, and you do not need to have weapon if you trust in system.

This is how I was thinking before this one event as well. Maybe the two guys who got killed also thought like this. It was early on, just a few days after the war came to our city.

I learned my lesson.

Death is ugly. Killing is bad, but it is a very natural thing for people when they fight for survival and resources. I think the problem of people who are against weapons is that they do not want to accept the facts of what can happen to them.

And then they are the ones who run away and have only a belt to fight with when they face bad people.

Survival Notes from Daisy:

Have you ever felt truly helpless? If so, then you can probably imagine to some degree Selco's feelings with only a belt to fight off armed attackers. It's important to understand that the worst-case scenario can happen to you, and if it does, you'll need every possible advantage to survive.

The Cost of Violence

I have been through the war with a lot of people. I spent a lot of a hard time with folks who in that time I could call friends or at least some kind of allies.

After that I lost contact with most of them. Sometimes I heard something about someone, or see some of them, but real "buddy" contact with people from that time is rare.

People who have not gone through experiences like war probably imagine that there is something like annual meetings of old buddies who used to shoot together and kill other folks, and on that meetings, there is huge barbecue and drinks...

They may think that at those meetings, we all have a laugh and remember how hard it was and we are lucky that we are alive. Actually, I did go to some similar meetings, but it was anything but fun, so I stopped with that.

People there mostly look at each other and we all see how destroyed we are. I have met many broken people there and the question is, has life screwed us or have we screwed up in life? And at the end, we all drink, but without music, we just look in fire from barbecue, angry because of some triviality and asking why we are here.

Actually, we do not have common topics to talk about after we spent time talking about all topics like whether or not a bad situation is in the country. Soon we know that at some point, some of us will start with, "do you remember how S. got killed?" or that famous "man, we are lucky to be alive."

But in reality, we all know how S. get killed. Nobody needs to asked, "do you remember?" Most of us think about how S. or M. or L. or whoever got killed every night at home, because many of us do not have families. Most of us are unable to have normal lives with someone close anymore.

And when we come home later, we drink alone, because people like us drink alone in most of the cases. Without false modesty, those of us who made it are the best of the best from that time, real survivors. We survived everything because stupidity got punished very hard back then, usually with death. It still has burned much out of us.

We are people without purpose and aim. One of us works at the parking lot. It is a job that barely can keep him alive with minimum money for food only. No wife, no kids, no real friends, no possessions except maybe weapons hidden somewhere, because you never know.

He was a lion once, a man without fear for his life and without respect for the enemy's life. I asked him once how he feels when he is charging for parking ticket to the guy who is 25, drives brand new BMW with couple of pretty drugged girls, who earned that by being a crooked politician and who looks at him like he is not even human. Or worse like he is invisible, like there is ghost who charges for tickets.

He said, "I try not to look, it is life, and I am too old anyway to care".

He is 45.

I think one day he will jump from 16 floors, or simply dig out his favorite TT gun and blow his brain out. One other guy is unemployed, officially unemployed, but he works at whatever needs to be done. To say it shortly, when a person needs to scare someone or harm someone, he is the guy for that.

He keeps telling me one story, actually, it is his dream or wishes more than a real story.

He said:

"I am dreaming and wishing that one morning I wake up and there is a decision inside me, one of the old feelings that I carried through the war.

You know what would I do? I would go to my place with my stuff, take two pistols and rifle and as much ammo I could take. I would put on my old combat vest, lucky boots, put on my armband that we used for recognition.

You know the government (local) building? I would go there, enter through the steel door, there are two security guys, I would use the pistol on them, two shots in the head, for each of them. Guys are young and inexperienced, full of steroids and stories from the GYM. Big chests and arms, but small brains and balls.

After that I am wishing that I could somehow weld that

steel door, with me inside, of course, so no soul can go out, me neither, but maybe I just somehow block it, or use explosive there.

You know the put steel bars to the windows, those crooked bastards, to feel safer, I would have them there where I want. And then, I would take off my rifle from the shoulder, and go slowly from the one office room to another. Everyone, every last greedy m*therf*cker of them would go down.

On some of the most important faces there I would use my knife, you know, faces that like to be on TV, like to take shots and interviews after doing some charities, or visiting schools and hugging the kids because good grades in front of the cameras, faces who earned their first million by selling baby food in war mixed with plaster, or taking someone's wife for two pieces of canned meat.

I would like to go slowly with them, piece by piece. I think I would be pretty much done before the special police squad would come to the place. Remember I was pretty quickly done with some of the buildings we took during the war?

After that I do not care what would happen, I think I would blow my brain out, or maybe I would take a few police guys with me too. They are young and full of movie ideas. Dirty games are something that is strange to them, it would not be a problem.

Every time we end up by laughing about his dream. He is saying all of this like it is a big joke, more or less.

But sometimes, I guess when he is feeling down too much or when he sees who is in charge today ruling over us or simply when memories get to him too much, I see something in his eyes and that is no joke.

There is a name for all this I wrote here. They label it with the words, PTSD. But the real point is that once violence enters your life, once it becomes part of you, you belong to that violence. For the rest of your life.

In the famous US series Dexter, he calls this "his dark passenger" and this dark side will stay with you.

There is nothing romantic about it. And every time when I see on TV or wherever some anniversaries of military events, when I see those guys under the banners and old flags, no matter what country or what war, they have the same expression on their faces.

They handshake with politicians, take pictures with them, kids take photos with them, they call them heroes and liberators and whatever. It might be the truth but probably means nothing to them.

When the politicians go away with their limousines and security, and when newspapers guy and TV crews leave with their stories, those guys stay alone with their thoughts and memories until next year when they get another pat on the back.

Two main lessons here.

First is that violence like this is glorified in action movies, games, and sometimes the media. It should not be done easily. If you might look at your weapons at home, you see them like that and pictures of shooting come up in your mind. If people who fought do this picture of bullet impacts on the human body come up.

The smell of people dying.

The sound of last breaths.

The mess someone leaves behind.

Every time you use violence the dark passenger in you grows and it will not leave. It is part of you.

So, if the SHTF and the internet and everything else are long gone, maybe you will remember this. Maybe you will tell yourself and the people around you that all this comes with a cost.

The second lesson here is that you should think about a time after the collapse. I have friends in the US army and I know some of the veteran services are bad, but at least they are there.

I have read in a history book that soldiers in earlier wars had less PTSD because they traveled together for a longer time from the area of conflict. If you lead a group of survivors during SHTF think about giving them rest. Think about sort of a debriefing time.

Survival Notes from Daisy:

People spend a lot of time romanticizing survival. We

read survival fiction and watch survival movies and it seems like everyone who survives lives happily ever after. But as Selco points out, there's a cost to survival and the price is too high for many people to live with.

The True Nature of Survival

If you are not eating right now, take moment and watch a video of a monkey eating a gazelle.

It feels very wrong for most people to look at this. This shows how much we are out of touch with nature. Most people want to eat meat but not kill it themselves for example. What happens to the gazelle is not good and not bad, it's nature. It simply is.

When you find yourself in a survival situation you get quickly in touch with nature again. **And nature is cruel, and the concept of fairness does not exist.**

It is hard to be prepared for that before you experience it. But understanding how nature really is and that we only live in a soft bubble protected from the true face of nature, is the first step.

Here is an experience I want to share.

When SHTF started, the great majority of us thought that what was going on around us was something like temporary rioting that got a bit out of control. The city services still worked in some areas and everybody was waiting for the madness to stop.

In that short period before the sh*t hit the fan with full

force, people usually lost their lives because they did not recognize the situation.

People were out rioting, stealing, fighting. But all that was still "moderate" in comparison to what was coming.

At that moment, people still were "inside" the system, so we all were trying to hide more or less when looting was going on in the neighborhood. The police were still arresting people and trying to control things. People were shooting each other yes, but it was not yet like full-scale shooting and violence. Most people were simply scaring each other with shootings.

One of my friends was involved in a shooting in those early days. After looting some stores, he got wounded. The wound was not too dangerous – he was shot in the foot.

As I said, most of the city services were still working and trying to bring order to that chaos. City ambulances came and picked him up and they rushed to the hospital with him.

About one kilometer from the place where he got picked up, the group of people that actually shot him stopped the ambulance with an improvised barricade. First, they shot the driver and then they killed my friend in the back of the ambulance. They killed him a little bit slower than the driver, and more painfully – they used knives. We got there a bit later, but it was too late for my friend.

Now this story may sound confusing to you. You may say "it happens in war." But for 95% of folks at that time it was not war – it was just violent rioting. And 95% of folks still trusted the system. They had trust in police and government that they were going to restore law and order. People still trusted that ambulances were "protected" and nobody would stop them, not to mention shooting at one.

In this story here, the wounded guy and the ambulance driver simply did not recognize the situation. He was a nice guy. Why would this happen to him? Back then, I probably would have gone with the ambulance as well if I was shot. It felt very wrong that this happened, but it was one of the first wakeup calls that fair and unfair were concepts of the past.

My friend, in the first place, should not have been there in that time of chaos. The ambulance driver should have said, "screw it" and taken valuable medicines and gone home at the first signs of real violence and total collapse. He did not. It is easy to call him a hero and maybe the day before or hours before he helped save the life of someone else – but it was still too high a risk to be out at this point in time.

It is easy to say that now but at first nobody realized what was happening.

But in those times, we all still called things by old names, police, trust, government, law, system, penalty...

If that happened maybe a day or two later my friend would have crawled off and treated his wounds alone, or the driver would have refused to drive, or...

A few days after that event, the sh*t hit the fan with real force, and nobody had illusions anymore that something temporary was going on or that things would quickly get back to normal.

The point is that lots of people died in that short period before realizing that things weren't the same. You should not still believe in the good of people around you, but most people did. This ambulance event was one of many that ended with similar deaths.

So next time, when some rioting erupts in your city, some violence after a football game or some protests because of high unemployment or similar, and you hear gunshots and screams, and words about people being killed on the streets, stores being looted, you need to hope that it is a temporary disturbance.

But you cannot trust in that.

Be suspicious, trust in your bug out bag, trust in your storage, trust in your weapon. Do not go out just "because everyone else goes out". Avoid being greedy and going looking to have a bit more, even if it sounds easy.

You prepare so you do not have to go out.

When you realize the random and brutal nature of violence, then you realize you do not prepare to be a hero. You prepare to survive. That ambulance guy could have helped many more people in later months when we were fighting for survival if he would not have died. But back then, we did not understand the situation.

Survival Notes from Daisy:

One of the most important lessons you can take from Selco's stories is the value of realizing what's going on early in the situation. If his friend had understood how dramatically things had changed, he probably would not have died in that ambulance. When the rules seem to be changing right before your eyes, believe what you're seeing. Not allowing cognitive dissonance to take over could save your life.

Raiders

Usually they would come during the night, but late (or very early) around 3 or 4 in the morning. They would not be come in silence. There was always with shooting, cursing and yelling. Sometimes they would just throw couple of hand grenades in front of the house, to kinda shock you. Even some tough and well- prepared guys would just run away if they had the chance.

It takes some guts and serious weapons to stand up to 10,15 or 20 armed guys, who are mostly drunk or high. Sometimes if people did not resist everything ended with just a few punches, a broken rib, or similar. They could just take what was interesting for them and leave.

On the other hand, they could also rape, kill, or torture.

In those situations, if you choose to resist, be sure that you can resist them, or just be sure to kill yourself before they get you alive. People just were not sure what to do, to resist and take chance, or to surrender and take chance.

One incident I can remember...

I will call him Dan, because of his privacy. His father was goldsmith, quite famous in town. The two of them just waited in the city and watched how everything was going to hell with the first months of chaos. The father could not survive all changes. The lack of medical care and every day uncertainty just finished him and his already sick heart.

Dan buried him with 2 neighbors one night in a nearby graveyard, while city was in flames and battles raged over the reasons that nobody actually cared about as soon as the TV news was gone with its propaganda stories. They had some large amount of gold in house and Dan buried that in the cemetery, too.

They came for Dan at 3 in the morning. They did not ask anything, they just searched the house in detail, beat him and took him to their prison. They ruled in that part of town. The prison was not like a real prison. It was a basement in the local mall.

After the 5th day of regular beatings, their leader came and said to him: "You will take us to the gold."

And he took them, he and two gang members spent 2 hours on rain in the middle of the night, while Dan was trying to remember where he is buried his father's gold in graveyard close to house.

After 2 hours he used the moment and hit the gang member with a shovel in the head. The other one was sleeping in house, he took him out too, and ran away.

I do not know what ways and connections he used then, but after 2 months in Croatia, he ended up in Germany. The war ended, and I did not hear too much about him, except that he was in Germany, and not doing so good, and that he is keep telling everyone that he was never coming back here.

But one day I heard that he was back.

I met him in a cafe close to his old house. We had some coffee, and he did not want to speak too much about old times. I asked him, "Why did you come back here?"

His answer was, "I remember where I buried my father's gold."

He also told me:

"Right after my father's death I took all his gold, put it in jars, and buried it in the graveyard. I did not use any map or anything like that, but I was perfectly aware of where I buried that. I memorized it very good.

After they put me in that prison, after they beat me, humiliated me, they took me to graveyard because I told them I buried the gold there. Standing in that graveyard, in the night, with two of them with their rifles just erased everything from my head. I was desperately trying to remember where I buried those jars, but nothing; my head was empty, blank page. I knew they going to shoot me if I do not find it, and maybe even if I find it, they shoot me.

So, I was digging like crazy, and suddenly I decided to hit him with shovel, I think it was not voluntary at all, something just woke up in me, like it was not me hitting him.

After I get to Germany I still could not remember where I buried that jars, so after few years I just stop thinking on that. And then few days ago I dreamed everything, like in fast forward motion, my father s death, killings, all atrocities, my prison, beatings, and I also dream about correct place of my jars, so I came here again

You know I think I was lucky because when they came in my house in 3 in morning they did not ask me anything, they just beat me and took me to prison, if they asked me the about gold, I am sure that I would tell them, I was scared to death, and if I told them then maybe after the took it they would have killed me at the place."

He did not want to talk anymore, so I left. I heard later that he suddenly "got rich" somewhere, and that he is doing fine now.

On that night when Dan was digging through a graveyard while two gang members were watching him, he was 17 years old.

USA: Looking in the Balkan Mirror?

For years I have been following news from the survival realm all over the internet. One thing is for sure: every day in those years when I read survival news, I could conclude, based on the headlines, that the world is going to chaos and end in the next week, next month or next year.

And still we are here discussing things while we have all the comforts and commodities. Let's say we are doing fine.

But now, for the first time, I have a feeling that the world is going to chaos really soon.

Too many things are seemingly moving inside global calculations, and this time we could be close to a "big one".

No matter how much food, ammo., training and skills you have, when SHTF you are gonna be surprised. Most of us have been in the mode of preparing for something that is not happening for years, and when it finally happens there is going to be a period of a shock for the folks, and in that period a LOT of people are going to die.

Since most of the folks who read my stuff and subscribe to my courses are from the US, things that are written here are meant for them mostly, but not exclusively for them.

Every now and then I get questions about similarities between the situation in the US and the Balkans before SHTF. And I have read a couple of good articles about the same topic lately.

Since I have a lot of people that I can call good friends, and they are from States, I am going to point out some things about my Balkan SHTF and possible US SHTF.

There are some serious and worrying parallels, even we are talking about two different systems.

The System

"The people have always some champion whom they set over them and nurse into greatness… This and no other is the root from which a tyrant springs; when he first appears above ground, he is a protector…having a mob entirely at his disposal…" – Plato

I have lived in a system and country where we believed that we are all equal. Different nationalities, different religions etc. Melted all together to make one "big and prosperous" nation, to be great and equal… united.

And then leverage of world forces simply changed, and suddenly we are being taught that differences between us are more important than similarities and "one nation." Old historic battles are been taught again, and one group suddenly is more important than other and so on and so on.

And then came "leaders" or saviors that led us against

others. After years of carnage, here we are again with almost the same leaders.

I have been through the war and met many folks on every side shooting because they have been told that the other side is evil, and yet all sides are the same at the end.

Rich are richer, poor are poorer. Nothing changed. Nobody learned anything.

Big Circles and Small Circles (and your decisions)

Again and again, there is a big circle and small circle. You may have the illusion that you are controlling things in a bigger circle, but it is only an illusion. What kind of government you're going to have and what kind of politics they use in the next years is not up to you, you just have been smartly led to believe that you can make the change.

It is like that…

In the end, it all comes to the matter of power and possession, and you are a just small piece of everything, you are a small part of the tool.

Over the years I have learned that it is more important to have one more month of food stored or one more skill learned than to waste time on worrying who is going be elected.

It is a waste of time. When the SHTF they are all gonna do the same, more or less, oppress people and take their rights and liberties very easily.

Your Rights

Living in a society where you have certain rights and freedoms for years is a good thing.

The bad thing is when the SHTF and you lose all those rights in a single day, you may find yourself so shocked that you simply do not know what next to do because you had those rights for many years, it became totally natural for you to own them.

Having lots of conversations with friends from the US, I concluded that the majority of common folks simply do not understand that all your rights can be lost in one day.

And not by the evil invaders from space, or Russians or whoever. Your government can take them. In one day.

The majority of folks simply do not see this as a possible option, and even preppers there who understand it may look like weirdos because of this viewpoint.

Do not get me wrong, I would love to live in a country where I can buy weapons easily, where I have rights to protect my home, where I can say freely, more or less, what I do not like.

I like that very much. Actually, I admire it.

What I do not like is the feeling that most of the people think it is written in the stone and it cannot be changed.

In short, the things that I like most about the US are going to be the biggest loss when the SHTF, and not only the US.

When the SHTF there is going to be a lot of surprised people, a lot of shocks.

Your Perception of Future SHTF and the Prepper Movement in the USA

I cannot get rid of the feeling, that majority of people see SHTF as big fun, shooting while drinking beer, with additional testing of all of their cool gear.

I see that in blogs, comments, forums, documentaries, movies…

I had more than one participant in my courses who told me, "This is not fun, it is hard, and not so pleasant."

I had people who have been preppers for 30 years and never considered the fact that when the SHTF, it is going to be smelly all around you.

There's been a man who advises a skateboard as a 'good' transport through a SHTF city, a man who thinks that 30 brand new gold coins are going to get him through problems on his bug out trip, and so on and so on.

Now I am not mocking the people who stated all the above. What I do not like is believing in "facts" that are not checked.

If you have never been through SHTF, you may not have the idea that it is quite hard and unpleasant. Where do you think people and dead animals are going to be buried? Where will the garbage be taken, human waste and everything else? A foul smell is going to be constant.

Don't you think offering someone a brand-new gold coin for safe passage will bring some "Ooh, maybe he has more of those interesting funny unusual gold things with him" attention?

Why don't you try to have 10 cheap gold rings in your pocket instead, and offer one at every checkpoint? One that you directly pull from your finger with the words, "Here, take my wedding ring. Just let me pass."

Is a guy going to think "oooh, maybe he has more of those his wedding rings in his pocket?"

The same things go with trade. Examples are numerous.

Common sense is something that is missing mostly in "mainstream" prepper movements, and I understand that it is a business. It is about money.

But folks, choose carefully what advice you are taking as a real.

For the average beginner prepper, the USA looks like paradise. A place where you can look and find the correct information, also look and find correct equipment for future SHTF, but that also brings risk because there are more false and wrong information and mindset than right.

Personally, I like what can be found in the US because, in most of the cases, I know what is good or bad, but for beginners, it is much, much harder.

Conclusion

I want to add kind of conclusion for this very hard topic, because it is wrong to put things right with a generalization:

It is going to be very ugly, much uglier than my SHTF experience here, simply because the 'fall' when the SHTF is going to be bigger. The distance between modern everyday life and life in SHTF for the USA is WAY bigger than in my time. The majority of folks are soft and too dependent on the system.

The survival movement is big business, and it has become more (much more) about selling items to make you *believe* that you are prepared than about learning and gaining knowledge.

Incorrect perceptions about the SHTF (or at least not checked and experienced beliefs) are rooted so hard, they have simply become the accepted truths. A LOT of these "truths" are simply false and there for earning money, not for actual survival.

A good thing is that you have many more options for choosing and owning weapons, but this option can bite you back if you have weapons, but the wrong mindset, "truths," and knowledge.

Because a whole bunch of bad people are going to have weapons too.

The majority of folks are not ready to bend the rules and

adapt. There is a lot of talk about adapting, but then suddenly you get the whole bunch of folks who are thinking "I'll do that" or "I'll never do that" instead of "I'll do what has to be done and adapt to the situation."

You need to work with other folks, to have friends, group, connections-before SHTF. Survival alone is for really tough motherf*ckers.

People think they prepare for the SHTF, but they don't, really. They are preparing for the romantic, movie version of SHTF. They want to feel cool and comfortable when SHTF, which is not a problem by itself. The problem is that they want that at the expense of real knowledge and covering of real basics.

So, you'll have a man who has a fancy and really cool rifle, but does not know how easy and fast in a real fight it is to use 500 rounds, so he ends up without ammo in a week. Or one who has a generator but does not have a clue how to light a fire, or the differences between fuels for a fire in terms of heating, smoking, etc.

There are many examples.

Do not look for higher reasons for the situation. You may have political options today, factions, candidates, government. But when the SHTF, all of those are empty words from some other distant time. When SHTF you will have yourself and people who want to harm you. That is it.

So, folks, make sure you are preparing for the realities. I

would encourage you to start 'fact checking' your plans and preps today...

Survival Notes from Toby:

Make sure your skills can stand up to the scrutiny of reality. Understand laws can and do change rapidly, especially when politically expedient, and these can have fast and far reaching effects.

Be aware of the 'bigger picture', but spend more time focusing on your local areas/issues as they will impact you more immediately...

Myth Busting: Knife Attacks

This article is written based on my experiences of seeing and dealing with knife attacks and wounds, both during the SHTF and during my work in the medical field. It is not written scientifically, or based on hard data, it is based on what I saw, or did... what I actually experienced.

Often, we find, some same topics are viewed differently by different people, and it is perfectly OK to be like that, but when it is come to knife wounds and killing, in the end, a wound is a wound and blood is blood.

Knife (blade)

There is something primal (can we say even mythical?) about a blade and I guess it comes from the fact that it has been used as a killing tool for many centuries, and to be honest, for me it is the scariest type of possible fight – to be forced to knife fight.

Having a knife in your hand and pushing it into someone's body is a scary thought. It is very personal, on many levels.

As always, thanks to the movie industry, people imagine a knife fight is like two guys doing a whole bunch of fancy moves. In reality, it is mostly about who pulled their knife first and stuck it into the other guy before other guy had a chance to pull his knife.

Knives and Common Sense

I know there are knife fighting experts out there, but I have never gone through some sort of experts training so I cannot say the full impact of this. But I know that if you are forced into a knife fight with someone when SHTF and by the chance you have a pistol with you, pull the gun and shoot the man twice... forget about 'honor' and 'movies'.

Knife fighting (equal terms) means that you (almost for sure) are going to get hurt. You will get at least a couple of cuts from your opponent. Remember even a small cut when SHTF can kill you.

Accepting the possibility that people on the internet will call me an idiot, I must say that choosing your knife for SHTF as a weapon ONLY is a HUGE resource waste.

A good knife means a working tool and a weapon.

Also accept there are more usable weapons and tools out there, like an ax for example, in terms of multi-use. A knife plays its part in the bigger picture.

What I am trying to say is, do not get yourself to romanticized into a certain type of knife- when it comes to stabbing and cutting in fights, most knives will do the job, with the possible exception of a really cheap one.

When it comes to tools, then you should aim to choose the higher quality ones (and multi-purpose if possible).

In one period of SHTF, most of the knife fights I saw were

done with simple kitchen knives, and I assure you those knives did the job bloody good.

The point here is to have the intention, and yes, to have guts for that. The type and style of knife are very much secondary to that...

Always you want to have common sense, and adaptability. For example, if you found yourself in a situation where a knife is your only weapon maybe it makes sense to make a spear out of it, to have some "distance and strength." You can't just assume there is only 'one way'.

Knives, Bleeding, and Statistics

There are numbers and data from years of the research about bleeding and death from knife wounds and blood loss, and it worth your time to read it, to know what is about and what you can expect.

On the other hand, there are real-life experiences and exceptions for everything, and you need to acknowledge that too.

You could see maybe in movies that if you silently move up on a guy from the rear, put your hand over his mouth and stab him with the knife in his back region or kidneys, he is gonna go down silently in two seconds.

Good luck with that. Stabbing someone is actually a very noisy job, and there are variables. Did you hit the correct place? Did you stab or slice? How long and sharp is your knife? Etc., etc.

On top of all this, you must understand that you will need to add a lot of force to whatever method you use, definitely not like in the movies. People will fight for their life – literally.

Depending on the situation, you could hit the correct place (carotid artery for example) but the wounded guy could still have enough time to strangulate you. I've seen it happen. Yes, he will die very fast from massive bleeding from a carotid artery – but the point is, he could still kill you before that happens.

So, you have an option of moving to the guy silently in order to kill him, great, but think, are you going to use your fancy knife in order to cut his carotid artery?

Maybe it can make more sense (and present better odds) to use a big rock and instantly crush his skull, with one strong blow, rather than take the chance of missing an artery and be faced with an alerted enemy with a knife?

If you do not have any good training about how to correctly use a knife, it is simply not very easy to achieve fast, effective kills.

More unpleasant facts about knife fighting

More unpleasant facts about a knife fight are that if you want to kill someone with a knife, there is going to be some serious requirement in terms of working with your knife.

For example, a simple stab or even multiple stabs to the

abdomen region will eventually kill the man, but not fast enough. It is a completely different story if you stab the man and then move your knife around – or dig, gouge and cut if you like. Messy job, but it works like that.

If you need to kill someone with a knife, and you get the chance to stab him, you need to be prepared that it will likely take multiple stab wounds. One stab rarely works unless you really know what you are doing.

The final sad truth is, that during the knife fight, when you get chance to stab your opponent, he has the same chances to stab you. So, there is a very good chance you will be hurt, too.

Make sure you are not oversimplifying your options and training. Many preppers I hear of carry things with them to kill folks or defend themselves. You need to understand your full range of defense options, train with your tools and train with an understanding of the realities of these things in mind.

Survival Notes from Toby:

Accepted wisdom is, "Charge a gun, run from a knife." Selco's up close and personal experience shows why. That said, while we will always recommend and endorse moving away from chaotic situations we have to accept and be prepared for standing and facing a threat, including edged weapon attacks.

There is entirely too much fantasy in the self-defense/ martial arts community on all matters around 'knife fighting', so again we need to be conscious, informed and aware of the training credibility and context we intend to engage in.

The Sweetest Treat I Have Ever Had

We all like to think about and imagine how SHTF will change us, but it is almost impossible to know how we will react to the whole set of new things that SHTF will bring to us.

People think that it will be something like a sharp cut and prompt change, like today it is SHTF and we are different people with different reactions. It would be cool, but it is not like that for most of us.

Some changes will happen over time, and we may not be aware of them at all.

One of the obvious changes (and probably the most interesting change for an online community of preppers because of movies) is a different relationship to violence issues. For example, over time you learn to react differently to violence, and to doing violence.

Another may be living with dirt. You will be dirtier and you will accept it. With each accepting of the above, you are losing your old life, becoming different.

Also, sometimes small things can provoke you to act like an animal, some things that remind you of your old and normal life.

I want to tell you about an experience I had during my time in the war.

It is about treats and pleasures.

Once, a few months after the sh*t hit the fan, during one of the constant tours to find anything useful, I stumbled across something special. And this will give you an idea of how low you go – or better how high our standards are now. It showed me how thin that layer is that makes us normal people.

It was around midnight and we chose a partially ruined house as a temporary shelter from the fire and rain outside. I was with a friend there. We chose one room inside the house which still had part of the ceiling above our heads to shelter from the rain.

We were smoking one cigarette passing it between us when I realized that I actually sat on some box that was partially buried under the rubble. We started to dig and clear trash from around it.

After a few minutes, we found out that it was a big military wooden box, used for long-term storing of various items. When SHTF and everything fell apart I remembered seeing people dragging similar boxes from army storages.

It was pretty heavy, obviously full of whatever.

Of course, we immediately started to imagine what could be inside, ammo, weapons, maybe uniforms… My friend whispered, "Man, imagine, new boots maybe?"

When we opened it, at the first moment in the dark I thought it was full of some small toys or similar because I saw a big pile of small plastic packages. But then I took few of those small items and I froze like someone had pointed the rifle in my face from that box.

It was full of small packaged cocoa spreads, kind of like cheap spreads that can be served in hotels with your breakfast. In this case, it was probably meant to be used for military meals or similar. Something that you could find in a version of MRE.

It was cheap stuff and not really tasty. In normal times I would not eat that stuff. It was like trying to chew sweetened sand.

At that moment I could barely remember when I last ate something sweet, something like junk sweet, chocolates, bars, candy, cakes or similar. If you ever go on a longer hiking trip and eat the same stuff every day for just 2 weeks and then come back to civilization and eat something different, you have experienced something like this.

Now imagine months.

My friend said, "Screw the boots, this is a jackpot."

I do not remember how much of that stuff I ate there in that room with a view of the half ceiling and half rainy night, but I remember seeing my friend eating that stuff by putting the whole thing inside his mouth, chewing the plastic package, eating the spread, then spitting out chewed plastic.

Probably I ate it in the same way. It helps that in the dark we did not see how dirty the packages were. And of course, neither of us ever remembered to check the expiration date.

I would have eaten even if "expired" was printed on it, or maybe even "Toxic from Chernobyl." It did not matter.

It was so sweet and good at that moment. It was not only food, calories, and energy. It was something like a drug for us. A reminder of normal days. With chewing it and eating it we were living a normal life for that moment in time, I guess.

I chewed it, and I knew that later I was probably gonna have some serious problems with my stomach because it forgot how to process stuff like that. But I did not care.

People say that in some moments you can be turned into an animal, you can be driven by simplest and maybe lowest instinct. And at the same time, they imagine that happens only in certain situations, combat, great fear or similar. That's not true.

I experienced before and later many similar events and feelings, many fights, blood, fears, you name it. But that event with those cocoa spreads was something weird.

Later while I was crouching outside my house, having diarrhea and throwing up at the same time, I felt like sh*t.

But I did not regret eating all of those cocoa spreads. I kept some for myself and from time to time I ate it in something like a ritual.

When all was finished, and the war was over I forgot about that. Years later, I found something very similar to that spread. I bought it and tried it. It didn't taste good at all, and I threw it away.

You never know how much you'll appreciate small things.

The point is that you never know how much you will appreciate things, until it is actually SHTF. So, for your preps, stock some "pleasure goods" like cocoa drink mixes in little sachets or coffee mix. They will be valuable.

For the holiday season take your meal or treats sometimes with you to a place that is quiet and without distraction and enjoy them. It is easy to forget what we have now, so I encourage everyone to be extra grateful in the good days we have.

Survival Notes from Daisy:

Never underestimate the value of preps that provide some normalcy. I keep some cake mix, frosting, and birthday candles put back so that we can celebrate the little things from our stockpile. These items will be a particularly special treat during difficult times.

The Temptation of Being Evil

Last week my friend Jay came home from driving somewhere at night and told me that he was not sure if he wouldn't get a power rush once the SHTF.

He asked me why I didn't do that – why I did not take advantage of the absence of law and order and play God in a post-collapse situation.

Because of a few reasons.

First, I am not a man like that.

And also, I have seen how some men get destroyed after doing things like that. Either he goes crazy or gets killed in a gruesome way.

So, my belief in destiny, karma and those things, helped me to stay away from the dark side. Not in a religious sense but its general principle that I saw repeating around me.

At the end, what you do eventually hits you back in the head. The situation was bad enough, so there was no need to make things worse.

To make things more understandable for you, I thought like Jay before the war, I mean about that thing. But as soon as you get involved in real sh*t, you see that real things are different.

I thought I would be the guy who makes decisions like a God (I mean like "I will kill rape, steal, have fun") but then I realized that when the SHTF you are able only to make decisions in that small circle around you. You just want to stay away from events like that. You do not want to risk anything or be part of creating more suffering.

In a real SHTF people get killed so easily. Somebody who was about to get shot and knew this tried to bite the guy who shot him. It failed, but still.

A few times I have mentioned young guys (and some older, too) on survival forums, who have opinion that when SHTF, it is something like a mix of a Mad Max movie and a video game. They seem to think all you have to do is to have a gun and go around and take stuff from people and kill them and that's it.

It is not like that in real life.

Committing acts of violence will shock you hard and depending on what kind of person you are deep inside and what kind of training you have, you must be prepared to suffer consequences because of what you did.

Why people do bad things is a question that is as old probably as mankind is.

The truth is that you do not know what kind of man you

are or how you will act before you find yourself in SHTF situation.

You must know that when times are bad, all kinds of scum crawl out to do their job. Kill, rape, torture, steal. But you may be surprised that the monster does not necessarily always look like a monster.

Gang members, criminals, addicts – they are all gonna prey on people when SHTF and you will expect that of course.

But also expect that your next-door neighbor who is a local bus driver for example, and your kids played with his kids, might turn out to be a sadistic maniac when the SHTF. SHTF may be his playground.

I knew a lot of psychopaths who became "important" in terms that they were deciding about the life and death of folks. And lot of them were nobody before SHTF, absolutely nobody, not even decent criminals.

The point is that they always were bad deep inside. They just waited for their chance.

In most of the situations, SHTF does not make bad people. It just pulls out the bad that is already in them. They already were bad but often too scared because of laws to let all the hate and anger and crazy ideas out.

I had many chances to make things go easier through my time in the war, but it would have required me to do very bad things. I did not do it because I am not that kind of man.

Did I do some bad stuff?

Sure, very often, but in order to survive and protect me and my family and not just for fun or to feel powerful.

Survival Notes from Daisy:

One of the things that may be shocking when the SHTF is the people you know who use the opportunity to live out their secret twisted fantasies. We never truly know who our neighbors and coworkers are until they're given the opportunity to act as they want without the risk of repercussions.

The Orlando Nightclub Attack: Some Thoughts

I hate to write articles following terrorist attacks, but here I am again. With how everything looks, I'm unfortunately anticipating writing more articles increasingly, based on the "newest terrorist attack."

What I'd like to discuss with you here and now is more about the core of these events, what is happening inside them, and what to do, or how to survive it.

Let's just cover some of the basics here, in terms of survival, if you find yourself in the middle of a similar attack.

Where Are You?

One of my favorite means of survival in any SHTF situation is not to be there. That goes for war and also for a terrorist attack inside some club.

Terrorism has as a goal to change our way of living, to instill fear in us, so we could be in constant expectation of attack. For me, they are succeeding in that.

Placing myself unarmed in a confined space with a whole bunch of unarmed people sounds like a very bad idea to me. The probability that a terrorist will attack a whole bunch of folks in a gun convention, or at a shooting range in Texas is very low, simply because their success there is likely to be very limited.

It is a bad time to be unarmed together with the whole bunch of another unarmed people, simply avoid that.

So that brings us to the next point:

Guns or No Guns?

Nearly all terrorist attacks end when good guys with guns come and kill bad guys with guns. So, one thing here is very clear: it is not about guns only, it is who has the guns.

"The only defense against evil, violent people is good people who are more skilled at violence." – Rory Miller

Clearly, if other good guys (victims) had guns, the chances for them to end that terrorist attack (to kill the terrorist) earlier would be much higher. Have a gun, be armed!

Terrorists, by nature, do not expect to meet active resistance (or firearms) from the victims.

They are there to shoot as many people as possible, and even one good man with a pistol could make a significant tactical change to everything.

Good people with guns brings us to the next point here:

Reality

I experienced and participated in shootings in closed

environments (inside buildings) with more persons inside, and it is nothing like practicing on a shooting range. It is something that you need to be prepared for.

Several gunshots from a rifle in an indoor environment are something that could (and did) make people literally sh*t themselves, or to be paralyzed in shock for some time.

Add to that, the complete chaos. Screams, panic and everything else – it is not sunset movie scene where there is an attacker and you only.

You will act how you are trained, so train for that.

A few thoughts here to consider:

The Building: Know the buildings that you entering and where you are going to spend some time, especially if there is going to be a crowd.

Entrances, exits, escape routes, obstacles, think where most of the folks will run, think where a possible attacker could come from and what is the best position for him, for you.

Cover and Concealment: Understand what is 'cover' and what is 'concealment'. You could read in some manual that concealment could be for example thick bush, you stand behind that and you are not visible, and for cover, there is a thick brick wall and behind it, no bullet can kill you.

With that knowledge you find yourself in the middle of terrorist attack inside the club and find out there is no bushes or thick walls and you suddenly have a flash of revelation that tells you did not learn enough about important things. There is a difference between knowledge and understanding.

Here I find movie industry very guilty for misinformation and lot of possible deaths. You know the movie scenes where people who were shot with a pistol, fly 10 meters through the air when they get hit, or, or guys who use wooden tables for cover in gunfights?

It is all wrong, you know.

A bullet from AK 47 (or any other similar characteristic rifle) can go through many things like doors, walls, shelves, cabinets, tables and kill you or even one more person. Even bullets from a pistol can go through a lot of stuff and kill you.

A good idea is to bring some stuff next time you go to the shooting range and test it. Shoot through those things so you have an idea.

After that exercise on the shooting range, whenever you go to your favorite places (malls, clubs, etc.) together with entrances, exits, route considerations, you need to think about, look for and identify real cover. (Can that big wooden bar take a rifle shot or that big refrigerator?)

Who Survives?

Mostly the guys who survived to tell the story about similar events were those who used the opportunity to flee at the right time, so I would not have any real deep thoughts about that. If you have a chance to run, then run and survive.

If you are there, at the place, armed and have a chance to make the change (to eliminate attacker) to save yourself, then no deep thoughts again, eliminate the threat!

But again, here is the catch. It is not a shooting range, with empty beer bottles. The attacker is shooting too, and most probably with a deadlier weapon than yours.

A slight advantage here is that the attacker is not expecting resistance in the form of a firearm.

Again, a few suggestions. Forget any thoughts of "honorable fighting." Scream while everybody else is screaming in horror, and then when he points in other direction shoot the asshole in back. Do some tactical thinking about his position and your position, angles of movement, corners, types of his weapon, and the time to it takes to reload. Use every opportunity to win.

Conclusion

It is a pretty dark conclusion since I strongly believe that even when you are entering the mall you need to think about possible exits, how thick is that glass in front, where can I find cover, and tactical movements in case of attack, but it is what it is.

Remember that attacks are happening where people are

not expecting it too much. That is also why are so many victims.

Be prepared.

Survival Notes from Toby:

Appropriate situational awareness should be maintained. Note 'appropriate', you can't have your 'head on a swivel', 'watch your six', and be at condition orange or red, ALL THE TIME, it simply doesn't work. Be aware of your surroundings, observe the physical layout of areas you are in, and as situations occur that increase risk, recognize and react to the best of your ability. Simply LEAVING should always be your first consideration and top priority.

Plans without Preps

I got asked a great question recently and thought I would answer it with an article.

A reader asks:

"I read your posts for years, I did not find myself survivalist all that time, I have read it because what you wrote about war times and similar... My question is simple, can you give a couple of simple advice's what to do in case of SHTF, without going into "prep for years" or "build your group for years and store pile of ammo" advice, what if SHTF tomorrow and I do not have anything like that?"

At the first, it looks like a simple question, something that any of us who are into prepping should answer easily, but again we are talking about a man who is not into prepping at all.

So, what to do?

Whole books are written about this answer, but let's try to be short and just stick to the basics here.

What Is Going On?

You see that something is happening outside, something big, let's say you notice that there is an emergency broadcasting on TV, and you see a huge number of law enforcement outside, and other than that you know nothing more.

Now, at this moment, you need to make some important decisions, and you'll have to make it based on what you know, so clearly the more information you can get, the better you can make decisions.

Two important points here you need to understand are:

1. **Look for the common elements.**

No matter what is the real reason for your particular SHTF event, there is some common elements of every SHTF event no matter if it's terrorist dirty bomb attack, solar EMP or Romulans attacking with spaceships.

Panic, disorder, rumors, looting, chaos. So just do not expect to collect all the information you want at that moment. Do not wait to find out what is really happening, or let's say do not wait to find out why things (shit) are happening. At this moment forget the 'why' and act.

2. **Collect information based on your small circle of options.**

That means (continuing from point A) that you do not need (most probably) to find out why there is looting in the street next to you, why there is police force in big numbers, why there is no TV signal, and why there is big black smoke visible from your office few kilometers away in the city.

What you need to know is how to avoid the looting mob, what kind of force the police are using there, and what way to travel to avoid that big black smoke.

Do not get me wrong, to know why things are happening is great, but to wait too long to find out is usually bad and it is often way better to solve things in small steps.

What to Actually Do?

Go back to the basics again. Simply try to stay away from the trouble. We said that you are not a prepper, and you are in the city.

Assess your situation and act.

Your "luck" probably at that moment is that people will probably look more how to take (steal) LCD TVs or laptops than things for shelter or defense.

Get yourself organized into a few simple categories.

We have 7 survival priorities:

- Fire
- Shelter
- Water
- Food
- Communication
- Medical
- Personal Safety

Try to cover each priority as much as you can.

Again, do not spend too much time covering each one at the expense of finding yourself in a worse situation.

As you are not a prepper, and you might find yourself in the middle of working day in the office when SHTF, look around yourself and see what you can use to cover each of the priorities.

For fire you can have only a lighter maybe, and, for now, you have that priority covered. For water you going to put several bottles of water in your bag.

For shelter, you are gonna steal a few more jackets, or emergency blankets or trash bags.

For food you're going to take energy bars from the vending machine. For communications you're going to take your cellphone with you (and hope there is still a signal/network). For medical you are going to "borrow" the first aid kit from the hallway in your office building, and for personal safety you will take a couple of knives from the kitchen or simply smash a chair and take a chair leg as an improvised baton.

So, there – all priorities are covered. Yes, it looks poor, but you covered sections with what you have. Improvising and adapting is key here...

Where to Go?

Should you bug out or bug in?

Simply go away from the trouble, that's it.

We are talking here about the city, so a huge possibility is that you are going to go outside of the city. More people mean more problems.

But the first thing to keep in mind is not to run from the city. It is to escape the trouble (think in small circles-steps). Rory Miller says it nicely, "Don't run away from danger, run towards safety."

If that means that you need to hunker down in an office building, or in a rolled over school bus or wherever, in the middle of the city for two days in order to safely leave the city, then you are going to do that.

The first and immediate task is to stay out of and avoid trouble in your goal to leave the city.

Maybe you are going to have to spend a week hiding somewhere in the city, waiting for the right moment to leave.

The point is to avoid trouble and adapt your plans accordingly to that.

Rules

Best advice for you is anticipating that there are simply no rules, but there *are* some common things for most situations, so:

1. **Stick to your plan up until to the moment when it is more dangerous to follow the plan**. Then improvise, adapt and modify your plan. Be ready that your plan

can fall apart right at the beginning (example: if you plan to leave the city through several pre-planned points and streets, and there is a danger on the way, you might choose to 'bend' your plan and use a long way instead)

2. **Avoid violence.** Avoid violence, simply like that. Violence means the chance to get yourself killed, or injured. Killed means your survival story is ended, and injured means much more trouble than in normal times, remember that a small cut can kill you in SHTF world.

3. **If you must use violence, use it without rules.** When there is no other way than to use violence, you have to use it in a quick and effective way, without hesitation, without rules. You'll think about what you did later if you have to.

4. **Things are (probably) not what they look like.** Police might not be police, the law is not law anymore, stealing is not stealing, honor is not honor. Survival changes things.

5. **Prioritize.** Systemic collapse, an especially first period of it, means a lot of chaos, that means a lot of distractions in your planned action. Always have in your mind what is your priority in the given moment. Getting from point A to point B might look easy today, but when SHTF you may find events problems and obstacles on that way that can fill one lifetime of the average peaceful citizen.

6. **Do not find yourself pulled into bad situations.** Going to the destroyed pharmacy seemed like a good chance to refill your medical kit, but also, it's a good

chance to meet a couple of high junkies inside who will stab you. Choose wisely what distraction you will take as a good chance.

Conclusion

As you can conclude, for the non-prepper, my advice would develop some plan and act. Also, that does not mean that the plan is to run like an idiot and get yourself killed. Sometimes what you need is just the will to survive, and based on that, you will adapt and build your plan.

Survival Notes from Toby:

Be adaptable, make the best decision you can, on the information available in the shortest time possible and ACT on that decision.

Post-Disaster Violence

Today I travel back in my mind. I write a lot about my preparations and assessments since the time I got trapped in my city and views on the future, but I will just now, write some about 'How It Was' back in that time.

Remember, we were all thrown into that situation with no preparation, and found often our allies were our enemies from one day to the next…

Violence is something that people like to talk about, giving theories and opinions, but at the same time few of us experience the real 'deep' face of violence, being trapped in a prolonged a deteriorating situation.

You may have experienced bar fights, or home invasions maybe, shooting somewhere and similar, and those events can be life-changing situations for sure (or life-taking). But I am talking here about violence on so large a scale and so long-lasting that it brings something like a 'new way of living', overwhelming violence that demands a complete change of mindset.

I often hear, and I often agree, that violence cannot solve anything, and that violence only brings more violence, but when you are faced with a man who wants to kill you, you are going to have to probably kill him in order to survive.

I hope that, at this moment, you will not care for philosophy, humanity or ethics, and that you just go do what you have to do and survive. Later you will cope with the other part of it; it is how things work.

As I get older, I realize more and more that violence is the wrong thing, but at the same time, I also realize that I have to be more and more ready and capable to do violence when the time comes.

It is a paradox maybe, but again it is how things works. I do not like that, but it is what it is.

Violence and You

It is too big topic even to try to explain it in one article, but here are some things I must try to show you.

There is a man, let's say we are talking about you here. An average citizen, a law-abiding person, and suddenly you are going to be thrown into a prolonged situation where you are going be forced to watch and use exceptional levels of violence.

Do you think that you are going to be able to operate in those conditions with the mindset you had from the time where you were average law-abiding citizen?

No of course not, you will have to jump into another mindset in order to survive.

Let's call it survival mode.

In survival mode, you'll have to not to forget what it was

like for you in normal times, but you will have to push those memories aside, in order to operate in a different mode – survival mode.

In a real-life situation that means, for example, that you'll maybe have to ignore panic, fear, smells, and noises in the middle of an attack and take the steps you must in order to survive.

Maybe you'll have to ignore the screaming, dying kid next to you. Maybe you'll have to ignore your pride and run, or maybe you'll have to ignore your normal mindset and you are going to have to kill the attacker from behind.

There is a list of priorities in normal life, and there is a list of priorities in survival mode.

Let just say that you are using your different faces and mindset during your normal life and everyday business with different people around you.

Just like that, when faced with violence you'll have to use a different mindset, a different face. Or another you.

Violence and Experience

There is a strange way of thinking here for me, but since I have lived through the time when a huge number of people did not die from old age, rather they died from violence, I have experience in this subject.

So, here are few thoughts.

Experiencing violence over a prolonged period of time

does not make you superman. Actually in some way it makes you a crippled man, a man with many problems, both psychological and physical.

But am I in a better position now than people who died next to me, or in front of me? You may call me a winner or survivor but many days that title sounds very hollow.

Am I lucky man? Yes.

Am I a happy man? No.

But we are not talking in terms of quality of life. We are talking in terms of surviving or not.

Ethics, psychology, and everything else here is a matter for a couple of books to be written, and even then, you are not going say anything new.

It is like that from the beginning of mankind.

What is more important about having experience in violence is that you simply KNOW how things work there. You simply know what you can expect. You know what chaos is. You know the best way of dealing with it. You know what it takes to do things.

Preparing for Violence

Again, there is nothing like real life experience.

But when you experience something like real violence, you keep that in yourself for the rest of your life. What is best next to that? Other people's real-life experience.

So, does it make sense to read about other folks' real-life experience? Of course, read a lot about that.

Training yourself physically is a great thing. You'll train to get yourself into the state where you are physically ready for hard tasks. So, of course, it makes sense to do that.

But training yourself mentally can be a hard thing.

You actually can only guess how it is going to be, how it is going to affect you.

I can tell you that it is hard, chaotic. I can describe to you a situation, but can I bring you the feeling of terror in your gut when you feel that you are going to sh*t yourself? Can I give you smell of fear, the smell of decaying bodies? Can I give you that feeling when you realize that "they" are coming for you?

No, of course, I cannot. You can read stories and real-life experiences and based on that you are going to build your possible mindset for violent situations.

You are going to build your survival mindset.

But there is a catch there. If you build it too firm, too strong, and then there is SHTF and everything that you imagined doesn't fit the given situation or scenario and you are still pursuing and acting in the way that you imagined dealing with it, you are going to have serious problems.

The situation will not adapt to your mindset. The situation

will kill you if you are sticking too firmly to your plan when it is not working.

You simply have to adapt.

It goes for any situations. If your plan and mindset say you are defending your home until you die, you are going to die probably.

Whenever I heard people saying "I'll do that when SHTF" or "I'll do this when SHTF" I feel sorry for them.

When SHTF you will adapt, and change your given plan accordingly to the situation.

It is same with violence.

Violence is a tool that you are going to use according to the situation. It is a tool, not a toy.

Now to finish with a final thought.

It can sound, from what I have written, that an SHTF situation is like a Mad Max movie. Everyone running around killing, hurting others, doing things with no consequences. In fact, this fantasy of a world 'Without Rule of Law' (WROL) is a big discussion in some circles.

For sure, the regular law has gone. There are no authorities or courts as we know them to deter or punish.

BUT, during an SHTF situation you will find out these things about violence.

It is (especially in the beginning) like everything is

possible. The law is gone, you could go outside and see people looting stores, groups organizing (by street, or other facts like the same job in a company for example) and they are trying to either defend part of the town, or bring more chaos just for fun. Sometimes you could not say what, but both could bring violence and death to you.

Over time, the violence becomes more organized and structured to start to achieve certain specific goals (although there is always chaos, as well).

After some time, you will look at the violence you encounter in two ways. Violence happening outside your group, or inside your group. It is quite certain you will need to be in some sort of group to stand any chance of surviving.

Outside your group, you just wish to be very 'small', invisible after some time, and not pay attention to anyone doing violence to others. Because, quite simply, you are still alive and want to stay that way. In terms of "I am still alive, I do not care what they do to that person, and how bad it is." Your will and judging of good and bad is broken; you just care for your own life.

Leaders of the "bad" group have best chances to stay leader if members fear him, so in fact, he is most dangerous, vicious, sick bastard, nothing like a reasonable man. Competition is huge in SHTF. Instilling discipline through fear and enforcing your rules are paramount to holding your position as leader.

Various groups were interacting with the outside world

and each other through fighting, exchange information, trading goods etc., but every group was more or less a closed world, with trust only for those inside the group.

The forming of a group was quick, mostly because nobody expected this situation was going to happen, and so we were not prepared, but very quickly were literally fighting for survival. Any problems were solved along the way (bad members, not skilled, not obeying etc.). Sometimes through discussion and agreement, but always with the threat of violence as an option.

To finish, and to educate, as opposed to shock you.

Many folks cannot think too clearly about being involved in the level of violence I am describing. Maybe you think SHTF is just like Black Friday shopping but every day. So, let me just give examples of the how far the world I lived in descended from 'normal'. Remember this was a regular city, in a nice country in Europe, less than 25 years ago.

- **People who never used violence before, committing 'hard' violence:** normal people, dads, and mums, killing folks in order to save their families.
- **Certain groups of people who looked like they just waited for the SHTF** so they can go out (crawl out from beneath some rock) and fulfill their own fantasies about being kings of the town, imprisoning people, raping women, torturing folks in the weirdest ways.
- **Strange groups organizing in whatever cause they choose to name it**, again only to gain power in order

to have more resources (sometimes simply "gangs" of 50 people, sometimes whole militias of thousands of people) through terror over other people or groups of people.
- **Irrational hate towards the "other"** whoever the "other" might be (other religion, group, street, town, nation) because it is very easy to manipulate groups of people through hate and fear from and towards "others." If someone manipulated you to believe that your kid is hungry because of the "others" he can do a lot with you.

Real life examples I saw:

- People burned alive inside their homes (And people 'enjoying' watching this)
- Private prisons were made where you could go and torture other folks for fun, or simply rape women as a "reward"
- Kids over 13 or 14 years of age were simply counted as grown-up people, and killed as an enemy
- The humiliation of people on all different ways in order to break their will, for example, forcing prisoners to have sex between same family (like father and daughter and similar)
- Violence was an everyday thing, you could go outside and get shot not because you were 'enemy', but only because sniper on other side want to test his rifle.

It is a needed, but depressing realization, that people, even regular folks can become so cruel, so fast. BUT it is a very important thing to be aware of for anyone truly involved in preparedness.

Survival Notes from Toby:

Reading, watching, listening to and researching real life experiences is to be considered an essential part of preparing.

A high percentage of the population have little or no experience with violence at all, and therefore risk a significant period of 'shock' (read inaction) as violence escalates in bad situations, which may prove to be a fatal delay.

As you become surrounded by violence you will have to use violence yourself on a regular basis, this comes with both a physical and mental cost.

The Human Side of Authorities

We do not need to label everything. All that matters is what impact it can have on us.

What I mean is that we do not need to know *why* something is happening right away. But we know something is going on and definitely we need to be prepared for results of that. Again, I do not want to judge right or wrong here, but just talk about some experiences and give you some things to maybe think about.

I read many times in comments and on different blogs and forums, questions and speculations about what the authorities are gonna do when SHTF, or how police are gonna react and what military is gonna do.

So, there is a whole different set of options and opinions, but a great majority of them are having the opinion based on the mindset that they are used to. They think like *before* the SHTF even though the SHTF changes everything into a real survival situation with a whole different set of rules.

And that makes big difference.

I had the idea to write about this because of the Chris Dorner[1] case. The case is interesting because of many things. It shows what trouble one person can make (and now imagine many Chris Dorners started fighting the authorities) and also how the authorities try to deal with the troublemaker.

If we are talking about police now, we can agree or disagree whether the police are there to serve and protect. That really depends on where you live, of course. In some countries, police are part of the problem but in general, law enforcement people are there to make difference between order and chaos.

In the case of Chris Dorner, when they cornered him in a small wooden cabin, they threw several hot tear gas grenades to get him out. Many people think this was on purpose to set fire to the cabin because these hot tear gas grenades are known to set things on fire. After having 4 of your colleagues killed, most people are not gonna be easy with the killer.

When people are under big emotional stress this is normal and in long-term survival scenario that happens to everyone.

I wanna tell you one story from my SHTF time.

It is about law-abiding citizens and special police force.

The first days of a collapse are the most chaotic in terms of panic and frightened people. Picture of a big number of people who do not know what to do, where to go, and what is gonna be. There is looting everywhere, and when folks realize that nobody is gonna punish them they just go wild.

One group of people (they all lived in the same apartment building) chose to hunker down or to a bug in, speaking in survival terms. There were a couple of days of chaos outside, but nobody touched them in that building.

When things get rougher they chose to move to a few apartments on the same floor and stay together. Anyway, after two or three weeks, there was some kind of peace outside. They were on watch at the windows, carefully checking what is going on, but they could not figure out anything.

A few hours later when dark start to fall, they noticed a group of some 30 policemen, with helmets, rifles, and everything. Special police were still around and in the first days after SHTF they made weak attempts of putting riots down.

They moved in order and formation. Guys from the building were so happy to see them after weeks of rioting and chaos outside. These police were the first sign that things maybe get back to normal.

The people in the building cheered and called them.

The police quickly stormed into the building and forced them out. They shot them after a quick search. After that, they searched apartments for useful stuff. One of the guys who realized what was happening fast and ran for his life survived and he told me his story. They were so quick and professional in killing that most of the people did not even have time to ask for mercy.

Now, what is the importance of this story?

Remember this: **When the SHTF, there are guys with guns and there are guys without guns.** Everything else is just labeled. Names like police, army, authority, government...

You cannot think in the terms that we think today. It is dangerous.

If you read between the lines in these stories, you also come to your own conclusions about how you can make changes to make your survival more likely if your group looks like official helpers. Of course, do not use this for bad things.

There is nothing deep and philosophic in this story.

The police force is just a bunch of guys with guns who are doing their job today. Some of them are good people; some of them are bad people. They are all just like us – they are gonna choose what they gonna do when the SHTF but when they are in big emotional stress or a fight for their survival, they might not be nice guys like before.

Even if they try to be good, they go around and anyone they see can be a Chris Dorner and in all the chaos, they do not know.

Guys who were hiding in the building were common law-abiding folks, and they did not realize that it was SHTF and that rules had changed. Actually, the rules were gone, so what was before did not matter much. Black can be white, bad can be good, or police force can be a simple gang.

Really getting this mindset is the main point of survival. Yes, there are lists with supplies and survival guides, but what I want you to see is how "not natural" it was. It feels like landing on a different planet when society changes like that but if you want to survive you have to be able to be almost comfortable with this.

Now do not get me wrong, I am not saying that we all need to go out and not obey the law. Nothing like that. But when the SHTF, it is a terrible mistake to act like a law-abiding citizen just because you are used to that. It just doesn't make sense and you have to question everything and everyone.

I had the advantage or dubious luck of seeing all that when the SHTF. Also, I am living in what I call an unorganized country, so I am perfectly aware that police here even in normal times are armed guys who also work for the people who pay more.

All of my problems I try to solve by myself with no real help from authorities. Maybe in your world, the situation is different, and you should be grateful for that.

I am not saying that all cops are bad. In your country, most cops could be very good. Just keep in mind that people who enforce law and order are humans too and when SHTF or in a major disaster that is followed by a long-term survival situation, they are living in a new world in which old rules do not mean much.

I know it is easy for me to say this because I have been in this situation but besides all the technical or logistical aspects of prepping, your mind has to be ready for the day when old labels, classification, and rules are not working anymore. Only then can you make the correct critical decisions that can make your chances to survive better.

I hope nobody reading this book has to ever go through such dark times but if you only know how bad it can get by reading what I write or listening to interviews then this can help prepare you for the worst-case scenario and that is what matters.

Do not live life scared and paranoid as some survivalists do, but also really understand how bad things can get or you maybe have best-organized food storage in your whole country but make the mistake of inviting the wrong guys over for dinner.

Survival Notes from Daisy:

The most important quote in the entire essay is this:

When the SHTF, there are guys with guns and there are guys without guns.

We'd do well to remember that we're all human beings, including so-called "authority figures." As such, nobody is immune to taking advantage of someone weaker in a survival situation. Don't let the pre-SHTF rules color your judgment when the SHTF occurs. Be prepared to treat everyone as a potential threat until they prove otherwise.

[1]   http://www.huffingtonpost.com/2013/02/12/dorner-manhunt-timeline_n_2672851.html

When More Chaos Helps for Survival

As I've mentioned, I work in the medical field, and a few days ago we got called to transport some guy who broke his back. A serious injury is nothing that unusual but this guy broke his back while trying to attack woman to maybe rob or rape her.

He attacked her on the staircase in the house where she lives.

Instead of resisting his attack from behind, the woman was just so shocked she fell backward on the guy and he fell down a staircase and broke his back.

That is what some might call a happy ending. The woman had just a few bruises and got away.

This reminded me of something that happened to my cousin during the war.

In this region here, Western type of culture was always more popular than Eastern. Especially for everyday things that young people do. So young folks here always like things that most of the people in the west like. Things like music, lifestyle, and all of that.

A few years before the war, that all became even more

popular, I guess thanks to the political changes and all of that.

A few months before the war, my cousin ordered from some small company military dog tags for himself. It looked just like original US ID tags, with those rubber covers.

It was some kind of fashion thing for him. He did not engrave his name on it, he engraved the name of the metal group he liked, and on another plate he engraved an eagle.

He was into the music, guitars, concerts, long hair and that kind of thing.

The important thing to mention is that the army here did not have ID tags, and even if they did, it looked completely different. It was actually one small metal plate, inside that plate were a name, unit numbers etc. on one small piece of paper (kind of thin plastic paper, waterproof)

In the first month, when everything still was confusing and when all kinds of people were on the street, some tried to run or hide somewhere. Others tried to take whatever they could in this chaos.

He found himself trying to run from his apartment to a safer place. All kinds of different armed groups were on the street, some on barricades, some others running through the city, doing raids.

They stopped him and a bunch of other guys at one

checkpoint and immediately started to beat them and search them for valuable things.

One guy pointed a pistol towards him and started to search him by ripping the pockets on his shirt. He said later in first moments of that he was scared to death and went completely numb and paralyzed, and that probably saved his life.

The guy who searched him saw his ID tags. He started to yell at him. The conversation as he can remember went something like this:

Gang member 1: "WTF is this, you idiot? Are you belonging to some group?" (slapping him)

Cousin:

Gang member 1: "I will blow your head off if you do not answer me."

Cousin:

Gang member 2: "What do you have there, white gold? Silver? Just take it from him."

Gang member 1: "No, it is something else, and he is playing deaf."

Gang member 2: "Let me see, shit, maybe he is French, I think it is in French."

At that moment my cousin realized that he needs to keep his mouth closed, not only because of fear.

Gang member 2: *"K.R.E.A.T.O.R. (spelling from the ID tags) IS YOUR NAME KREATOR?" (yelling in local language)*

In the background my cousin heard a few shots, he did not turn his head to check who was shot or why.

Gang member 2: *"Anybody here speaks French?" (asking other group members)*

My cousin said luckily those guys looked like they barely could speak their native language. Most of the time they just yelled, grunted, and moaned, like a bunch of apes.

Gang member 1: *(yelling) UN? NEWSPAPERS? BBC? SPAIN? REPORTER?*

Gang member 2: *"OK just leave the idiot, we do not want any troubles."*

Gang member 1: *"GO, GO, YOU CAN GO" (waving with his hands on my cousin)*

Gang member 3: *"Maybe he could write a story about us, our group."*

Gang member 2: *"Shut up you idiot!"*

My cousin just slowly moved away from them, and after 100 meters started to run. He said one of the guys said to him few times "nice, nice" in English, probably trying to say to him that he can go, but probably that words were only English words that he knew.

I asked him why he did not start to speak English because

I knew that he knows some basic English. He said, "At that moment I forgot how to speak my native language, not to mention English."

Not to mention that he had in the back of his pocket some documents that clearly stated he was local. The guys just did not make it to his pocket.

The survival lesson from these stories is that **when you are outnumbered or clearly in a weaker position, often it helps to introduce more chaos and confusion**.

The woman did not plan to fall back on the guy but just was shocked and then because of falling the cards were mixed anew. She could have gotten hurt or her attacker could have. Luckily, her attacker got hurt more.

Same with my cousin. He did not plan for this but by having this ID he made a straightforward situation for the gang members more confusing. It is hard to unkill someone, so he was let go because they did not know how to react in this situation.

Both my cousin and the woman did not do what they did on purpose. They got lucky.

But if you ever find yourself in a hopeless situation keep in mind that if something nobody expects happens or you make it happen, the cards are mixed anew and your chances for survival might have increased.

Shuffling cards new is better than sure death.

Survival Notes from Daisy:

When you are in a dangerous situation, sometimes you can change it in your favor by adding confusion to the mix. This may happen accidentally, so be prepared to take your opportunity if the chance arises.

Dogs in Violent Survival Situations

I did not have a pet when SHTF and I did not have one later. Most of the people who had them when SHTF let them go or in some cases probably ate them.

I want to clear up some things I believe are myths.

Dogs for protection did work but not because a dog guards you and fights for you. When human life matters little, nobody has problems shooting a dog. Dogs were sometimes shot for "fun."

So, leaving the family at home with dogs as protection is a bad idea.

In civilized times, somebody who breaks in the house and never killed a human might wait long enough before shooting the dog that they get attacked, but in our case, nobody waited.

People who waited and did not shoot, did not live more than first few weeks after SHTF. Or if they did survive and if they could not get themselves to shoot at living beings, they were just hiding somewhere.

Some families just locked dog out and never let them in again. Food was only for humans after some point in time for most.

About eating dogs, there is not much to say about this. Dogs are animals and hunger can make people eat anything. There were some people who nobody knew what they ate and how they got food. The most "exotic" meat I had was a rat, some sort of big water rat. I'm not sure if I would have touched dog.

I say not sure because of course I'm against eating a dog now, but once it is a matter of your life or that of a dog, an opinion can change.

One of the guys from my street had and kept his dog through all of that. The dog lived a few years after all was over with them. I did not think too much about that dog, his importance for that family or burden or whatever.

But after many questions about pets when SHTF via email and in my course I decided to ask that guy about his dog and their SHTF time.

They got dog a few years before the war, an ordinary mixed puppy, I mean no famous breed. Small dog, we call it house dog or kid's dog here. They called it Rino. Kids paid attention to Rino, but after few years when kids were grown up into teenagers, they stopped paying too much attention to him.

The oldest guy in the family took him as something like a best friend, so it was normal to see Grandpa walking through the street with that dog.

When everything started, the family pretty much forgot about the dog. I mean a lot more important stuff was on their schedule. Some other folks moved into the house and it was crowded, with many problems, food, hygiene and all that our survival situation brought.

The dog still stayed with Grandpa mostly. He shared some of his food with him. Some of the family members had an opinion that giving food to the dog in that time was not such a smart idea.

Anyway, the old guy got sick. He was pretty old and had problems with high blood pressure and heart, and the stress and the overall bad situation just sped up things. He lost his strength and fell into the bed.

For two months he was laying in the bed with Rino beneath his legs. That dog did not want to move from him. Grandpa and that dog became something like best friends. The guy from the street told me that it was like they both felt that they are not so useful in the whole situation, so they just move very close to each other.

Nobody ever said anything bad to the old guy, or acted like he was a burden because he was sick, but being old does not mean stupid. The old guy felt useless.

A neighbor said it was at the same time so sad to see them together always. Like a picture of things breaking down.

Grandpa died in the middle of the hardest period when hostilities and hunger were worst, and nobody knows what tomorrow was gonna be.

My neighbor also said, and he swore to me it is the truth,

that the night before Grandpa died that dog was howling all night. He said that dogs can smell death when is approaching the house. I do not know, but when he told me that I got chills.

Dogs saved themselves from recent tsunamis before they came so they seem to have some sort of sense for things.

In the morning they found Grandpa dead, they buried him in the park, and they kept the dog. In next few days they noticed that the dog was blind. Nobody knew when or how that happened. The neighbor said nobody paid too much attention in those days what dog is eating or how clean it is, so anything was possible.

But he also noticed something else: when bad guys came onto the street, some 150 meters maybe, that dog always would run and tried to hide. When somebody friendly came on the street dog would stand next to the window frame with front two legs up there.

So, they learned that and they use it as some kind of early warning sign. He said that dog actually probably saved their lives a couple of times.

When everything ended dog had a special place in that house. He something like a special decorated war hero, best food, best care, best everything.

My neighbor told me at the end of the story that they found dog dead one morning, in the exact place where Grandpa was lying for months and where he died at the end.

I do not know too much about dogs, and I do not know if things from the story are possible, but my neighbor swore to me it was the truth a couple of times. He even cried at the end of his story.

He told me that story while we had few beers in a café. Across the café was the park where his grandpa is buried. They did not exhume people from the park, too many graves, too many problems, and authorities after the war just turn that park officially into a graveyard with everything that goes with any other normal graveyard.

So, in short, no, dogs will not be great fighters by your side when weapons are commonly used but dogs can help you with their senses.

Deciding What to Do

When the SHTF, making the wrong decision can cost more than you will ever realize, so advice on what to do and what not to do should be sought out and heeded.

You see many articles like "Ten Things to do When SHTF" or "The 5 most likely situations..." or similar.

The truth is that these articles, while a great way to learn something (I've written posts like that too) are, very often, oversimplifying situations or scenarios that most likely when SHTF is going to be dynamic and probably complex…

It is essential that you are ready to adapt because there are many variables about what to do or not to do when the SHTF. So read these lists but be careful of how attached you get to them.

My main point here is this: there is only one thing worse than being without a plan when the SHTF. And that thing is having a plan and sticking to that plan so tightly that you simply end up dead because your plan is not working for that particular SHTF situation.

So, what to do (or not to do) when the SHTF? Let's look at two sides of a couple of things:

Panic: Side One

Panic is a plan-killer. Panic is a fearsome enemy. You may have a very good plan and preparations and end up dead, simply because you failed to understand how bad panic is going to affect you.

There is research that says that 74 % of people, in a case of disaster and being forced to quickly leave their home, would forget to take a lighter and something that they could boil water in to disinfect it.

We could say that research is for non-preppers, but be aware that in the case of panic and fear (and we are all are going to experience some level of that for sure) you are going to make mistakes. Be ready to accept, adapt and overcome this.

Panic: The Other Side:

Fear of, or when in, danger is a powerful thing and you need to not deny it, rather go into a mindset like, "Sh*t, of course, I am afraid just like everybody else. Let me use that fear and do something smart."

The good thing here is that most of the people around you are going to be in some kind of panic or state of fear and confusion. Let's work on the basis that you, as a prepper, are going to be in a lesser state of panic than these other folks.

So, suddenly, panic and fear can become friends in some situations. Use it in your favor.

For example, while everybody else is in a panic still figuring out what really happened, use the moment for a last run to the grocery shop for more food, or use it to simply to get away from the danger.

There is also one important moment here to recognize. Some researchers conclude that people actually panic much less than we imagine.

So, they stated that in cases of some catastrophes (disasters in sports stadiums, factory disasters and similar) the first reactions of a number of people is not to panic, but rather to help other injured people.

I agree with this, but only to a certain extent. If you find yourself in the street and see a building collapse suddenly, and hear screams from rubble, most people's reaction who just saw the event is to go there and help injured people. But if you see or hear other buildings continue to collapse, you're going to panic, and other people are going to panic.

It is an example only, but in the case of a serious SHTF event, expect panic and simply use it in your favor, however you can.

Changing the rules: Side One

I'll try to explain this "change the rules" rule with one small, short but serious real-life experience.

Just after the sh*t hit the fan here, a man went out to seek help. He saw a police officer, he ran towards the officer and cried for help because his wife was wounded at home. The police officer just shot him in the head and robbed him.

End of story.

The story could be – and actually is – longer because I should go through the events leading to that, panic on street, no information on what is going on and much blah blah blah.

But the point of the story here is that the dead guy simply failed to change rules from the mentality of "there is a police officer" to "there is an armed dude in a police uniform."

When the SHTF, rules are changing, all rules. Rules like "the police are going to help us, the government is going to take care of us, there is help at the hospital," etc., will change.

You simply do not know it, but the rules are gone.

Changing the Rules: The Other Side

Nobody said that you cannot be a guy in a police uniform when SHTF. I am not saying that you have to put on a police uniform when the SHTF and go out and shoot innocent people.

I am saying that you may use other people's lack of knowledge and adaption to the new rules and, for example, wear an EMT uniform on the first day of chaos in order to go through some part of the city or a police uniform, or act like a rescue worker or whatever you think makes sense in your particular situation at the moment.

Switch yourself to the SHTF situation thinking in all ways and means.

ABCs (Go Back to Basics)

It is again about big and small circles.

People tend to think too much and it actually can be bad when the SHTF initially. They overthink simply because there is no real information.

You need to look for the right information, of course, and try to figure what is happening. But in the meantime, if you do not know what to do because you do not know what is going on, use that moment to go for your basics.

That means if suddenly something bad is happening (SHTF) and you do not know what to do, do something that is useful. Why don't you use that moment and go to fill your bathtub with water, for example?

Most probably you're going to need it.

Or go through your equipment, or check your weapon?

Just go through the 'basics' if you do not know what to do when lacking real information.

Survival Notes from Toby:

There are pros and cons to every plan, every decision. Be aware of them, be adaptable but do make decisions and carry them out.

The Different Faces of Fear

Fear was constant.

Sometimes it moved you and made decisions for you. Sometimes was just as a reminder in the back of your head. Fear of the unknown, fear of pain, fear of minor things that can become a disaster, things like the cold or an injury.

Just like with most things when the SHTF, there are no rules, so fear is different for different kinds of people, and not everybody reacts the same. Some say that fear can kill you, and yes, I agree, but also fear can save your life.

Fear can "do" things instead of you.

I've seen people doing some weird and crazy things just because they were terrified for their life or lives of their families. I saw a man who beat two armed men with a rifle, he was driven mad with fear, fear for his family over what those two men were gonna do to them. He did not even try to shoot; he just used his rifle as some kind of stick or baton and beat those two guys almost to death.

He was not something like Chuck Norris or anything similar. He was a terrified father. Fear just turned him into a monster.

When you find yourself in a situation of life and death, fear can just overwhelm you.

I was in a situation where I needed to stay low and quiet while a group of men went past me. It was matter of life and death and I knew it. I remember my heart was bumping so loud that I was thinking, "Those guys are gonna hear me. They are gonna hear my heart."

I was breathing normally I guess but I remember that I thought I breathed so loud and I was turning around and checking because I thought someone else was breathing behind me.

Later it got much easier. In the first few situations, fear controls you. After a few times you slowly learn that you need to control fear. If you survive and have enough time for learning that.

Again, different people react differently. But fear is always there. Over the time you learn sometimes to control it and use it in your favor, as an extra power actually, as some kind of adrenaline jump starter. So, you can do some things faster and better. This is the point you want to get to.

I am talking about an ordinary man, not prepared, not trained.

What I learned about fear

What I learned for sure and what is pretty much obvious is the fact that people did not get killed because they feared a lot. They get killed mostly because they reacted wrong and fear paralyzed them.

It is good when fear pushes you to act, run or fight, do something, do anything. It is bad when you get paralyzed.

The first time when a gang came in some bigger numbers, in some form of attack I think the hardest thing for us was to realize the fact that they have bad intentions, that they want to hurt us or kill us.

After that, fear took place, and that fear moved us to defend and to fight.

As I say later, we all more or less learned to control fear and to somehow use it in our favor. Some did that better than others, some learned, and some did not want to.

Another man's experience with fear

One of my neighbors was a normal guy with a normal life.

He just could not understand that the sh*t had hit the fan, and nothing was normal anymore. He was a guy who just paid too much attention to being a law-abiding citizen. He never drove too fast. He always used a seat belt, paid his taxes, watched his language, and trusted the government.

Anyway, when the SHTF, all kind of "police forces" popped up. Suddenly there were all kind of armed groups going through town and doing things in the name of the law or in the name of the "cause" or whatever.

They robbed, killed, and mobilized people to fight for

them. In those days for some people, it was just hard to understand that the law was gone, and that it was something like "each man for himself."

Each one of these groups claimed that they had the right to use force in the name of the law and in the cause of protecting the people. Of course, those armed groups were mostly just gangs, more or less.

During our discussions in the first days of chaos, he stated to me that he cannot go against the law. In other words, he was saying to me that if some police force came to his door and wanted something from him, he could not refuse it. Because those guys are the law, and he just could not go against the law.

I had another opinion. Mine was more like whoever is armed and wants to enter my house is my enemy.

He just did not accept the fact that times had changed. He was afraid to accept it, he wanted to believe that everything was fine, and someone would take things into hand instead of him. He was this sort of "the government will take care of us; some higher power will sort thing out" guy.

When guys came to his door "in the name of the law" he just opened the door and went with them, for "a talk at headquarters."

After they robbed him, he spent a few months in their prison, working for them. I know that he was armed when they came, and I know that he could have tried to resist them. They probably, in that case, would have turned back and found some easier target. But he chose to listen to them, he chose to trust them because they were the law. He chose to believe that they were doing what was best for him.

I think he was just paralyzed by fear of the fact that he can somehow not abide by the law.

Deep inside he probably knew that those guys were not any kind of law, he maybe just wanted to believe that everything was gonna be fine.

People see what they want to see and especially when things get tough, they try to look for good things in a bad situation.

Unfortunately, even if there are no good things some still convince themselves there are.

On a "Good Day"....

Most of the people will understand what I write only in the proper way after they experience some serious event. Only then can you put it in the correct perspective.

There is nothing like learning from real-life experience.

And there is nothing wrong about changing your survival system. I do it too when I figure that something works better than plan or equipment that I have.

If you have been a prepper for years and you did not change your setup and plan from day one of your prepping until now, then usually something is wrong with your philosophy.

On a good day I can...

I think it was on some forum or in some blog comments, the discussion was about some particular weapon as far as I remember, and some guy said something along the lines of "when SHTF, on a good day I can shoot and kill..."

In that short statement "on a good day" is condensed one of the biggest mistakes about prepping in survival movement.

There are not too many good days when SHTF. It is simple like that.

In short, people are prepping based on imaginary

perspective how the SHTF's gonna look, and that alone is not the problem. You do not necessarily have to go through serious SHTF event in order to be good prepper-survivalist. The problem is that people stick so hard to their imaginary perspective of what the SHTF is gonna look like, and what they need for it, that they are simply not willing to change their plans.

They are sure.

Whenever I read that someone has changed their plans based on an experience or thinking and that he recognizes that, in my articles or courses, where he was wrong, I feel great.

By the way, on a good day, you can sit down and shoot 6 magazines from AK in 5 minutes and shoot 5 people who want to break in your home while you are singing "Hey Joe" without too many problems.

You are fed, secured, comfortable, warm, healthy, police are probably gonna come in 10 minutes, you'll get professional psychological help later, and maybe you'll even end up in the local newspaper as a hero...

On an ordinary day during a real collapse, though, chances are that you'll be tired from days and nights of not sleeping well, more or less hungry, maybe you gonna have weird and painful infection in your groin from lack of proper hygiene and serious case of diarrhea, your younger kid has pneumonia and of course the doctors are gone, and your friend who is a veterinarian gave you some pills and you are not sure they're working, your wife had nervous breakdown and you do not have clue what to do with her...

You were listening to screams from town for weeks while gangs were killing and raping, and your bones melted from horror.

Several times the strange idea of killing your family and then yourself struck your mind because listening to screams for weeks put pictures of what kind of things are happening out there, and you cannot cope with those pictures.

Then, there are five people attacking your home. They even yell that they gonna spare all of you if you give them your supplies, but you're thinking about those screams, but still maybe they will spare you...

It is definitely not your "good day."

You need to *hope* for good days when SHTF, but you need to *be prepared* for bad days when SHTF.

Survival Notes from Daisy:

It's pretty easy to come up with detailed plans when life is good, you're not hungry, your central heating works, and you have a laptop for research at your fingertips. It's entirely different to put those plans into action when the situation is total chaos and you are cold, hungry, and sick. It's all about your perspective at the particular moment in time. Don't get so tied to your plans that you are unwilling to accept that your situation is not what you expected and that it's time for a new plan. Don't expect a shiny, sanitized version of SHTF because the reality is entirely different.

Heat

It is an equation that takes into consideration your skills, preps, event, circumstances... and adds heat (SHTF).

If you show me a man who can have all prepared perfectly well for any kind of possible scenario, I will bow to him, but, from my experience, it is simply impossible.

If you understand that, then you'll understand two things:

- You'll need constantly to adapt to the given situation
- You'll have bad days and fails

But you'll still have a good chance to survive. To show that in an example I'll use a very widespread and popular topic: Bug Out Bags

It is something like the holy grail of survival, and it is like a minefield to go into those topics against widespread and popular opinions in survival community, but that's okay. You just need to think about it.

So here goes...

Bug-Out Bags and Equipment)

A bug-out bag is something that is considered an "absolutely must-have or otherwise you are not a prepper."

So, there you have a situation where people have a bug-out bags. Each member of the family has his own BOB.

Yours might weigh 25 kilos. You have everything there, food for three days, toilet paper, ax and knife, tarp and small stove, extra ammo, first aid kit and a lot of antibiotics.

You have maps and radios.

It is heavy duty military grade backpack, waterproof.

All members of your family have BOB with good and usable stuff inside.

And then the city erupts in violent protests for whatever reason and you need to bug out immediately.

You all grab your BOBs go out and get shot after 300 meters because you have such good and cool looking stuff on you (and in huge amounts). Or you drown in the river because your backpack is too big.

I understand that this example is very rudimentary, but you need to stop thinking that you can cover everything for every scenario. Otherwise you end up covering nothing.

The BOB has become almost a burden because we are being bombarded with information on "what we really need to have in order to survive and thrive" or "you must have this or otherwise you will end up dead for sure."

It really needs to be about necessity, not comfort.

There is "prepackaged first aid kit" for your BOB with nonsense inside. There are stoves that are heavy and give your position away to everybody from a 2-km distance. There are ways to start your fire that take like a half an hour and require 1000 calories of your work… doesn't anybody use lighter anymore for starting a fire?

"What if the lighter fails?" people say.

Can't you have 2-3 lighters for that case?

There are powerful flashlights that make "night look like day" for only such and such amount of money…and if I want to read my map in the middle of nowhere using that torch I'll be blind for the next half hour, and if there is anybody within 3 km of my position they all will know where I am.

Again, all above are examples, and flashlights and flints are great stuff. They have their place (I have them too) but did you think to also include lighters and microlights?

An example of a solution would be "shelf "system. You need to have a lot of stuff ready to take quickly but based on a given scenario.

Some things can cover all scenarios, basic things, but why in the name of everything covered would anybody drag a big heavy bag when you need speed and blending in?

Does having a sports bag for a given scenario not make more sense than a camping backpack or military type backpack? Is carrying a rifle in your hand having more sense than hiding undercoat in a given moment in the scenario?

Maybe a simple sleeping mat being visible on your backpack clearly points you as a target in a given moment? Maybe the moment demands only heavy-duty trash bag in your pocket (as a mean for sleeping on the way to your BOL) These are only examples, but hopefully, you get my point.

Sit down, pull all your gear out, and think about 5 possible SHTF scenarios, and that you have 10 minutes to choose only 30 percent of your BOB stuff. See the difference in equipment selection for each scenario.

It is a good practice.

It is a reality – you cannot have everything.

Find the Balance

You may find that in the end it is about balance how much preps you have in your home (or are willing to carry) with you.

Sometimes it affects your mobility and adaptability. Sometimes you grow a huge connection with your stuff and you are not willing to leave everything and run to save your life because you have valuable things.

Sometimes all your cool preps will save your life.

A metal container with 300 dollars' worth of preps inside that you took and buried in the woods as your secret stash can be worth much more than $50,000 worth of preps inside your home, simply because you maybe had to leave your home in 10 minutes to survive.

It is a balance that cannot be taught because you need to put it in perspective of your given circumstances.

There is no magical solution to "survive and thrive when SHTF for only $99.99." There is no "prepackaged perfect solution" products.

YOU need to pack your solution.

Survival Notes from Toby:

Survival psychology is one of the most overlooked areas within the Preppersphere. Even those addressing it are often, at best misunderstanding the basics and more, at worse convincing themselves and others they are far 'stronger' than they actually are.

The general lack of training commitment and avoidance of discomfort further compounds the problem. Education from credible texts and training in context is key here.

Following directly on from this and in those credible and contextual information footsteps will also greatly improve your ability to effectively select (and hopefully use) the right equipment.

A Lesson in Survival and Dying

Last week at my job in the medical field, we had an emergency that reminded me of something I first learned in my SHTF time. It was a lesson in survival even if it helps also with dying.

During my SHTF time, the night this happened started normally.

I left my house right after dark. That night there was a lot of shelling. I had a bad feeling, I remember that. Not that it was not normal to have a bad feeling going out, but this night I remember it was worse.

Before a shell hits, depending on the shell, you may have a bit time to hide. Not much, seconds at best. So, you hide to stay not seen and when you hear the sound of artillery you try to make yourself even smaller. Usually you jump behind the next pile of rubble or whatever is there.

Early that night I came to a bigger street and some shells came down in front of me. I was still in a ruined building hiding, so no problem. I made it across the street a bit later and then saw the mess. A woman, I do not know what age, had caught shrapnel to her body and face.

She had somehow crawled or dragged herself to the entrance of a house and was lying there in shock.

It looked bad. I did not know what to do. She tried to touch her face but there was not much left. She kept on saying she cannot see. I told her to be calm and that help was coming. It was not, but I did not know what else to say. There was nobody to help and the only hospital with a few doctors and a few medications was in different part of the city.

Then I took her hand so that she would stop touching her face. She became quieter, almost relaxed. So, I sat there, holding her hand and she started talking about how nice the place was before the war. We sat and talked for maybe twenty minutes. I'm not sure if she really heard me, and then she was gone.

I thought that holding hands had helped make her last journey more relaxed.

I saw many people dying in my time during the war and always tried to give them gentle touch if they wanted. It usually has the same effect. They get more relaxed and peaceful. Some want to roll up and be left alone, but many more do not want to be alone.

Now that I work in emergency services, I know how important that is. Last week we had a terrible car accident with an older married couple involved. The man ended up dead right away, and the woman survived. I held her hand on the way to the hospital and a few days later she remembered and thanked me for that.

This is not only for a woman who is dying, but for a man too. If you still see and are in shock, you might feel like you are stuck in a bad dream. Someone holding your hand can help you bring you closer to normal.

So, if you can do anything to help, do it. If you know first aid and nobody else is already doing it, do it. Other than that, show them that they are not alone. Holding someone's hand can work wonders. They are scared and do not want to be left alone.

This can make big difference for someone even if it is in the last minutes of their life.

Survival Notes from Daisy:

Don't let the SHTF take away your humanity. If you can make someone less frightened in their last moments of life without risking your own, take the time and do it.

In at The Deep End...

There is a whole range of situations that look completely different in real life than in the survival realm on YouTube.

It is normal that you cannot bring the full scale of reality to a training situation but still some things need to be shown more realistically than they are shown in the usual shows on the internet.

I watched a few days ago a couple videos and read some stuff about safe river crossing in survival situations and noticed some things.

I will mention the most important:

Common sense (yes, common sense... again)

First a majority of those videos and articles describe river crossings in wilderness survival situations, and while some of those are pretty good and give you good advice about basic stuff like how deep, how wide, what kind of ground under the water, how fast, safest places to cross etc. they forget to mention urban river crossings.

In urban river crossing, there is a whole new set of things to think about like polluted water, garbage and different kinds of stuff in (like a car wreck, for example) in the river bed that can give you lot of troubles.

Also, videos usually show rivers that are up to your waist

deep, or rivers not too wide so you can use a fallen log to cross it.

But just like with all other internet survival, there is one *major* thing in those scenarios is missing – other people.

If your survival situation includes a river crossing in the middle of the day in peaceful country settings, where there is no single soul with possible bad intentions to you, and the only noise is birds singing etc. you are a lucky man, but most probably it is not gonna be like that.

Forget about videos of shooting anchor with a rope over the river and crossing it like that unless you are an SAS member in good condition. In reality, most of us cannot do that.

Also, most of the rivers in urban settings (and a lot of in wilderness settings) cannot be crossed by a handy fallen log.

Either there is no fallen log, or you do not have time to look for it, or it is pitch dark, or simply river is too wide for a f*cking fallen log.

Instead of looking for a fancy solution of survival river-crossing immediately I suggest you go from the start, from the very basic.

Check your survival plans (you bug out route for example) and see what kind of rivers there are. Do not forget to include areas that may be your secondary or tertiary choice for bugging out, remember that the plan is only that – a plan.

Now see what kind of rivers there on your way are, what kind of river beds, what banks there are. Remember sometimes what it looks like a good approach to the river may be mud hell where you can at least lose your shoes if not even something more important.

There are huge differences between wild rivers and rivers in urban settings where the river bed is controlled and paved or similar. Walking through those rivers require a different approach too.

Good advice is to think about the bridge as the first and easiest crossing over the river, take that as a start and then check possible pros and cons for crossing the particular river over the particular bridge.

In other words, do not go and drown yourself because you try to swim over the dangerous river just because you felt very "survivalist" while there is a bridge standing close without any danger to passing over that bridge.

Forget being fancy. Use common sense and choose the least danger in a particular situation.

Internet survival techniques

A lot of techniques that work beautifully on the internet turn into sh*t in real life. The reason for that is simple: most of the internet survival techniques are based on philosophical or fictional scenarios and cannot include all possible real-life factors.

Simply – reality can throw at you many factors that you did not think about.

Still, it is no reason not to learn and prepare for different situations.

I can share with you my experiences with "survival river crossings," my experience is quite different, and actually not smart at all, but I think there are lessons to be learned.

Swimming

It was around 3 am and I was in the part of the town where I should not be at that time of the night, because I should be home earlier than that.

I would like to say that I was there to trade, find food, scavenge or fight – it would sound more "survivalist" for the sake of this article and blog but the truth was that I was there to see a girl that I liked a lot.

On my way back, I found myself in one of the sudden raids. A 50-man group attacked the street and I ran from them through ruined houses and found myself on the bank of the river

I always kinda hated that river- I liked how it looked but I hated how cold, fast and treacherous that river could be.

It was pitch dark and I crawled downhill some 20 meters through small willow trees, and bushes on huge stones that stand on the bank. There was no f*cking fallen log there, just so you know.

I crawled through something smelly and soft, I felt like everything was rotten within that bush.

I could see the river. Small waves were wetting my shoes, and I was standing on a slippery stone holding a willow branch with one hand.

The riverbed was a mix of huge stones and sand, and depth went from 30 cm to 3 meters – depending on size of stones. The stones were very steep so you could actually swim under the stone (and probably drown there) or a strange current and whirlpool would do that for you, roll you and pull you under the stone and drown you there, or simply throw you on the stone and smash your head.

It can be a dangerous river for an experienced swimmer in broad daylight and a swimming suit.

I tried to see what was on other bank-some 20-25 meters far, tracer round flashes reflected on my eyes and all I could see was darkness on other bank and something moving in darkness. Was it the same willow trees or people with rifles, or maybe my imagination? At that time and situation seeing a guy selling popcorn on the other side would not be surprising, given how my imagination worked.

I expected any moment that enemy would shoot me, so adrenaline worked hard.

I had a backpack which was almost empty, a 22-rifle which was duct-taped

(two screws that holding steel part together with the wooden part were "worn off" so it was duct-taped to hold it together), a tobacco box, and some 15 bullets in my pockets.

As I heard a guy approaching my place, I hesitated for a second or two thinking what to do then I put rifle over my chest and jumped into the river. And I immediately started to drown.

The shock of the freezing river somehow turned off my adrenaline surge, and my thought was, "I am gonna die now."

In the next second, the river took me and rolled me all over and I felt my rifle sling was choking me. If I had enough voice and strength I would have yelled "help" to the guys that I wanted to run from. But at that time, I simply had no voice.

Crossing that river was not swimming – it was drowning. It took maybe 20 seconds for me to get to the other side, but it felt way longer for me, and I ended up some 100 meters downstream.

Several times the river threw me onto those big stones. I was trying to loosen my rifle sling all the time and when I finally managed to grab stone with my hands and stop the crazy movement, I was not even sure if I was on the same river bank or if I actually crossed river onto the other bank.

I was holding the stone for 10 minutes, probably, then I slowly crawled from the river.

I was on the other bank. I was frantically holding rifle sling. The rifle was falling apart, the steel part separated from the wooden part.

I lost my backpack, and my tobacco box too. I did not see from one eye because it was full of blood from a big wound on my forehead.

Later I figured out that I broke two fingers and a rib too.

But I was alive and on the other side. I had huge luck.

The point of the story is that sometimes crossing the river may look much more complicated and dangerous than finding the fallen log.

And very often crossing river is like a lot of situations in real survival – be ready to leave everything and take just your life. Or things that you like may pull you down and drown you.

Or is the point of the story to carry heavy duty trash bag with you all the time, so you can use it to put all your stuff inside and try to swim then?

Survival Notes from Toby:

River crossings are one of a great many examples of the

difference between 'internet wisdom' and reality. All techniques have limitations, and as Selco highlights what may work in one situation can well not work in another. On higher risk activities, such as this one, it is easy to get focused and fixated on the 'main risk' (in this case drowning) and forget about ALL the other risks that actually need to be identified, assessed and factored into the decision-making process. It is essential, that as individuals, when you are looking at 'life threatening' parts of your plans and preparations it is done so from a position of (true) understanding and **grounded in reality.**

Old Guys...

My great uncle was a drinking man. He would drink heavily from the moment he woke up until the moment he went to bed. But I do not remember ever seeing him stumbling, walking funny, or having problems with his speech.

When he was at home, his favorite spot was on the couch in the corner of the room, just next to the wood stove which was running always except on really hot days.

He drank from very small glasses (shot glasses). The bottle was never visible – he kept it behind the couch. On the table there was the silver box for cigarettes, with tobacco and papers for cigarette rolling inside, and his shot glass.

The table was an old type table with a glass plate on top of it, and under that glass, he kept the paper that says that government and state recognize him as a member and organizer of the early resistance movement against the German and Italian occupation during WW2.

The table, his cigarette box, his rakija, and everything else in his room was off limits for us kids. He lived with my grandparents, he never married, and he had no kids.

Actually, now when I remember, he himself was pretty much off limits for us kids. The only person who ever had some influence over him was my grandmother – his sister.

She was the only one who could tell him sometimes that he needed to do something.

He was one tough and dangerous old dude, sitting in that room. Drinking and staring in the spot where the wall connects to the ceiling.

Sometimes we kids snuck into the room, seeking stories or money from him. In return we would bring firewood from the shed for his never-ending stove fire.

He would give us money often from his big "veteran warrior" pension. Stories were rare.

Often the kids just sat there, talking about something. He would occasionally say "uhm" or "hmm" and stare in empty space.

He did not go out very much, except for his regular chess meetings in the local community hall, which was a war veteran organization and heavy drinking joint all in one.

People called it "half leg" because of several handicapped folks who were there all the time.

And I was a kid who often went with him there, my grandmother often would tell me "go with him there and wait for him." I guess she was worried for him.

The place was a big hall with old tables with games like chess and checkers on them. Great Uncle would sit down usually with same folks there, his old war comrades.

They would play chess, drink heavy booze, and over time they would usually forget that I was even there.

In that time, I was taught in the school that we were living in great socialistic and communistic society, where all people are equal, and that we got to that point through the heroic and noble fighting of the working class in WW2.

War and fights were something noble, heroic and full of sacrifice. Our war vets were clean; they were people who sacrificed themselves for our motherland – for a socialistic society.

I was taught like that. In my young mind, all was black and white.

Over time, I realized that folks at that table together with my great uncle had a different picture about war and fighting and honor.

They talked about everything, but with heavy slang and in what looked to me in that time as codes, and a lot of "remember the Mora (mountain) and how we ate our shoes?" and the answer would be "Yeah, f*ck it, and how many bodies there were."

A lot of that was not understandable to me. I did a lot of head nodding,

One of those chess games stayed in my mind over several decades of the time since I heard it at that table:

The man who played chess with my great uncle had

pieces of shell in his body. I think it was not an option to remove it so he grew old with that in his body. He had a couple of pieces in his arm and fingers, and while he was thinking about his next chess move, he would squeeze his fist and fingers and the pieces of shell in his fingers were producing a sound like something was chewing inside his hand.

It was fascinating to me at that time.

What I understood from their story was this:

He and my great uncle found themselves in some heavy fighting during WW2.

Their unit was carrying a lot of heavily wounded together with a lot of civilians who were running from German forces. A sudden attack of Germans made chaos and they together with a couple of guys got separated from the unit.

They manage to break out from the encirclement, then they hid inside some cave for a couple of days. They ate tree bark.

Days later they went out and wandered through woods trying to get to the safe territory. And then they stumbled onto members of their unit.

Actually, a pile of them.

In one small clear place in the woods, there were hundreds of bodies in a big pile, and the man with the "chewing" in his fist said he never before or later saw anything like that.

Soldiers and civilians were shot and put into a big pile of bodies in the middle of nowhere, and he said that lot of them were heavily wounded but still alive. Actually, they were put there intentionally still alive, to suffer more before they die.

They found a couple of women tied to the trees...Dead.

They quickly moved away from there, scared.

Later that night while they were resting, they heard noises. They quietly went to check and find out German soldier sitting down and bandaging wound on his leg, probably lost and separated from his unit.

They killed him with a bayonet, and as I understand they killed him slowly. That story terrified me to the bones, and I think I heard it only because they were pretty drunk and did not even realize I was with them.

My great uncle died a long time ago. He was a heavy drinker to the last breath.

At his funeral, there were flags and speech about honor and sacrifice, even his medals.

We never found his wartime machine gun, "Major," (an MP-40) that he hid somewhere after the war never giving up to anyone where it was. As I am older, I feel sorry I did not hear more about his experiences.

I am sure he cared a lot more for that machine gun than for speeches flags and medals.

I do not remember him as a war hero, and I am sure he did not think of himself as a war hero.

He was scared often while he was in a survival situation. He often did things that he did not like. He was not invincible, and he was ready for trouble again all the time.

He was a survivalist.

The point of this article (just like a lot of my articles) is the memory of something, in this case, the memory of my great uncle.

And there is one more point for you that is even more important:

Talk with old folks, with veterans, old or young. There is nothing like real life experience. Be patient. The best (or worst) stories are hardest to get, but it is precious knowledge.

It is a better prepper investment to hear how (and what) tree bark to eat then to buy 10 MREs.

Many years after my great-uncle experiences and events, I experienced similar things, hunger, fighting, piles of bodies…

It is in human nature, things like this are happening and will happen again…

Survival Notes from Toby

To anticipate the future, you MUST study the past. Neglecting to learn from others real life experiences whether by reading, watching interviews or talking with them in person is one of the most negligent activities those preparing can engage in. Studying real experiences, whether current or ancient, will reveal many of the essential truths you need to know to truly 'prepare'. It is that simple

How We Celebrated During the SHTF

I will write here a bit about how we celebrated.

Actually, we did not celebrate anything particular, like birthdays or Christmas or anything similar. Maybe we celebrated the fact that we are alive.

If we managed to have something like a safe house to fix something as a party, we just brought whatever we had and partied there. Usually it was two things, heavy homemade drinks and marijuana (everyone was growing that at the time). There was music sometimes. Sometimes music was in the form of some kind of musical instruments, or sometimes in very rare occasions in the form of a battery-powered stereo or boom box.

To understand how that looks, you first need to understand what all of it meant to us.

Every occasion for any kind of party was a chance to get away from rude and harsh reality. So, whenever I attended some kind of party it was a special. With very few things, it was great.

Sometimes a few cigarettes, a bottle of drink, and the good company of 3 friends was the best party that I ever attended, even before and after all of that.

And when somebody brought boombox and we listened to music, it was not like we listen to music today. It was like we listened to music for real, like we had never listened to music before or after. Magical. We felt that music, we felt those few cigarettes and alcohol.

It is actually a precious and special feeling. Simple things just meant a lot. Music alone was enough to get you "high." When you are so deprived of special things, things like that become very intense.

It is much easier to bond with people on an occasion like that. I could say it is spiritual and weird.

An important thing to mention also is that feelings and customs about getting together with girls and sex are moved on the scale.

If I wanted to speak in today's terms, if you attended some party and you had the will, a few joints or a bottle of alcohol, you had a great time, because boys and girls in those parties lived for that moment only. Nobody was sure if tomorrow was gonna come for them.

So, in reality if you attended some kind of party where we had 10-15 people including women, it was not like in parties before and after that. I guess it comes from fact that life was not worth too much so due to that, connections between man and woman could be made more easily than in normal times, much more easily.

If a girl wanted to connect with you, or you wanted to connect with a girl, you just asked. Some things just became easier to do, with lots of shortcuts. People just did things without regretting them because times were hard and so unpredictable.

Nobody wanted to have too many missed chances.

Every part of town, every street had something like a "safe house" for parties. Sometimes the houses changed, but mostly not. Young people still tried to get together, to do what most of the young people do. Party.

Friendship were made fast. Relationships were made fast and broken fast. Fun was fast and unpredictable.

One good thing which came from all of that was the fact that we did not have enough time to pretend in our ways of expressing emotions, for example, expressing our love. It was fast and very powerful. I guess the true nature of people is visible in hard times. Emotions can be expressed easily if you are aware that maybe you are gonna die tomorrow.

One place I remember was the basement of a partially burned house. In the small windows were bags of dirt, with very small openings for ventilation. The basement was divided into two big "rooms" with some old furniture, and all kinds of junk, like the engine cover from a ruined car, that we put on cinder blocks and used as a table. In other room there was a part which is separated with an old curtain and made like more private for "love" purposes.

The air was congested with smoke, so much you actually

did not need to ask for a joint. You just needed to breath inside and you gonna be fine.

We are all best friends for that night, because tomorrow may not come. We already speak stories that we are normally not going to speak because of the same reason. The music is giving you a feeling that there is a reason and sense for life. I am looking for a girl, so I can spend that night with her there, talk nonsense or story of my life, and she is looking for that too.

The parties were our little escapes and helped us to keep a bit normalcy in these hard times. Music was very powerful, so you might want to add a small music player to your preps if you do not have already.

15 or 20 years later sometimes, in rare occasions when I meet some of the girls from those parties, we just share a small smile. We do not talk.

Skills and Training

I have just finished delivering another 'Mile in My Shoes' (MIMS) down here in the Balkans. As always, it was a great event with many insights both for the students and me. Having finished the course, I got to thinking more about training in the survival and preparedness community.

Learning real survival skills in the field is something that cannot be substituted with anything else, but I see people often trying to do that.

Another mistake in learning skills is because they are often (almost always) taken out of context, or even more often, there is no context at all.

So, as a result, there is a whole bunch of people learning skills without the mindset of where and when to use it, or not to use it. I agree it is better to have skills even without context than not to have them at all, but that sounds more like an excuse than a justification.

Prepping is a BIG industry, and for lot of people it just needs to be "sugar coated" in order to be consumed.

Levels…

Two examples here:

When you say to me "SHTF" my first thought is the partial or complete collapse of the system and its services, so my second thought is about the lack of resources, and other people realizing that fact. My third thought is about fighting with other people for the resources still left.

That is *my* thought when you say SHTF.

For some people when they heard "SHTF" their first thought is, let's say a power outage that's going to last for about 12 hours. Their second thought is that they need to be comfortable for those 12 hours because after that government system and services will jump in and fix things.

For them, the SHTF is 12 hours without electricity...

Now what is clear here, I firmly believe that there will be event of complete prolonged absence of the system, (law, medical services, food distribution chain...) and some of the reasons could be new pandemics, economic problems, ethnic race, religious reasons, chaos, or simply some worldwide event.

Important thing is that people believing in any of these two levels have a lot to learn, but the starting point should be different.

For example, for the folks who think that it is impossible to meet anything more complicated then short disturbances in the electrical supply there is not too much use in throwing to them war scenarios and tactical shooting courses. For them it is maybe going to be fun, but there is no context there for them, no understanding.

It is more useful for them to read history books, speak with war veterans to try to understand that sh*t happens, even in most modern societies where similar things did not happen for generations.

That is the starting point for them.

Skills and Using Skills in Context

The real danger here is not about learning skills (which is again a great thing to do). It is about not understanding how to put it in the correct context in a real-life situation.

If you putting skills-learning into good, practical multi-day courses of basic primitive skills or wilderness skills and play it like that it is perfectly good and useful.

But again there are courses, books, publications, media, and YouTube videos of "how to survive end of the days", austere medicine courses, or simply "buy this and you will survive and thrive when SHTF" and inside are skills, and lists of items to learn or buy without connection to real situations, it is not only a scam, more or less – it is quite dangerous.

What I am trying to explain is best to show through an example.

Let's say there is "where there is no doctor" or "austere medicine course", and it is "advanced" too.

In short part of the course goes like this:

- Students start with drinking coffee and getting know

- each other
- It is nice, the weather is fine, there are snacks and food available, all students feel really comfortable
- They are injuring a pig (or other good-sized live animal) and then trying to stitch the pig or stop the bleeding in different ways
- The pig does not survive, and they learned something about stopping the bleeding, and they feel stronger (and disgusted) because of the amount of blood and screams and how 'real' the training was.

Good things here that students get some feeling about blood, and they learned something about bleeding and ways to stop it.

But the bad thing here is that they have been told that now they are ready for SHTF in terms of the bleeding and how to stop it.

In reality, they are not even close to being ready.

Preferably this is how this part of the course should look:

- No coffee on the course
- No food that day
- Bad weather is preferred
- Students are divided into two groups
- Preferable one at least one student in each group should be slowed down (let say evil instructor will "somehow" cause one of the students to have a serious case of diarrhea)
- Students in each group separately are instructed to

carry the pig 5 kilometers to a near mountain or a specified place using compass and map only
- Halfway to the mountain each group has been instructed to stab the pig, stop the bleeding and carry the pig to the mountain again (while the pig is screaming)
- Groups should hide one from another
- The group who get first to the mountaintop with a living pig is the winner

Now this is a very basic example, and it is here only in terms of an example, but the point here is to understand – there is no sense only from learning skills without putting and testing those skills in scenarios that need to be as close to real-life as possible.

I mean, if we are learning about stopping bleeding on someone when serious SHTF do you really believe that you'll be well-fed, healthy, in a good mental state, and perfectly capable for that?

There is a huge probability that you'll be in poor condition while you trying to stop someone's bleeding. Remember it is the SHTF. Actually, you may be in a condition where you may not be able to stop someone's bleeding at all.

What is the point of testing yourself if you do not push yourself at least close to the limits while testing?

It is much more important after some course, book, or YouTube clip to understand and realize that you are not yet ready, and to know your current limits than to be sure "you are ready for full SHTF" because your instructor told you that, or a book tells you that, while clearly, you are not.

If you know your current limits you know what more to learn or practice or achieve, and that is good. I learn something almost every day, and in many fields, there are unknown things for me and there is nothing wrong with that.

Remember…

"We don't rise to the level of our expectations; we fall to the level of our training."

~ Archilochus

Survival Notes from Toby:

If many preppers spent a fraction of their overall budget on credible contextual training as opposed to 'stockpiling', there would be many different and improved conversations happening on the realities of preparedness throughout media, forums and so on.

This is such a serious and significant topic it will actually be the result of a separate and specific book, as opposed to being reduced to a bullet point here.

Consistently the feedback we receive from students having completed our physical courses is one of overwhelming shock and surprised at how unaware or misinformed they were on many issues, some even the most basic and foundation principles that they have, to date, built all of their plans on.

The most important takeaway here and now though is **context is key.**

Under Pressure

A month or two ago, I made a promise to myself that I would write posts on my blog more often, because of a few reasons. First and most important is that you folks react positively to posts and want to read new posts more often. Other reasons are simply because there are always good topics for writing, and I simply want to write more often.

But just like with a lot of other good decisions, very often, real life jumps in and asks for all your time and attention. Life pressure gets you and you are simply living day by day under it.

Pressure dictates all your actions because you have to live, and sometimes writing a blog post is a fine luxury.

The point of this short intro is that I have learned, a long time ago, how to operate under the pressure. It is simply about switching off some of your functions and pushing on and on until you get again into the position of normal.

It is one of the most valuable lessons of surviving the SHTF, because if you do not do that when SHTF you will fail to operate properly and that will get you dead.

Anyway, now I finally have some time to write a post, I want to share with you this story.

The guy was about 45 years old when I met him. The

SHTF maybe two months before that, and I met him while we were trying to make sense of some military power generator that we found in abandoned army storage.

It was a hopeless attempt to make it useful. We did not have any clue about how that thing worked, what fuel was used, or even how to drag that beast to our home.

Even if we solved all those problems, starting it at home was like an invitation for bad folks. But we did not know any of that at that moment.

That guy was something like the "guy who knows stuff," because decades ago he served in the Army and his duty was to operate those things, so he was there to explain to us what we actually found.

The generator was partially buried under the rubble of a collapsed roof and all kind of junk and we spent a lot of time cleaning all that away. He helped us, and while he did that, he was murmuring something all the time, like he was talking with someone, or arguing about something with someone. I did not pay attention to that.

And when he started to explain to me what we had there, he talked slowly. I could see that he knew that stuff.

But then he went quiet and turn his head like he carefully listening to something. My senses immediately went up. I crouched and looked at him and whispered to him, "What, WHAT?" because I thought he heard someone that was coming which could easily mean danger.

He raised his hand to me wanting me to be quiet, and I went quiet. Then he kept his head in that position for a couple of seconds then said to me, "All good, man." Then he continued with an explanation about the generator.

A couple of minutes after that, he again went quiet and raised his hand giving me ae sign to be quiet and turned his head like he is hearing something suspicious.

I started to sweat, something was moving in my guts and I felt like we are gonna be jumped by someone. I almost wanted the shooting to start just to have a target to break down the fear.

Then he continued and asked me, "You do not hear anything?"

I said, "No, man." But actually, I heard a lot of things. The water pouring somewhere inside, ruins tapping very slowly, probably from the destroyed roof on some piece of broken glass, some piece of metal shivering somewhere in the wind, shots in the distance, explosions somewhere far.

But I did not hear anything suspicious or I was not sure.

He said, "Sorry man, I often hear things. Now I hear someone calling my name."

At that moment I froze, and a tingling slowly went over my back.

Here we were in the middle of a huge military complex, in almost pitch darkness. All kinds of noises that you have in destroyed buildings are there. Probably other folks are somewhere scavenging for useful things. Everyone has some kind of weapon, something smells awful – clearly there are corpses. There is no law and no punishment and I am sitting in middle of that with a psychopath?

He was smoking a big, fat, handmade cigarette and when he pulled the smoke, I could see his face. It was completely peaceful, but all that I could think was did he have ae knife close to him?

I remembered seeing that knife while it was still a little bit light from the dying day, it was on his belt, a big kitchen knife.

My friend was somewhere around scavenging. I was alone with this guy.

The guy continued, "Sometimes I hear music, but mostly I hear people calling me. Usually I know and I am aware it is only in my head, but from time to time, I just have to ask if someone else is hearing it, because it is so real and I know I am not crazy. I like when I hear music, usually there are my favorite songs."

I said, smartly, "All good man, it happens." But in my head, I was waiting for my friend to come back and I was thinking "F*ck the generator, f*ck the barracks, this dude is crazy!"

Then the guy said, "Yeah, forget it, you do not hear it" and continued with explanations.

My friend got back, and we moved from there. And anyway, the generator was junk.

I was angry at my friend because he connected us with that crazy dude. I yelled at him, "I almost sh*t myself there in the pitch dark with him and the voices in his head."

My friend said, "Oh, he is fine, do not worry. He is a fine guy; he was an electrical engineer when the war started and the militia imprisoned him for a week and beat him all the time for fun."

Every day they would bring him in front of the prison and put a blindfold on his eyes and make a firing squad and acted to the last moment like they gonna shoot him. After one week they released him. He then started to hear voices. He was a genius, but with a bunch of people inside his head."

After that story, I just said, "Sh*t."

Months later, I was on the upper floor of my house, drinking and smoking, and having a moment of some kind of weird personal peace.

Noises of explosions and gunfire were there, mostly in distance. The moment was fine for me.

And then I heard music, and it was one of my favorite songs actually.

My first thought was, "Great, my favorite song!"

5 seconds after that I jumped as if someone had stabbed me, remembering and thinking, "Oh God, I am losing my mind, oh no, please!"

I ran down, entered my house, scared my family, and pulled my relative out from the house asking him, "Do you hear it? Do you f*cking hear it, man?"

He was angry at me because I pulled him out violently. He said, "Do I hear what?"

"The song, do you hear the song?"

He said, "Yes, it is a Drago, man. They are probably drunk there."

I was staring at him, not understanding what he is trying to say. Then slowly I realized things:

Drago was the nickname for Army Armored Personnel Carrier (APC) with speakers on it – a propaganda vehicle. Usually, they blew our brains out with propaganda all the time, public declarations, calls to surrender, all kinds of junk, sometimes patriotic songs, insults and threats of what they were gonna do to us all the time, but never good music.

It looked like someone in that APC got bored from propaganda and junk and finally put on some good music, or simply he got stoned.

I asked him again, "You hear it?"

He said, "Yes man, I hear it, you are fine, you are just drunk."

I repeated to myself, "Thank you, thank you, thank you/ I am not going crazy."

Later, in the next couple of months, I met more folks who lost it. A couple of times I personally heard strange things and saw people who were not there, usually when times got really bad.

Pressure on the human body and particularly human mind in a real SHTF is usually huge and you can expect weird things sometimes. The brain will play tricks on you, and sometimes you can just lose it.

Prepare not to lose it.

In my physical courses, I pointed out often that real survival things and skills are tested best in circumstances when you are scared, and when you think that you saw something that is not there or hear something.

I am trying to test you in those circumstances.

That usually means you are so overwhelmed with events, and pressure is at the highest level, and the real art is to perform perfectly on that level.

It is up to you and your well-prepared mindset whether you are gonna "lose it" or not.

In the shortest summary, you need to prepare bullets, beans, band-aids, and *brains* (mindset).

Survival Notes from Toby:

Do your very best to know how you, your loved ones, and anyone you intend to have around you in tough times reacts to stress, both short term and in prolonged situations.

Group dynamics can affect any and all plans either in a positive or EXTREMELY negative way.

It is essential that you are honest and objective in your assessments on how you and others actually react. Once you are 'in the moment' t is too late to do anything about this, so this topic fits heavily into the 'forewarned is forearmed' category.

Survival Situation – Action Wins

Usually we take for granted what we see on TV or other media. You can say, "No, I am always suspicious and do not believe all this" but most of us are forming our opinions unconsciously. Over time, we have some opinions, and we are just certain about some situations and solutions. We believe some things just work like that because we saw it so often. Even if we are not experiencing that in real life, or even if we are not spending much time thinking about these things.

You see an action movie and people just shoot each other like it's no big deal.

As I have said before, the act of shooting is not so hard, actually it is pretty easy. But the decision to shoot someone is much harder. And a great majority of people have problems with that decision in real life.

At one of the local meeting during our hard time, people tried to organize some stuff like how to protect homes, to set up some kind of neighborhood watch, or something like that. Most of the guys on one side were armed with guns or some other kind of weapon. On the other side mostly all the people were without previous experience with guns or weapons.

One guy who had a rifle was a taxi driver in normal times. He bought the rifle a few days before everything started. He was probably just getting know about the basics of gun handling, but he was trying to look dangerous and relaxed at same time. In the middle of some kind of meeting and yelling he somehow got into an argument with another guy, who had a hunting knife on his belt.

Very soon the argument was out of control and the man took his knife out of the belt and started to approach the guy with rifle. It was not something like a jump or sudden attack. It was more like a slow threatening walk with knife toward the man. The ex-taxi driver had enough time to raise his rifle and simply shoot the guy with knife, but he did not.

Instead, he got finished off, stabbed multiple times.

People just left the area and moved on. The ex-taxi driver guy was left there. I guess his relatives picked him up some time later, because the body was gone the next day.

It was not about his speed or anything like that. I guess he was just stuck with the whole situation. He hesitated too much. He was not prepared for that threat. He was not ready. Call it as you like.

Now when you look at it, the whole situation looks strange that the guy did not just raise the rifle and fire. But to do that you need first to cross over some things in your mind. That change takes time.

I have seen more situations like this one. Sometimes seconds count, and your will to do things.

My ex-coworker bled to death because his wife froze when heavy caliber bullets cut off his arm. Even though she had some kind of tourniquet and some bandages close to her, she did not use anything. She just screamed while blood was pouring all around him.

It is hard to get your mind into a state where you do not think too much, instead of just acting accordingly. It is hard to do that especially in not-normal times. Hard times can teach people to act like that, but it is a hard school, and a lot of people failed.

The great majority of us are the same as that taxi driver. Only a few of us are like the guy with knife.

This is not about becoming a killer, or the toughest man. **It is about acting instead of freezing.** Hopefully your SHTF situation will not be as violent as mine. But remember that human reaction to act or freeze can happen to all of us. Prepare people around you to not freeze but act by practicing drills.

There is reason why you do "boring" airplane and ship rescue drills. It teaches you to act and this might make difference between life and death.

An 'Ordinary Day'

A lot of people wonder what an 'ordinary day' was like during the SHTF. I was thinking about this and remembered this day. I think it is a good illustration and answers this question. It's odd to say but we were often glad of ordinary days when nothing too bad happened.

The rain had been falling down for days, and we all felt wet and soaked with it.

Moisture was in our pores, our clothes, and kind of in our heads too.

It was the kind of weather that pushes down and back the smoke from your stove, back into your room instead of through the chimney.

Holes in our roof were plugged, more or less, in the way that we managed to channel the leaks into numerous pots and canisters, in order to keep ourselves dry and also to collect water.

Being dirty is bad, but being dirty and smelly during several days of rainy weather is simply awful.

We dried our clothes above the stove, evaporation of dirty clothes together with smell of dirty bodies, bad "tobacco" (we had discovered some new tree leaves which we used as a substitute for tobacco), handmade oil lamps, and tea boiling on stove (we called it sometimes 'soup', other times 'tea') made a mixture of smells which simply added to the depression of the whole situation.

In days like that alcohol intake would go up high.

When the weather was fine, I liked to go on the second floor, remove the tarp and plywood "setup" from roof hole that was made with mortar shell a few months before, sit under it, watch the blue sky, and drink.

Other folks would say, "He is up there again waiting for mortar shell to land on his head" but it was nice and peaceful to do it, and sometimes I just did not care.

Even that weird relaxation was not an option because of the endless rain. In days like that, we were the closest to animals as we could be.

We ate potatoes for days, we managed to get it through one UN convoy that somehow entered city months ago, and it was a mess to get those bags of potatoes because while UN forces tried to organize some kind of delivery system- like small bag of potatoes to each family that showed up folks simply overrun them and started to fight each other over it.

Several people got killed then, but we managed to bring home quite a stash of it.

We were happy because of the potatoes, but a few days later rumors exploded that potatoes that we got were poisoned, actually that they were not for human use. The rumor was that the potatoes were meant for seed only or something like that and apparently, they were treated with very harsh chemicals.

We continued to eat them; the only difference was that we were not so happy anymore about it.

And then a trade opportunity came to us.

It was my turn to go to visit the guy who "had some stuff for sale or trade" or at least that was information that we get it.

The good thing about this guy was the fact that I knew him a little bit prior SHTF and when SHTF he had strong connections and had interesting stuff from time to time. He was something like a "trustful" trader, he kept his stuff in his house and did trades there, which usually meant either he is stupid or very protected, and he was not stupid.

"Gogo" was his nickname, and we felt good because we are going to trade with him because his reputation was pretty big and he (we thought) could not afford too many bad stories about trading with him.

It was as safe a trade as it could be in those days.

My relative showed me our possessions for trade while we were preparing for trip – it was 10 packs of Kent cigarettes, and when I saw that, it was like I saw UFO landing in the backyard, with aliens bringing to us food, water, candies, and safety, and flying me then to a rock concert.

In that period cigarettes were rare, sometimes impossible

to find and we were even lucky to have tobacco-which was not actually tobacco but ground "tree" of the tobacco plant, or simply all kind of tree leaves that we experimented with.

White filter Kent cigarettes at that moment were something like a wet dream of every smoker.

It was a pleasure to even see them, to smoke them meant pure happiness.

I asked him where he got the Kents. He answered "from some mercenaries" and I did not want to ask more, I did not care.

We started our way to Gogo's house around midnight because the plan was to be at the most dangerous place around 0100 hrs.

On our way back we would choose a different way.

That dangerous place was a big opening between houses, some 100-150 meters of space where we were completely open to the nearby hill where the Anti-Aircraft gun and few M-84 machine guns were located.

That machine gun was nicknamed "sijac smrti" which translates from my language to English as a "death seeder" or "death bringer" or something similar, and when I first heard that nickname my thoughts were: "oh c'mon somebody is watching too many movies, it is a bombastic nickname for an ordinary weapon."

Later when I was targeted first time from that weapon

when they shot at me, I corrected myself and I thought something like "Death seeder? It is more, much more, it is Satan, it is hell, it is pure horror…"

And much later I also realized it is more or less common nickname for some other similar weapons.

So, I built pretty fast my respect for "*sijac smrti.*" That sh*t was way too fast and deadly. It sounded like a whole bunch of small deaths flying directly at you while they scream.

(Years later, after my SHTF ended and all things go back to some kind of let's say normal, I was watching a member of a Serbian elite parachute unit, while he was trying to explain his battle experience to another guy.

He and his small unit were holding position in dense woods on some hill during NATO bombing of Serbia. It was on Kosovo, and they were attacked by Albanians. The Albanians were much stronger by numbers, but poorly trained, as he said, and he and his comrades did pretty well. Morale was high; they were tough guys.

And then he said airplanes came. He said planes were firing from cannons, destroying the hundreds-of-years-old trees like simple matches and obliterating his unit.

But he said that was not the scariest thing. The pure horror was the sounds of the planes and cannons while they were firing down on them, while he was trying to explain that he opened his eyes wide and said, "It sounded like there are 10 big cows in the air flying to you and they are screaming because they are being slaughtered."

Another guy was watching him probably not understanding what is so scary about that sound to terrified big strong elite dude.

And I said to myself, "Oh man, I know that horror.")

Anyway, we came to that open space without too many problems.

Nobody knows what kind of view they had there on the hill, but during the night they fired often, without real cause, on that opening, so it was a matter of luck. Sometimes you are going to be shot. And somehow it was a myth that it is safest to cross it around 0100hrs.

At that time there were many openings like that in the city with different weapons and different tactics for crossing it and different myths about it how to cross it safely.

A lot of folks find God and faith on openings like that while they run or crawl over it.

Of course, a lot of folks ended up dead there, too.

I have seen guys being shot dead there while they ran as fast as they could. I saw some crazy dudes walking slowly there and nothing happened. Some guys were wounded and screamed there for hours with their guts hanging out until they died… There were no rules.

We sat down behind the wall next to the opening and I told my relative, "Okay, give me the cigarettes."

He said, "It is not smart; it is for trade."

I did not care, so he gave me one pack, I opened it and smoked a cigarette.

It was so cool to smoke it, a white paper cigarette with a white filter, after a long time of smoking trash tobacco in any kind of paper that we could get.

It smelled like perfume to me at that moment.

I finished it and said to him, "Okay, I can die now if I need to."

He answered to me, "F*ck you, man."

We ran across that space while rain was pouring down and nothing happened. Not a single shot on us.

Gogo's house was close by after that, and nothing dangerous happened until we came to his home.

After some guy shows up to us in the yard, we were allowed to enter the house with a weapon, which was a good feeling but not necessarily a good sign. But when we saw Gogo, he recognized us, and after some casual conversation which included people that we together knew, we started to feel better.

We entered a small room, two of us and two of them, sat down and had a drink.

Rakija (a strong, locally brewed spirit) was available then, so it was not a surprise when he gave us two glasses with that drink.

Numerous different kinds of that drink were circulating around. Most often it was pure poison, simply not a finished product from a destroyed distillery diluted with water, but this was soft and nice.

The room where we sat was something like a weird version of a display room for customers, so we could see all kind of different stuff around in bags or open cabinets.

I saw a pack of beer, even couple of bottles of coke, and the room strangely smelled of coffee which was a high luxury in that time. Everything there was set up for turning your senses to want stuff.

Bags full of something were lying everywhere and a steel cabinet from army barracks was locked in one corner.

After some chatting, he put down his hand under the table and put a *Zolja* (wasp) single-use RPG on the table and said to us, "This is good stuff for you folks, and it is cheap."

I take it and said to him. "It is an empty man, fired, useless."

He opens his mouth laughed with joy and said, "Okay, man, okay. You know that and I know that, but how many idiots outside know that? You could paint a water pipe in green and state it is an RPG and 90 percent of folks would trust you in the dark. This looks real, man. Just fill it with something, point that thing at someone and ask the right questions."

"Yea, and then I can be killed by the guy who knows that weapon was fired a long time ago. He could choke me slowly with his bare hands, so no thanks."

He said, "Okay, okay. I agree, but here is the right one," and then he pulled out brand new one, the same type, not used.

We said, "No, man, we do not need weapons right now."

He said, "Okay, okay, I have this too, I sell a lot of these and everyone is a satisfied man."

Then his buddy opened a wood cabinet behind his head and gave him a wooden box, the size of a shoebox, a bit smaller.

I look at my relative and look back at me with short surprised expressions.

It was a wooden engraved box, pretty common in households in this region prior the war, something that you would put as a display in your living room, and when you opened it there was a small wooden bird with the mechanism inside, the mechanism was activated by opening box, and melody would start, like birds singing…

Is he trying to sell us a wooden singing bird in the middle of the civil war?

Then he opened the box and pushed it to me.

The wooden bird was not inside, the box was full – maybe some 25 vials of penicillin. It was pretty expensive stuff.

I took one bottle and checked it. The expiration dates were good, a Serbian manufacturer, the labels looked originally "glued" on bottles.

But on the top of the bottles, some of those were missing a small thin metal "cap" that is covering rubber sealed "plug" (through that rubber Penicillin powder is being diluted and aspirated into the syringe).

The first thought was that some those of the bottles could be used and then filled with flour.

He noticed what I was checking and said, "Yeah, some of the caps are missing man. It is being transported through some rough situations before they came to me, but they are good."

I said, "Cool stuff man, but we do not need it." It was bit suspicious stuff and way too expensive for us at that moment.

He asked finally what we want.

And I said, "Meat, man!"

He leaves the room and gets back with one can, and I know he finally meant business because he brought only one can, without showing how much he actually has of it.

He put it on the table and said: "I have it, it is *konj* (horse)."

In that time, different kinds of canned food was circulating around, a lot of expired stuff, broken, spoiled… But popular was "horse."

The horse had good and bad sides, but better than bad sides.

It was canned meat, stamped label on the tin was saying only something like "help from EU" or "help from UNHCR." I do not remember exactly.

Funny thing was that under the marking "type of meat" was written "meat." Just that: "meat." It was kind of partially cooked meat with a huge amount of grease inside that looked like snow.

If we ate grease alone it induced bad cases of diarrhea, but you could use it for cooking, melt it and use as oil for the lamp, or simply folks stated that it is good to put it in places where you have pain, like an ointment ("bad knees pain – horse grease, rifle butt to the head – horse grease…)

The meat alone did not have any particular taste, it was unrecognizable, and people simply after some time said it is horse meat because nobody had a clue what exactly it was.

So that can was nicknamed "horse."

There were attempts to call it "kangaroo" but "horse" just stuck to it.

Simply put, it was usable.

He asked what we have, and I took out one pack of Kents. He said "nice" without too much enthusiasm, but his buddy stood up and said, "Where you get these, man? Cool."

And at that moment I knew we were gonna get a good deal because they were interested. They just kind of "blinked."

Gogo said to his buddy, "Sit down a man and shut up. You smoked too much pot." (Use of cannabis was rampant during the war.)

And he asked how much of these we have, I answered it depends how much horse he has and the bargaining started.

In the end, we agreed that we were gonna gave him 9 packs for 15 cans.

It was great to deal for us, and probably a cool deal for him because he knew folks who would appreciate those cigarettes a lot, I guess.

After setting up a deal, and after we exchanged stuff, we chatted for a bit and he offered me a handmade cigarette.

He gave me a small tin box with hand-rolled cigarettes.

I looked into the box, it used to be a small box for cigarillos I think and I looked at the box. I liked it very much.

We carried our tobacco in all kinds of different bags, boxes, foils or whatever, but that tin box simply was laying down in my hand so cool. It was foreign stuff, clearly.

It somehow clicked and perfectly laid in my hand when I took it.

I gave it back to him asked where he got that, and he clearly saw that I "blinked" this time.

He said, "Offer something. It is a nice box, man."

I only had that one more pack of Kents, with a missing cigarette inside (which I wanted originally to keep for myself).

I pull it out from my pocket, gave it to him, he said "ok, I'll give the cigarette box for this pack"

It was outrageous price, and I could almost feel my relative sending thoughts to me like "You fucking idiot, a pack of cigarettes for the tin box? We could get more meat for that!"

But I liked the box.

Then Gogo said, "Wait for the second, cigarettes are missing from the pack. It is opened."

I said, "Yes, but still a man, only one is missing and this is Kent, real cigarettes."

Then he opens a drawer from the desk and pulls the hammer from it. We almost jumped ready for a fight, but he took a hammer and hit the tin box.

Then he said, "Okay, one cigarette is missing in your pack, the box is a little bit damaged on one end now, but still working, now it is a fair deal. We need to keep some rules in our business. It is reputation, man!"

I was looking at him, realizing that he had kind of lost it, just like most of us did at that time.

But we made the deal done, and all went well.

We got home in one piece, we ate those cans mixed with herbs and potatoes. An older member of the family was happy with the grease on his knees for some time… I heard a lot of b*tching because of that tin box trade, but I survived.

The war ended and years went by. I lost the tin cigarette box, Gogo moved to Canada, and I heard he has an apartment decorating business, and sometimes play guitar in some clubs, and has drugs issues.

Then one year, my wife and I were doing the big renovation in my old house, and in some box, with all kind of mess she pulls out that tin box and said to me, "Oh it is some box for cigarettes, are we gonna throw it away or do you need it?"

Then she opened it, and inside she read the small words that I wrote a long time ago "GOGO" and date of the trade.

She asked me, "What is it? Who is Gogo? Is it a man or woman?"

From all of the explanation that I could give her somehow

words that came from my mouth were "Yep, I could have got maybe two horses instead of that box during the war if I were smart."

"You had horses during the war? Did you ride it? I thought this was a city siege! Where in the world did you get horses?" she said looking suspiciously at me. She had spent the war years in Germany without too much clue how it was here in reality.

I said smartly, "No, no. I didn't ride horses. We ate them, it was good stuff."

Then she looks at me with horror stating "You killed and ate horses! How could you? They are beautiful animals!"

And then finally I said, "You know what, forget it. It is a long story, just throw away that box, it is useless."

Still, for a week or so she had suspicious looks at me from time to time.

Survival Notes from Toby

There is a fascination, to the point of obsession, it seems, on people's interest in 'Barter and Trade' during tough times. This article gives some great detail on how messy, complicated and fraught the process during disastrous times bartering and trading really is and how some of the hardest trades will be for the most basic of supplies... This article, more than anything, offers a great 'reality check' for the reader...

You Get What You Give – But Different

Some things about mentality and about morality changed drastically.

Every man changed in some way, some of us more, other less. Some people welcomed that change in their thoughts and saw whole new situation as some chance to do things that they could not do in normal times, not without punishment from system.

Most of the people accepted some things over the time almost without noticing it. For example, you might wake up one day with thoughts that to steal things had become almost normal, useful. It became a "must-do" thing.

Even with some newly-accepted behavior, people still had some judgment about what is bad and what is okay.

It was distorted, but it still was there.

The easiest way to explain it would be to say that almost everyone did things that normal people in normal times could not accept as a normal behavior but comparing to some other people's actions it was nothing. It was like the scale of what is good or bad was moved all together for everyone. Facing all the killing and misery, smoking marijuana became accepted by everyone. Humans look for an escape and alcohol was too precious.

But one thing is for sure, whenever I hear these days somebody says: "I will not do that if SHTF" or "I'll do only that if SHTF" – whenever I hear that I feel sick.

Wait and see...

The truth is this: **You never know how far you are going to go in order to survive. There is no way to know that before SHTF.**

Everything else is only talking and discussing in front of PC, in nice and warm room, safe, not hungry or thirsty and not under fire or with the high chance of losing one's life or the likelihood that loved ones are going to get murdered at any time...

And to make things clear, I am not approving of those things that I wrote about. I am not advocating some actions. Everyone has to find the line and choose his own "good or bad" actions. I am just sharing what happened and how I experienced it.

It is one thing to suggest what kind of medicines you must have in storage, but for some other things there is no advice. It is all on you. It is a mindset thing and no equipment can help.

Most of the people, a great majority of people, are ready to say instantly, "I am a good man, and I'll do only good things when SHTF."

The truth is, when SHTF, a lot of those good and nice people forget those strong decisions, mostly after the first few close gunshots or explosions, or after finding out that the local food store is gone, just like any other store.

I, like most of you, (I guess) want to believe in fact that some kind of punishment gonna catch up to all the people who did or who are gonna do bad things.

Here is what might have caught up with one guy.

Before SHTF, this man was a small thief, a pickpocket guy who steals wallet, and does some small cons to naive people at the market, maybe smuggling some things. He was not even a big criminal, actually he was nobody. When SHTF he recognized his chance and in a short time he had changed from nobody to become a powerful man with group of some 200 well-armed man.

He was something like strong charismatic leader, the kind of man who would know how to organize small groups of people from lowest aspects of life. He was like a God to them.

In some time, he was in control of some vital functions, like the organizing of food coming into that area, through some convoys. In that time, you could be rich with a few bags of flour, so imagine the amount of power and control if you get all the flour from convoys of trucks full with flour.

When everything ended, he was a rich and powerful man, a man with his own enterprise, and his own people everywhere.

He did not leave area when everything ended. He was

even more powerful. He became active in public life. Some people would have given everything to be close to him. Media even called him a philanthropist, helping the poor, giving contributions to orphanages, or giving donations to rebuilding schools.

People whispered in cafés about his famous parties which lasted for days and nights, filled with women and drugs. He was a powerful and untouchable man.

And then one morning the maid found him hanging from some window knob, naked, with his swollen blue tongue out, and his own waste beneath him. Rumor was that he had nightmares for years. Nobody knows for sure.

But I remember a story from some other time when baby food for newborn babies was very hard to find, and even when you find it to trade then trader could ask a lot of things for that. Well in that time this man just kept baby food from aid and sold it for astronomical amounts, and even he mixed that food with some things when it becomes very rare, things not good for babies to make it seem like more, and then sold it to people.

I like to think there is a reason why he died like that: alone, naked, and dirty.

So, keep in mind even if the scale or level of what is ok and what not shifts it still makes sense to only do what you have to do. Accept the new reality quickly, adapt to it, and do what you have to do to survive.

People easily get seduced by the dark side and many will fall for it.

Some Thoughts on 'Reality' TV

A long time ago, (years ago now), I wrote a blog post on something like a 'review' of one of the popular survival shows, and I kind of "crushed" that show because it was full of techniques that looked cool on TV but will get you killed in reality. Later I decided that I will not do anything like "show reviews" because it is an industry that you cannot beat.

That said, I have to say my piece again!

I read a few days ago (maybe some of you read it too?) about the newest survival show that's supposed to start. This time in Russia.

It is gonna be set *"on a large island in the Ob River, the seventh longest in the world, chasing a 100 million-ruble ($1.7 million) prize on a nine-month survival mission in winter temperatures as low as minus 50C."*

And he continues: *"Everything is allowed. Fighting, alcohol, murder, rape, smoking, anything."*

And: *"The survival rate on the island will be filmed and broadcast 24 hours a day on an internet TV channel,"* Pyatkovsky said.

While I do understand how survival shows attract

attention and earn good money, simply because they are interesting, (I guess) to average folks who do not have a chance to test their survival skills, I still do not understand the amount of stupidity in the majority of them and lack of common sense.

Does anyone have the thought that people are gonna die because they learned something the wrong way from those survival shows?

This newest Russian show I think beats them all. Do they think it is game? Rape? Have we gone so deep down as a society and humanity that we throw in rape as an option in a survival show? And we put it down on the same level of "wrong" as an alcohol and smoking? (*"Everything is allowed. Fighting, alcohol, murder, rape, smoking, anything."*)

Anyway, I do not have high hopes in survival shows when it comes to learning something, from a whole bunch of shows there are a couple of shows that are usable, and people in those shows do not run, jump too much, or do things the 'hard way' (when there is a clearly easier way).

People in good shows are usually showing good survival techniques for survival, not fancy and dangerous that attract views and numbers (and earn a lot of money).

Also, "real survival shows" that are recorded and broadcast all over the internet live are not real, people usually do not act real when they live all over the internet. It is a pure show, not survival, folks somehow tend to forget that.

One more interesting thing about this Russian survival show is that one of the possible contestants says: "*I want to do something so mad and unforgettable so that people later say "do you remember that girl"... We only live once and we must make the best of our lives. I am ready*"

Mad and unforgettable? Best of your lives? You are ready?

Some things cannot be part of the game, not even in hints...

My friend told me a story a long time ago.

...He was a part of a small squad unit who got ambushed in street and shelled with mortars.

A house wall collapsed on him and he lost consciousness.

He woke up in the middle of the night, under the rubble of the wall, alone if you do not count his fellow next to him – his buddy that had the only torso, everything below his belly was gone. He was dead, of course.

Everything was peaceful. Nobody else was there. His comrades from the squad were not to be seen or heard.

He started to try and dig himself out of the rubble when he heard noises of people approaching.

Group of some 20 enemy men, together with 5-6 women approached and entered house across the ruined house where he was lying.

The only thing that separated him not to be seen is a

partially destroyed the wall with a window opening on it and the fact that it was the night.

Behind that opening, he was lying under the rubble.

He said that armed men together with imprisoned women entered house leaving one guy in front of the house.

After some 20 minutes screams started from the house, together with the laughter of the men, it was clear that they were torturing and raping women inside the house.

My friend said he heard comments like "bring her here" or "move her on the table" and stuff like that, and then a few gunshots.

It continued like that for a couple of hours. My friend tried to remove dirt and rubble from him, but it was impossible, a piece of concrete wall was on his legs, and he was afraid to death to make too much noise, the guy on guard in front of the house was standing maybe 10 -15 meters from him.

His mouth was full of pieces of dirt from the wall and broken teeth, and he said that night he suddenly become a man of faith-he prayed so hard not to cough, not to be heard, because he knows he would be shot to death maybe tortured before.

Out of a couple of women, he remembers one of them refused to "cooperate" – they gave extra attention to her, he said probably with a knife...

He had rifle next to him, and he said that he started to pray to God to give him the strength to shoot himself because he could not stand it anymore. But he did not have the courage for that.

Then he wanted to use the rifle to shoot the guard and to try to shoot at the others when they rush out, but he was even afraid for that because he would end up dead.

Then he cried silently.

He says he was listening to screams almost all night, he also said that he literally shit and pissed in his pants out of the horror from the screams, and out of fear for his life.

Then he heard a couple more gunshots from the house. Guys went out from the house, and left the area without noticing him.

He said everything went calm, the only sound at that moment was the very distant sound of jet planes very high (NATO coalition regularly had high attitude flights in order to maintain no flight zone above war territory).

Before he passes out, probably because shock and loss of blood, he said two thoughts formed in my head, first was "I am a coward" and second was "thank you, God, because I am alive."

He woke up a couple of hours later in a British UN forces field hospital. Their unit found him in the morning and took him inside an armored vehicle. War ended, he took down his uniform and left rifle.

He married and had a kid, he went through a serious drinking period, he "touched" some drugs too, he divorced, lost his job. He became more or less a not-functional man.

But he never forgot that night when "God gave him life again" but also when he realized that he was coward too. And what he did not say is that night actually destroyed his life.

By now, you have probably realized that some of my articles are just memories, without a clear message or point. It is up to you to draw point or see the message.

It is like that with real life – often there is no sense and message, or there is a different message for each one of you.

But real survival usually is not the "best time of your lives" and you may conclude that you are simply not ready for some things.

Some things cannot be "played" before you experienced it in reality.

Survival Notes from Toby:

As prepping becomes more popular and increasingly mainstream, it in turn becomes more attractive and lucrative to different market sectors, including various media outlets and platforms. This is a very problematic situation, as it takes an industry that already has massive problems with the credibility of a lot of the information circulated and further dilutes and muddies the information down. It is essential readers begin to discern and differentiate the difference between entertainment (in the media sense) and educational content (in terms of useful, credible, contextual information).

Any and all 'reality' shows are driven by agendas, and it is relatively safe to say none of those agendas will ever be to show the truth of good and accurate preparedness. Again, be aware of what information you place your trust and faith in...

Some Thoughts on Food...

OK, I want to look at something very specific.

As you know I like looking at the aspects of the survival mindset. I agree that you may have the mindset of a warrior or really hard survivalist but still some basics need to be covered.

Basics like food.

Food

Food is something that you cannot live without, and just like about any other basic survival topic, a whole bunch of books have been written about it, what food to get and how to store, prepare it, etc.

While I am not going to write a book about food, I will mention a few basic things that you need to consider, based on my SHTF experience.

Have What You Like to Eat?

Yes, it makes sense to store food that you kind of like to eat. But on the other hand, if you hate canned tuna, for example, and there is a sudden huge discount of canned tuna why not buy it and store it, you can trade it, or simply (trust me) you will eat it if you have to.

Do not miss a great deal just because you do not like some food (or you think you do not like it).

Another point here is that SHTF is stress for your body (and mind), huge stress.

Your body will need food that is balanced and good for you more than ever. So, if you have the wrong eating habits and eat too much unhealthy food, maybe it is the time to change your habits, learn some stuff, start to eat good food, and start to store it.

When SHTF you will need your maximum strength, and since you "are what you eat," you can conclude that stuff in your pantry will have a big role in how tough you are going to be when THE SHTF.

What Food?

It is a matter of being practical or having common sense (again).

You are storing food for the SHTF, so it makes sense to think about few things that food needs to cover.

1. It needs to be in amounts large enough to cover your or your family's needs over a certain period of time. Do some calculations in order to have a clear picture what amount of food will get you through how long a period of time
2. It needs to be packaged in a way that gives you options to move it quickly and hide it in different places. Small packaging, cans, vacuum sealed, MREs,

sealed buckets, small packages of sugar, and similar packaging is preferable. You also want packaging that gives you less chances of spoiling whole storage if something goes wrong (water, infestation, etc.).
3. Preparation of the stored food preferably needs to be as simple as possible, not time consuming. It also needs to have as little impact as possible on your other resources. For example, if you store food that needs a lot of time to be prepared and a lot of wood to burn in order to make it ready for eating you are doing something wrong. MREs are a good example of foods that require minimal preparation.

In a lot of cases, you will have just enough time to eat something quickly, not to spend a couple of hours making complicated meals.

"Fancy" items

Yes and no. If you are preparing on a budget then forget about fancy items, stuff like junk food items, useless candy, and similar.

On the other hand, if you have covered your basics really well, then why not? Have things that you can use for trade because in any situation there are always going to be people with extra money or resources who will want to spend it on "fancy" things.

Also, think about items that may be kind of comfort food for you and have some of that stored too. There will be days when a piece of food like that will make a huge difference for you.

I just want to be clear, make sure you have all of the basics well-covered before you worry about adding 'fancy' items to your food supplies.

"It Is All in Your Head"

Do not forget about the mental aspect of everything.

Here is one small memory from the war, from the first period of adapting to it. It is not a pleasant memory, but I cannot erase it. Let's try to use it here in order to make my point more understandable for you.

I was visiting my buddy; his father had broken ribs as a result of being partially buried under the rubble after a shell hit the house.

After I checked his ribs and gave some advice, they offered me a meal, and of course, I took it.

My buddy and I went out at the yard with two bowls of macaroni. We sat down in pitch darkness with our backs to the house wall and we ate and look at the city with sporadic explosions and fires in it.

At the moment we had a Czech 22 sniper rifle so we were trying to see something in dark, hopeless, but we simply were eating in the dark, chatting, scoping... some kind of weird SHTF break, I guess.

It was hot summer weather, and when you close eyes and

catch a break between explosions and gunfire you could almost imagine barbecue and beer.

And then I felt something weird in my mouth, I was paralyzed for a second, then I moved to the corner of the yard in order not be visible when I let my lighter, and I checked what exactly is in the bowl.

Bowl was almost empty, some macaroni was left there in the water, but also together with that, there were a bunch of worms floating there.

I checked again, yes-bunch of small grey worms, I was not sure but I could swear that some of them were still alive.

I felt immediate urge to throw up. I close my eyes and remembered that I did not eat the whole day, that macaroni was my first and only meal that day, and I started to repeat to myself, "Do not throw up, do not throw up, I need that full stomach, do not throw up…" And in next second I throw up everything.

I walk to my friend and asked him, "What the f*ck you gave me to eat, it is full of worms!"

He answered me, "I know man. All that I have is infested with it, it is like that for weeks. I do not mind, and I thought you not gonna notice it in the dark."

I was angry. For a moment, I felt the urge to shoot him in the face, then I was angry at myself because I did not check the food.

And then a minute later I was angry because I saw the

worms, I checked what I was eating, and now my stomach was empty.

The biggest highlight was that my stomach was empty.

It was in the let's say "adapting" period of SHTF.

Later, I learned to eat what was available. Expired food, infested food, raw food, weird food.

Over time, you simply want to fill your stomach with something. The hunger gets into your pores somehow and you do not mind some things.

Often, I would intentionally go into the dark with my bowl, just so as not to check too much in case there was anything else inside.

I assure you, as the situation deteriorates, you will eat a lot of stuff that you would not usually eat.

Survival Notes from Toby:

Preparation is as much psychological as it is physical. In these modern days of 'over sanitization' of food, people disposing of perfectly good food because of some arbitrary date on a label, many being completely disconnected form the realities of how the food chain actually works and more, means this area, more than most is going to be one of the first and foremost 'shocks' people will have in tough times.

Fortunately, it's one that you can easily be more prepared for, so long as you are aware. Stockpile food, by all means, but also miss some meals, try new dishes, try and build tolerances to foods you don't 'like'. Most importantly try and eat healthy NOW and reduce dependency on poor dietary choices.

The fuel you put in your car seriously affects how the engine will run. Even more so the fuel you put in your body.

Under The Bridge...

After maybe 6 months of horrible violence in the city and life without enough food, water, or electricity... After months of shelling, shooting, screaming and crying, and after months of collecting wood for the fire, plugging holes in what's left of my roof, I stumbled upon on a piece of normal life.

Through some contacts of mine, I managed to meet some guys from some kind of international force.

I need to mention here, in the wartime there were all kind of strangers in the city, going in and out, through smugglers routes or with rare international convoys.

Some of them were UN forces, other were mercenaries, spies, or simply folks who want to earn money in bad times.

Anyway, one evening I met these guys from Spain. Three big guys with even bigger smiles on their faces. Actually, they stated they are from Spain, we did not care even if they came from the moon as long as they were of some use to us.

I was with two relatives. The Spanish guys knew some English language and we knew some, and we waved with our hands a lot as an addition in communication.

They wanted to know where they could find drugs and

women, just like most of the outsiders wanted, together with what they called "war souvenirs." They wanted weapons of war and stuff that was interesting to them, or I guess, exotic to them: flags with blood, knives, personalized weapons, etc.

They had small assault rifles that they carried under their jackets, pretty fancy for us in that time, but what caught my attention was a small portable Walkman on one of the guy's belt and the headphones around his neck.

I asked him, "Can I take that for a second and check it out?" and he said sure.

I put headphones on my ears, started the machine and when the music started, I just had to sit down.

It was so powerful to me at that moment that I kind of lost it. It was like I was drugged.

I was sitting down and listened to the whole song, while Spanish guys looked at me. I guess to them I looked like some savage who never saw a Walkman before.

They could not get it.

There I was, dirty and smelly, I could feel my toes in boots are sticky because water got in. I had a weird rash on my neck, handmade cigarette smell like hell... but I sat there, smiling like an idiot.

Music brought me back all that I had lost in the last 6 months. It brought me peace of mind for a moment, memories of normal life, cafes, girls, the beach and fun.

Somehow, I forgot that in only 6 months' time I had turned myself to survival mode only, which was not bad, but at the same time, I had lost part of me.

A few days before I met those Spanish guys, one of my friends got killed. He found himself in the open during the sudden shelling.

He panicked and froze behind some telephone pole, instead of jumping behind the wall of a ruined house a few meters from that spot.

A piece of shell got half of his head almost with surgical precision. The upper half. Scary sight.

And that morning before we met the Spanish guys, we were already making fun out of his death. I said something like, "Can you believe that idiot tried to take cover behind a pole like this is a cartoon?" And we laughed like idiots and drank.

I had no emotions about his death.

After we ended our deal with the Spanish guys, we went home, and I felt like I was gonna cry. Because of the stupid death of my friend. Because I wanted to listen to music, not to shoot. Because I guess music reminded me of normal times and the fact that I *have* to be sorry because the death of my friend, not to make fun of it.

And at the same time, I was angry with myself at how one song could turn me into a sissy.

Later I had the same feeling when I found a whole bunch

of books and brought them home to burn on the fire, and took one and started to read.

Funny thing.

The point is that no matter how bad the situation is, you just need to have some connection with "normal" otherwise you'll simply turn yourself into an animal.

It can be a book, it can be a guitar and music, or simply chatting with friends – no matter how hard the sh*t hits the fan.

Do not forget that you are human and you need to have and express emotions. Or simply, you may burn out.

Today I heard that song on the car radio, and it brought me back to those times and feelings. I sat down and wrote this post without too much thinking.

It was the Red Hot Chili Peppers "Under the bridge" song.

Survival Notes from Toby:

Mental welfare including 'Psychological First Aid' is another significantly overlooked area of many peoples' preps. When it is regarded, often, it is concluded that medication is key, which can sometimes compound the problem more than solve it. Learning and applying simple techniques and therapies to help cope with or minimize stress and stress reactions are a very worthwhile investment of time and energy.

A Way Out of Town

There were a few possible ways out of the town.

First let me point out if I had recognized what was coming, I would have run away from town for sure, no matter where. Some signs were there, but I did not notice them. From this point of view, I was fool because I did not figure what was going to happen.

During the SHTF, one way out from the town was that you pay a local gang leader some huge amount in foreign currency to get you out of the city. I guess now something like $15,000-$20,000, for us here it is a fortune. I've heard of agreements where people gave everything what they had: jewelry, guns, everything.

Some of the gangs had power and connections to do that, to smuggle you through enemy lines, but, as I remember the probability that they would just take your money and shoot you was very high. I think the chance for success was something like 50%. Not a good number if we are talking about life.

But yes, there were some cases of success that I heard later.

A different way was to use another smuggling route to get out of the city. That other way was through the mountains. It was used sometimes to take some wounded defenders out on horses. Also, it was one of the ways to get things from the other city, some 50 miles. It was a long trip. Depending on the weather and enemy movements it usually took 5-10 days.

There was not any kind of road or path. Just a big mountain standing between two cities. There was narrow "passage" between enemy lines, maybe 1 mile or something like that. So, it was a real art to get there and back, through hard environments, landmines, hostilities, and absence of any order.

The situation in the other town was slightly better, so you could bring some useful things home, maybe. But it was so hard and dangerous that probably worth only to mention here as way out.

I took that trip once, in January. I think it was something like -15 C, with freezing wind and blizzards. It was like swimming through snow, not to mention that nobody had clue where exactly mines and other traps were.

I was a city guy. I liked to watch snow from warm room or on idyllic postcards for New Year. But to walk many miles in deep snow at freezing temperatures, in military boots made probably for dry weather only, and to eat snow (yes, I made that mistake) it was nightmare.

The local myth was that if you were going to take that trip, you need to have sugar and few liters of alcohol. During the trip we mixed alcohol and sugar and drink that, it was supposed to give us energy for long walk in freezing temperatures. To be honest, though it sounds ridiculous, I finished that trip. I'm not sure is it because that mix. I just know that most of the time on that trip I was half drunk and walked like a zombie.

Sometimes people took that trip only to try to get some specific medicine.

Again, rumors raged, there was a story that some folks went through the sewage systems and managed to get out.

I do not know for sure that is true. It was a system about 100 years old, combined with newer sections, so it looked like labyrinth to me. I think now it would be great idea to have map, blueprints of that.

There were a few people who tried to get in, too.

I remember also a few times some of the international aid workers, or some foreign news reporters tried to sneak into the town, or be smuggled into the town. They wanted to help or have an interesting story, I guess.

Also, I met two foreign soldiers, mercenaries, I think from the UK. I did not have a clue how they came into the city, but I know that they "worked" with a sniper weapon for those who paid more. The urban legend about them was that when they take position to shoot, they did not move several hours, and that they eat only chocolate bars when they were on the job.

In one occasion I spoke with them, and they were nice guys. I think for them it was a job like any other job. They did not even look like "tough guys."

The International Red Cross tried a few times to get into the town with food, but were mostly unsuccessful. Even when they got in, they had such small amounts, it did not mean anything much.

Going it Alone... Some Things To Consider.

I've written numerous posts about the advantage of having a trusted group when SHTF.

Still, I get questions about how to actually survive alone when SHTF, or how to be a lone wolf. So, it makes sense to write about it. Yes, some people managed to survive alone when SHTF, but in much lower percentage and at the much higher price and effort.

So, this is based on my experiences of what I saw, and what kind of folks survived alone and how.

Here's some advice for all you lone wolves out there.

Mental Strength – Having A Cause

Being alone in hard times gives you much more chances to find yourself without emotional or psychological support when you need it.

An SHTF situation will have a huge impact on your mental state, your emotional strength, and since you are going to be alone, you will lack the everyday small and big support from your family and friends in the group.

Do not underestimate the effects of this. If you forget, over time you may well just turn into an animal, or simply get yourself in a state where you are going to make some basic mistake and end up dead.

I was in a group during my SHTF, and I had support from other family members. But still I had moments when I had doubts about everything, when I was so deep down that I could not see any sense and reason to move on. I had my own methods for coping with that, together with support from close family and friends.

What you can do if you are alone?

Find yourself a cause and purpose in the chaos that will unfold around you.

If you are a believer, a religious man or woman you may have an advantage here that can give you strength and sense in everything.

Other things help also. Be sure to find out what helps in your case before SHTF because remember – **you are going to be alone with your fears and doubts**.

I knew a man who was alone during the SHTF, and he wrote every day in a journal about the things that happened around him. He told me later that he started with that without any plan. Over some time, it became almost a way to make sense of everything, to carefully monitor all of what was happening and to preserve it in written form.

Mobility

I already mentioned that if you are planning to be alone when SHTF you need to be mobile, very much

What does that mean?

It means that you need to be ready to move more, much more than if you had a group.

Acquiring information, getting resources, scouting, etc. – it all comes to you only. You are everything in your survival circle.

That can change a lot of things.

For example, how much firepower you can have alone in defending your home against invaders? Let's say, against 15 invaders?

It simply means that there is much more of a chance that you cannot defend your home because you are one man. That means there is much more chance that you'll be forced to leave (run) from your home.

All that means is that you must be ready to have *more*. More than one shelter, more than one secret stash with ammo, weapons, food, etc. You must have more than one option for almost everything.

You need more options because you are alone.

It is simple – a lone wolf needs to pay attention to the same things as any other group of survivalists, but much more and much deeper. Because you will pay for your mistakes at a much higher cost, and usually only once and then you are gone.

Skills

Every survivalist needs to have certain skills, group or no group. Lone wolf survivalists need to have skills too, but again on a much deeper level.

He needs to be an expert in at least one relevant field. As a lone wolf, you'll be forced (especially in a prolonged SHTF) to form some kind of alliances to get stuff, or simply you'll be forced to join (for shorter or longer periods) some group.

When all your other valuables are gone (and you have more chances for them to be gone because you are alone), you will have that precious skill as a bartering value. Your skill will be much more important to you because you are alone.

Choose today, before SHTF, some skill that you feel best suits you and learn everything about it. Think about weapon repairing, gardening, medical skills, herbal knowledge. Become a real master of it.

One more thing about being alone and skills. The simple fact that you are alone is asking from you much more effort and skills than having trusted friends or group, and it goes like that for every aspect of survival.

It takes much more time to gather firewood, start a fire, and prepare food for you alone than if two or three men do that. Not to mention how many skills have three men combined together compared to one survivalist.

Let me give you an example, and it is real life experience based. If two survivalists travel through the urban area and decide to spend a night or few hours resting in some ruin it is more or less, they choose a building, check it, and take rest with one man on watch.

If you travel alone, you will look for the building, you will do that with more effort, it will take more time, you will look for a bit different type of building because there is only one defender (you), you will have to make some traps (warning or killing ones) which will take more time, and you'll sleep with "one eye open" and so on...

As I said, both examples are from my experience and my SHTF. Being alone is not impossible. It simply requires more effort and skills.

Other People and You

You may be a lone wolf, but you will be forced to deal with other folks, that is for sure. You will come into situations in which you have to cooperate with other people, or to trust other people.

My survival philosophy when it comes to urban survival is that urban SHTF means more people, and more people means more problems because you'll have to deal with people in order to survive.

That "dealing with other people" when you are a lone wolf

is much more dangerous than dealing with them while you are in a group.

It is simply because you are more vulnerable, less protected.

For example, if you are going to trade or deal, it is much more dangerous for you alone to make a safe trade setup, as opposed to having you and two more group members with you.

With that in mind, you come to the point where you may conclude that you'll be forced much more to avoid people because you are a lone wolf. It is simply safer like that.

Aftermath and Consequences

Again, let me explain through my experience and my example.

I survived the SHTF.

I have had PTSD for years, which drives my mind everywhere, from thoughts of 'reasons for still being in this world' up to thoughts of writing a book.

I can say that I am pretty much not capable of living a normal everyday life. I cannot stand crowded places. In nice cafes I look for possible exits. In exchange for this pain, I am completely sure and ready for another SHTF.

But again, that does not give me the ease of living a normal life. I lost that ability a long time ago because I went through SHTF.

I forget the names of people, or streets or places. I even sometimes forget when exactly my kid was born.

But I remember so clearly how grown-up people cried before they died, gaping wounds and blood that always gave me "how much blood is there" thoughts, the smell of buildings on fire, the crackling noise of those fires and the glowing that mesmerized me.

And I remember much worse things. They are carved in my brain.

I am all that and I remember all that, even though I had support through my group of family members. We cared about each other, about the mental state of each one of us.

I feel sorry for the lone wolf who will survive SHTF. He is going to be a mess.

There is a reason why most of the lone wolves who survived SHTF were kind of weirdos who avoided people before and have a terrible time with the aftermath after...

As you might conclude by now, there is no magic formula about how to survive alone when SHTF.

The rules of survival are mostly the same as being in a group, but much harder or sharper, with much fewer margins for error.

Survival Notes from Toby:

Selco raises a REALLY important point about the 'aftermath'.

So many of us are focused on surviving bad times, but we have to think, what 'price' will that journey cost?

One of the reasons we do so many of our physical courses in the Balkans is to clearly show people the aftermath of such events. Even now, 25 years after the war, you will see people, regular people, just wandering in the streets and the towns, still clearly struggling with what they went through. It is normal in this area.

Every village, every town, has the people that are known (by the locals) to be 'still fighting the war in their mind.' To visiting outsiders it is often shocking, a very clear and sobering indicator of the cost of living through terrible times... ***This is an aspect you cannot afford to overlook****.*

'Lone Wolf' Life Expectancy

Over the last couple of years, I get many questions about "what to do when SHTF if you are alone, without a network of people." Most of my answers were pretty much grim about the perspective of being alone when SHTF.

It is not impossible, but it is very, VERY hard. One reader asked specifically:

"*Selco, what is your advice to people who have no family or many friends in their immediate areas if disaster strikes? Bug in where you are safest and meet people? Bug out in the wild where supply is limited, harsh weather and the slow decline of sanity? There are people out there without a support network. I look at it this way. If you are alone now with people around you then when disaster strikes then bugging in is really the best option. Why? Because you can pull resources together and form a group. Your sanity can be stable, you can learn new skills, have a structure to protect against weather, trade and can reduce caloric intake. What do you think the options are for the lone man? I think he is going to have to stay put.*"

But that discussion draws other interesting topics, and from the statement that "being alone when SHTF" lot of folks might conclude wrong things or wrong ideas, so again let's (again) consider few problems here if you think you are gonna be alone when SHTF (urban).

Being Alone When SHTF in Urban Settings

I must point out here, again and again, the difference between the romantic view of surviving in the city and reality first.

Every city is a complex mix of services that need to operate in perfect (more or less) harmony in order to let the ordinary man live in it.

When those services go away, it is not a city anymore, at least not as you understand it.

It is a big pile of people, inside a big pile of not-operating buildings and houses. To make it simpler to understand, when SHTF, cities become too small to support that number of citizens. Suddenly you realize that there are way too many people around you and far too little water, power, food, security, medicines etc.

It becomes a complex death trap and it will ask from you to implement your strength, your skills, your view of morals and right and wrong so badly that it is hard to imagine right now.

Of course, people will survive it, nothing new, but sometimes at very high prices.

Or to bring it to the examples for a moment.

You are alone, and your home is under threat. How long

are you going to be able to be on guard, watching for the threat?

One night? A day and night? How long before you are going to see things that are not there, or even worse, not see things that *are* there?

Now add to the problem that you might be forced to be on guard for 48 hours while you are having diarrhea or a fever.

Who is going to watch over your place when you are out looking for resources or information for example?

Bugging Out "Into the Wild "

Maybe it is only me, but as I see it, only a few can go out in the wild and survive for a prolonged period of time.

Bugging out in the wilderness is not like a camping trip, because a camping trip is just that – a trip. You go out in the wild with resources and you are going back into normal life in 5 days, 10 days or a month – but you are going back.

Surviving in the wilderness for a prolonged period of time is something completely different because you are going to start a new life in a way.

The range of skills plus physical and mental strength needed for that is way beyond the skills of the average prepper. Most of the people could not last too long in the wilderness.

Most of the folks who bug out into the wilderness without huge prior preparations (including a BOL) will end up dead or simply as unsuccessful scavengers and solo raiders.

Forming A Group

I am a big advocate of building a network of trusted people. Simply because I saw what it means when you have someone that you can really rely on when the SHTF.

Now there is a difference between forming the group before SHTF and after SHTF because for a good group, you need to have enough time to build confidence and have all things set up for SHTF.

Common sense because that is what you need to build a group *before* the SHTF. It takes time.

Building a group after SHTF usually means that you form "alliances" with people that you do not know well enough. That equals the fact that you simply never know when they are going to turn against you.

Conclusion

As an answer to the original question at the beginning of this post –

Robert,

If you asked me several years ago what to do, I would advise you to bug out into wilderness and take your chances, but after years of learning about wilderness, there is only one possible choice for you here – bug in.

No friends, no network, no family, no BOL, no absolutely perfect skills and knowledge and perfect mindset for wilderness you just have to take your chance by bugging in.

But consider the mentality that you need to be really flexible and ready to be really mobile in the city. Staying bugged in one shelter is quite hard.

You need to consider alternative shelters close to your place, secret stashes with preps (food, ammo etc.), people that you will use as a help, not trusted network of people, but kind of 'associates' in order to get what you need to get.

Do not expect to find 6 good people on the second day of SHTF. Use people from situation to situation. Do not trust anyone.

My advice here, in short, is to bug in, but not the type of bugging in that people imagine, with tons of everything ready to die for that. You are going to need to be highly mobile, with lots of choices prepared for where to spend the night.

Survival Notes from Toby:

Sometimes there is no 'perfect' answer. In fact, often we are less working in black and white answers. Instead we have many and various shades of grey. Anyone *answering a complicated question like this one with a clear, simple statement – "do this and you'll be OK" – is selling you something.*

Having a community and group to rely on is fantastic, but not achievable for everyone. When it comes down to it, you have to deal with the situation you are in, with what you have got. Flexibility, modularity, and mobility go a long way toward solving some of the more complicated problems we expect to encounter in disaster situations...

If I was in America, I would…

And then one day, finally, real democracy came!

We were feeling that after a long time of the same old politicians who cared only for themselves or their own circles and families, suddenly there is a man (or people) who will bring something new for us, pride, strength, wealth or whatever.

Media was full of high hopes and praising, in order to bring new world for us, jobs, security and what not.

New factories are promised, new liberties, patriotism and love for the country exploded.

Something beautiful was expected. We felt like it is the dawn of a new era…

What a bunch of fucking idiots we were.

Then the polarization started. In the beginning, it was something like "there are people FOR and there are folks AGAINST it" whatever that "IT" was.

Pretty soon we were "thrown" into a situation where you have two families, they are neighbors, friends for years, decades even, but over the political reasons they started to see each other with kind of 'bad blood'.

And then one morning, SHTF and I found myself standing in my backyard like an idiot, still trying to find out what happened with great words of a new era and better life...?

People were shot dead on the street for fun or wrong words, fire trucks were driven by stoned teenagers in weird uniforms, police cars burning, men with assault rifles walking on the street in cowboy boots and metal band T-shirt acting like self-proclaimed government forces, every group who had more than 15 guys and 5 rifles was self-proclaimed police force doing whatever they want to do...

A whole bunch of people who had dreamed of times where and when they can do whatever they want to emerge.

I forget together with a bunch of other people high hopes and big words, all that was left is pure survival, day by day.

America

I got an email from one of my readers (thank you Mike!), and I really liked it. Mike and I share some opinions – I will cite his message here:

"My nation, America, is being abruptly dragged out of a deep and prolonged state of subconscious anxiety and depression. It is being assaulted with hope and this is beginning to produce a state of relief which will be managed into uncritical nationalism if at all possible. This euphoric state of national mind is the perfect cover from *which to ambush a nation. The pressing for a one world government did not die under Trump, it simply got a new face. The danger to America and to the other nations of the world are more real now than ever. Extreme sobriety is warranted at this time. Most people I have spoken with cannot see this. They need to. Perhaps you could bring this to their attention. Mike"*

Yes, America is being "attacked" with hope, changes, trust in a better life, new jobs, pride. At the same time, the media is on the run for making "demons" out of people or political options, and polarization is there. It all looks (sadly) *VERY familiar* to me.

It is looking so familiar to me that I have to say I am afraid for the future of Americans. The stage there is perfect for violent changes and SHTF. Stay sober and operate in your small circles. You will appreciate that effort when the SHTF.

What Can You Do?

In terms of the big picture, you cannot do anything.

It is like that, if big players are set to make shit, then it will happen, and timing and climate there in the US is perfect for that, so no matter how hard I hate to shovel "fear", you have to be afraid if that will at least mean you get into motion.

And again, and again – think in **small circles.**

For example, I can say for myself that I am for human

rights, protecting the weak and people who have suffered, but more, I am about respecting my way of living. If there is a bunch of people who want to change my way of living with force because they are so different, I want them out of my country.

Now, this sounds nice and normal, decent.

But it does not have too much to do with storing food and ammo, learning new skills, knowing how to purify water or simply working on your survival group.

When real SHTF there are no Democrats, Republicans, political options, moral or wrong, left or right.

Everything is kind of blurred and at the end, there are YOU and OTHERS.

You will find yourself standing somewhere, maybe in a similar backyard to mine, 25 years ago, asking yourself where everything has gone and how suddenly a bottle of water is more important than the whole bunch of political options, parties, opinions, solutions, etc.

And you had such high hopes of a better life!

Stay on the right track of prepping. Do not be mesmerized by current events. Monitor events, of course, but stay on track, and please do not have high hopes that "everything is gonna be OK".

Also note, while America is the greatest example of this problem right now, other countries are, and will, experience very, very, similar things... Don't believe it can't happen where you are.

Survival Notes from Toby:

Remaining objective to politics in general, and media agenda in particular is difficult but ESSENTIAL. Stay aware and informed but avoid being distracted by whatever engineered headline dominates the news cycle. Approach your preparations in a calm, logical and thorough manner. Do allow yourself to see the situation(s) develop and deteriorate however.

The 4 Types of Real Survivalists

During the SHTF, I was a jack of all trades.

Resource gatherer, fighter and defender for my family, and also just the young man who wanted to enjoy life as much as possible in these problematic times.

In this section, I want to talk about different types of real survivalists. I don't want to judge here. If you have lived a normal life, you maybe only know a glimpse of your survivor mindset – what kind of person you will be when SHTF and you fight for survival. What is important to know is that people show very different faces or mindsets when it comes to real survival.

Normal people like to think that everything can be solved with doing good, so they are trying to do good. Here it is not important whether we are talking about people who believe in God or not.

We have all seen TV shows where preppers are showing their stuff, talking about their plans for a time when SHTF.

I have seen a lady who is preparing for some possible scenario and showing her food storage and talking about her plans when SHTF. She is storing a whole lot of everything, much more than she and her family need because as she explains there is gonna be a whole lot of people who have lost everything, and her plan is to help them.

I hope everything the best for her. She is a great person. Someone who wants to help other people is a good person, period.

But when the SHTF, she is going down.

Sorry for being so negative but when people have to decide whether they die, or this nice lady does, for many the answer is easy.

When SHTF, things are upside down, so it will not work as people imagine. We are all living our lives today aware that bad people exist, but that bad and evil is more or less (depending on where we are living) controlled or locked away from society. So, we are actually not aware of how many bad folks are around us.

You might be living with one… yourself.

When the SHTF, I was rudely awakened from the illusion. Actually, my illusion was shattered to pieces when I saw what "normal" people did to just survive. Bad people *will* be around.

#1) The Bad Man

I knew a guy before the SHTF who was a nobody. An ordinary worker from one of the industrial machine parts factories.

Actually, I did not really know him than the usual "hello"

on the street, or football discussion sometimes in the neighborhood.

He lived alone, looked decent, and had a typical work and afterward "coffee house/bar with friends" life. If someone asked me to describe him, I would say "just a guy from the neighborhood" or a typical "normal dude".

When the SHTF, he emerged as one of the leaders of a local group. And he was popular, he had something that made people want to follow him. The problem was that he had something that made bad kinds of people follow him. He was pretty much something like a psychopath.

Murders, rape, robbing and everything else that goes with that was their way of life in that time. And to make things clear here, I need to say that whenever I met him and his group out on the street I would go and hide even I knew him from his former life as a "normal guy."

This guy was now someone very different.

It was not like a movie. I was prepared to confront them and fight only as a last option, but Batman was not living in the city in that time. Even if he was there, he probably would have given up, so the chances of a superhero versus a group of bad guys were not realistic.

How bad?

Sometimes he liked to catch a guy and make him run across the open space where snipers were active. If the guy survived that (rarely) then they shot at him. If he survived that shooting too, then he would live. He called that, "God will decide are you going to live or die."

Some people have a certain type of charisma, and he had a lot of it. When you add the fact that he was bad, or evil if you like, you got an explosive combination. He was something like a bad kind of hero, the man who weak people want to follow. And they would obey his commands. Also, when you add the fact that he provided security and food for them, that counted too.

I was once in their nest, or headquarters, if you like to call it like that. It was like a place taken from weird fairy tales, or like some drug-induced nightmare.

On the ceiling, there was a big disco ball. On the wall, there was a big target drawn with paint with holes from bullets. Some women were laying on the couch giggling, drunk or high, watching me.

On the floor in one corner, one man was laying. I was not sure if he was dead, drunk or just sleeping. I passed around him carefully. I was wearing my "I do not care" look because in a situation like that, if you showed fear you may find yourself in a bad situation. For example, these guys could make a practicing target out of you just for fun.

Also, to look too bold was not a good idea.

He was sitting in a bus seat taken from somewhere, and he had a hat on his head, the kind that you wear with a tuxedo. If that all was in a movie that I was watching I would laugh a lot.

But it was not a movie and I did not laugh.

My friend who brought me there introduced me to him and told him that I needed MREs. That friend was supposed to be my protection or something similar, but very soon I realized that, I, just like everyone else there, was dependent on his good will.

His first question to me was, "Are you going to her concert?"

I was confused, then he showed me a poster on the wall announcing some folk concert that happened a year ago in some different world. I did not know what to say.

He said, "I can get you tickets."

And I said, "OK thanks".

Nobody smiled. Some guy behind him was taking apart a machine gun and cleaning it with oil.

Anyway, we finished our deal, and I went home. While I was leaving, he said, "Do not forget to pick up your tickets" with a big fat smile.

I thought that he was crazy, but actually, he was not crazy at all. He just had a big great time since SHTF and enjoyed terrifying people to feel his power. He lived his dream where everything is allowed, where there is no punishment from society other than some other stronger and more wicked guy.

There is nothing deep and philosophical in that guy's

behavior and mindset. He was just a normal guy who turned bad because he loved power and was in a world without rules where he could play.

He lived on the bad side and lived a fast and evil life. He liked that SHTF situation.

But SHTF did not create that guy. He was there all the time. His real character just waited for SHTF to come out and play.

After some time, he ended up stabbed to death and then burned. I also knew the guy who did that, and he was even worse than the first bad man.

Now, this guy was not alone. When the SHTF, a whole bunch of weird and sick folks emerged. The point is that you never know what kind of people are living around you, or even with you.

And to make things worse, as I said, this guy was something like "normal" guy before SHTF.

Besides those normal guys who turned bad, there is a whole army of scum and criminals who are just waiting for the SHTF to happen, so they can go out and be something like small dictators.

You can be sure that they are perfectly prepared for that. They already live in their own version of criminal SHTF, with their rules. When real SHTF they gonna be ready for it, they just gonna jump out fully organized and ready to take over. They are gonna go open and be very mean.

I was surprised, though. I was like, "Why are there so many mean and bad folks suddenly?"

The answer is actually simple. Bad people are all around us. Some of them are aware of the fact that they are bad like organized crime members, gangs etc. Others are gonna see SHTF like their chance to fulfill their secret wishes and indulge in power over others.

So, no doubt once the SHTF you'll run into a bad man from time to time, too.

#2. The Chameleon

Most of the folks who have been through some serious and life-threatening situations and survive are gonna tell you one thing: they survive it with mental strength.

Also, all survival instructors are going say that first thing in any survival situation to have is the will to survive.

It is easy to say today "I will survive" but a great majority of people do not know what the will to survive actually means.

In my time I did see some folks who just laid down and had lost the will for life. They just gave up.

When it comes to survival you have to focus on what you are good at, and some people are just good at working with other people or maybe dealing or playing with other people. The mainstream media gives everyone a picture how real survivalist need to look and act, but they're wrong.

The Chameleon is a smart type of real survivalist.

When SHTF, the word deception has a whole other meaning and becomes powerful.

It is used in many different situations and for many different reasons. It helps some to survive but also helps to take lives.

Never form your opinion about what kind of man is dangerous based on popular images. When the SHTF, you can end up dead because some 70-year-old lady blows your head off with a shotgun.

This is how you should think, but the average man – the sheeple – don't.

So, you can be sure that when the time comes, you'll need to look stronger than you are. But also, sometimes you gonna need to look much weaker than you are. More options are always better.

And for all who are preparing with the attitude, "let them come," you need to change it to "let them not come".

There was a guy in town in that time who was very good to know if you needed to figure out where you could find something useful, or to find out what is going on.

If I needed to find something particular, for example, if I needed 10 liters of diesel fuel for something, I would first check people in my vicinity. I'd check a few guys out, do they have that or do they know someone who has that. In short, I would go out and try my luck.

But there was also that guy who always had good information about sources for trade or any other information.

The guy was shrouded in some kind of rumors, or it was more like a myth. So, you could hear all kinds of stories like, "he has important friends" or "he has some sources from the outside" or "somebody powerful is protecting him." After all of those stories, you could easily conclude that the guy was powerful, even before you saw him.

He alone did not look mean or powerful or anything similar, but he carried this mean-looking, old-style, heavy machine gun all the time, with bullet strips over his shoulders and chest.

Anytime when I would go and visit him, I got something useful for trade or some useful information where I could go and find something.

He survived the war and I did not see him for several years. Then I met him in the mall, when he was buying some toys for his grandson. I started a conversation with him, and we got some coffee.

I asked him what he is doing now. He said he is a lawyer. I was surprised. Then he told me that he was a lawyer before the SHTF. For some reasons, I could not connect that man from the war period with a lawyer, but soon some things were clearer for me.

He invited me to his house for more coffee, and after some

time he went to the basement and dragged up a big wooden box with locks on it out.

He opened it and I saw that old machine gun inside. Of course, I wanted to check it. When I took it, I saw that barrel was full of melted iron, in order to make weapon unusable.

I was surprised and asked the man why he did that. I mean, you never know when you gonna need weapon ready. He laughed and said, "It was always like that, unusable".

Now I was completely confused, and then he started to talk.

He was a lawyer before SHTF, he never fired a shot from any weapon, and violence was completely strange to him. When SHTF in the chaos he found himself on the street, looking at how a bunch of folks were breaking into malls and shops, taking whatever is useful.

In 5 minutes, he was inside a local museum with some young people who were breaking stuff and taking whatever useful things they could. He said, "When I saw a local policeman completely drunk trying to take a German uniform and helmet for fun, I realized that we were starting to live in interesting times."

He took the machine gun from a glass box, together with some bullets strips and went home.

Ten days later some punks tried to loot his home armed with knives and screwdrivers:

"I put those bullet strips on me, took the machine gun, stood in front of them and yelled that if they do not disappear that moment, I am gonna massacre them."

And of course, they disappeared.

He said, even if that thing worked, he was not sure if he would be able to shoot at them. But he realized one thing. **It is not important how things really are – it is important what things look like.**

When all the different groups in town started to use signs – I mean small colored bands on the shoulder in order to make clear who belonged to their group – he got *all* those bands and markings.

When all of those groups started with some system, when to wear what, he bribed guys in order to know that system.

So, if one group was controlling some part of the town and they used red bands on shoulders on Monday and Wednesday, and a black one on Sunday on Saturday he would know that.

He used that for moving through the city, because in all that chaos if you were moving through the city during the night, and you needed to go through an area that was controlled by some group, it was very useful to have some of their signs or code.

So, he was a member of multiple groups and all those

groups shared information with him. As a result, he was everywhere in the city, and he always had correct information about important things.

He knew what was gonna have a high price, or when new food aid might come in. I asked him, "How were you able to know all the information about so much stuff?" Because it sounded just too complicated for me.

He said, "What I did not know I just made up in my head".

Actually, he was playing with prices, with demand, and the needs of the people. He *dictated* the prices.

After some time, because of all of his information, he became so popular that if he said that "cans are gonna be very hard to find in next month," people believed it.

So, it was easy for him to distribute all cans at higher prices. Of course, not personally, but at the same time, he would, of course, know a man who had cans right now at a cheap price. His man. He got a cut out of most deals and that helped him to survive.

Through his network of people, he put the word out that "powerful people were protecting him." Another illusion but together with fact that people did not want to have problems with a man who had always good information, he survived.

Also, one other thing helped. In the first period, he collected 5-6 bodies, badly dismembered by shells and put them in front of his house. He put word on the street that "some guys messed with him, but he called his powerful friends and those friends made examples of the guys to not mess with him."

If some really strong group caused danger to him, he just left the house and waited for them to leave.

No problem, he did not have anything valuable in his house. Trading goods he kept with his "associates" and his main value was information.

His main value actually was his brain.

Keep that in mind. Before you give up because you have nothing, use your brain and try to play the system with deception. Chaotic urban survival situations offer lots of opportunity for that.

#3. Slaves and Servants

Drug dealers, prostitutes, thieves, addicts, homeless people, family people, believers… good people, bad people… we like to call people by names in order to judge them and live our lives easier.

Most of the time we judge them so easily and form our opinion about them as we go without too much thought. It is easier like that. We see people doing something and think it is because of how they are. We often do not consider all the things that make them do what they do.

We see something, give that a name, and that's it. Sometimes there is much more behind it. Someone who is bad might just have had circumstances in life that being like that is the only thing which made sense for that person. Yes, their whole way of thinking might be "wrong" or he might not act badly because he is bad, but because his kids are dying.

People judge too fast.

Not to mention that when the SHTF, it is dangerous to sort people in the easy and fast way. It can lead us to form the wrong opinion, which can lead to a lot of bad things. I learned not to judge people right away. A future friend might behave terribly the first time you meet, and a future enemy might be very nice to you.

I want to say this before writing about the type of real survivalist that I write about now. You encounter slaves and servants in a long-term survival situation because even though they go a very different way from a brave fighter… they are real survivalists and just make things work.

Many lone fighters died, and many servants suffered but survived. It's not like a movie.

A lady who was my colleague before SHTF lived with her husband and two kids. She was in her 30s, a very nice and easy person to work with. She was my friend and we shared a lot of great moments at the job. I never saw or heard anything bad about her. I knew her husband, I knew her kids.

When the SHTF I lost contact with her in all that chaos,

and to be honest I completely forgot about her. I had more important things to worry about.

A few months later on the trip that almost killed me out of town over the mountains to get some things we desperately needed, I had the opportunity to meet her again.

We already passed the most dangerous parts of the trip – mines, mountains, woods, and no man's land – and came into a small part of territory controlled by one of the numerous militias, loosely tied to bigger (again numerous) factions.

The guys did not give us any problems, other than very short checking of who we were and where we were going.

We had already paid for passage to "a guy who knows a guy," so everything went smooth. We took a small rest in one of the shacks and drank hot "tea." Actually, the exact description would be "hot dirty melted snow, with added alcohol."

Then I saw her, my ex-colleague.

If I learned anything since SHTF that was fact that you need to hide your feelings and body language until you figure out what is really going on.

So, I did not say anything to her, and I acted like I did not know her, even though I wanted very much to jump up, hug her, and ask about everything, about her, her family, etc.

She put some rice on the table, and more alcohol in front of one group member. She was one woman in a group of some 30 men, who were armed, wasted, and pretty dangerous. Most of them did not know too much about literature but they know enough about violence.

She did not look like a prisoner, and also, she did not look scared or beaten. She also did not recognize me (or maybe did not *want* to recognize me.)

Anyway, about a half hour later, one of the men from the group offered me her, for a price, explaining to me that "she is the property of the leader, but also if anybody is willing to pay, she can belong to them for half an hour."

Now if that was a movie, probably you would expect from me to shoot all of them and save her, so we could ride into the sunset.

But it was not a movie, and I could get maybe three of them down before someone blows off my head and takes my boots and rifle. And even if I could save her, she would probably tell me that she does not want to be saved.

We went through that piece of land without any problems, and I did not see her again, ever. And no, I did not pay the price to buy her for half an hour, and I did not try to start a conversation with her.

Later I found out the whole story.

When SHTF people did a lot of different things in order

to survive. She became the mistress of one of the small group leaders, and also the prostitute of that group.

She was not a prisoner, well not obviously, but you also need to understand that if she left that group, she and her family would lose protection and the steady income of goods. And her kids needed to eat something.

I do not know what her husband thought about all that (he was a bit of weak guy before SHTF) but rumors were that he agreed with it, in order to survive.

So, it lasted like that for months. And they survived.

So, is that good or bad? It's nothing. It's survival. Blame her husband? No… because they survived. If he would have become the fighter he might have died and with him, his family.

This does not mean people should let their wives become prostitutes (there were male prostitutes too, by the way). Everyone makes their own decisions and later you always know better.

Again, here comes in not judging.

Of course, when peace and normal life came, they could not stand to live here, not after everything. So, they chose to immigrate. As I heard it, they are living somewhere in South America under different names.

Here is some more background to that.

Prostitution here was something different than in other countries, and before

SHTF you had to be a member of very rich and higher class of society or higher ranks of the political elite to be able to get into the contact with one. It was illegal and also it was traditionally very "wrong."

So, prostitution was rare. To be a known prostitute was rare. To be a normal family woman and become a prostitute was unbelievable and almost impossible.

But when SHTF, lots of things changed.

There were prostitutes all around, not to mention women who were held as some kind of half slaves. Their position was not always the same, so some of them were not more than slaves, another one was almost powerful as the gang leader who they belonged to. There were also men who were just mascots or servants for more powerful people – but overall this was a more common way for a woman to survive.

Not all women were prostitutes, of course. Just like men, they all chose how to survive. Some were prostitutes, while others were more dangerous with a rifle than a lot of men.

But most of them chose just to stay home with their family and care for the kids. It was not something like – they need to do that – it was just that they did what they did best and what was needed, just like most of the folks in that period.

That woman I spoke about was much closer to an equal gang member than to a slave. They did not force her into prostitution. Actually, she "belonged" to the group leader, but also, she sold herself for goods, some of which she kept for herself and family, and some went to members of the gang. It was her "trade." While other men risked their lives, she overcome her dignity and did that.

She had protection and food, and also her family home had some kind of protection from that group as well as food and other things.

She was there mainly for the fun of the group leader, and sometimes other members and customers when she wanted.

They survived.

We can now judge them and talk about what every one of us would do in their situation, but we should not.

This may also be a lesson for normal times.

I worked for years in emergency services and see daily people living at the borders of normal society or even far from those borders in a different, very dark and nasty world.

It's not that all of them are bad but sometimes in life, you have to do what you have to do, even if it only makes sense to you at that moment. It is not an excuse but it helps to remember that when your existence is under threat you might do very different things too.

I'm sure only a very few (maybe sexually very open people) really plan on going that way when SHTF. But plans, they change.

#4. The Good Boss

The last type of survivalist I will write about is about a typical leader who knew how to handle our survival situation during the war.

He was a police officer. We called him "Boss" because of his look and stance. He had 30 years of service and I do not think that he used a gun too much. But he had a palm like a shovel and he used that a lot dealing with problematic teenagers.

He was the grumpy guy with whom you do not want to have too much business. If you got caught for some minor thing, theft or whatever, he did not talk too much with you, but his look talked stories, and his hands too.

He gave people justice on the spot and got respect for that too. He made a difference for our neighborhood and was a type of police officer that in my opinion does not exist today anymore.

He and his colleagues had a patrol in a better part of the city when the SHTF, and in the beginning, they tried to restore some order in all that. But when they saw that an ambulance vehicle on call got shredded with shots, they realized that a new time had come.

They did not discuss too much but they were sure that law

and order was something that was gone now, and to act like law keepers just did not make sense anymore.

They went back to the police station and took more weapons and equipment. Then they used a police van and went to army storage and took more weapons.

They separated and took that to their homes. His colleagues shook his hand and left, each fighting their own fight. He pushed the police van out of the street and went home.

He lived alone for many years before SHTF, and also being the police officer for years gave him the advantage of knowing something about mob mentality and power over people. So, he did not have too many problems in dealing with issues in those beginning days. He was alone and that was a problem. But he was smart and that made a difference.

In these days, everything fell apart in the city, all that makes life normal, and institutions were falling apart too.

Local correction youth center, something like an open type jail for teenagers was falling apart too, so young folks were leaving there.

He went there and took 7 guys from there. He used to be something like their "watcher" in normal times. He had arrested them for small-time burglaries, cons etc. He also kept eye on them when they were out of the correction facility and on streets again. Because of how he did things, he was like a father who gave them slaps here and there.

They all were kids without families. That correction center was their home or they were on the streets. Anyway, he took them to his home and took care of them in that chaos, and after some time they took care of him too. They all were around 16-17 years old at that time when all hell broke loose.

He taught them to shoot, to defend themselves, to trade, and to recognize problematic people. The fact that they been that problematic person once only helped in process of teaching. Those kids were street smart. And he was not too soft in process of teaching, in other words, he used his "shovels" a lot in process of "making people of them" as he called it.

But he also taught them never to take from someone else. He was still a policeman and kept his ideals. They never turned against him. I saw many times that real sons turn against their fathers in that time or brother against brother, but they were perfectly loyal to each other, a real family. I guess it was because they knew that only in this group could they survive.

They did pretty well because of the starting "capital" he took from the army barracks. They were people that you could visit and get a rifle in a fair trade, without danger that you would be shot in the back. Also, they were the people that you did not want to f*ck with because violence was not a problem for them at all.

"Boss" died a few months before peace came, from wound infection. All seven of his "boys" survived and I never heard that they did something bad in that time. OK, bad in a little bit different terms, maybe. Not atrocities, nothing about unnecessary violence. What was necessary is a different question of course, but all of us who survived were not the most gentle folks at that time.

One of them later in peace went into organized crime and ended up shot dead, but all 6 of the rest of them grew up and became proud and strong family people. The type of men that you would want to have for a friend.

They all refer to Boss as their father. They live today in different cities and countries, some of them even on another continent, but once every two years, they have met, all together in his memory.

And that guy from the beginning of the story, that colleague of the Boss?

He used his share of the loot from the barracks to form a gang, and they did a lot of bad stuff to the people. He finished dead, stabbed more than 30 times. Nobody remembers him or wants to remember him. It is like he did not exist at all.

In a survival scenario, you want people around you who know why the group matters. Just like early humans who knew not to fight each other or cause problems for the survival of the whole group. In the case of a Boss, the street kids already knew about survival and he was the perfect leader for them who also knew what kind of leadership style worked with them.

Now I could say nice things about how to choose your group and of course include that annoying drama person that maybe your brother or sister married because "he/she is part of the family".

But I speak from my experience and if you want to survive, like in any other "team" your group has to work. Having a strong leader like Boss helps a lot.

Normal laws and norms of society are gone in a long-term survival situation so people who still do things because it looks good are at disadvantage compared to people who do what works and make the team stronger and not weaker. If someone makes my team weaker on purpose (not because of sickness or age) he is not part of it.

When you think about your survival group, think about who makes the best boss. Who knows how to lead the people? What works? Prepare for that too, and you are far ahead of many other preppers who think they can buy safety with money and having the most preps and gear.

Survival Notes from Daisy:

When you read Selco's descriptions above about the different types of survivalists, which kind seems the most like you? Which kind seems the most like other people in your group? It's good to have an idea of this well before the SHTF strikes because it can help you find your way when times are difficult.

Reality Check: What You May Be Doing Wrong and How It Will Get You Killed

Over the years being in the prepper and survivalist community, I realized that my favorite topics to write about are survival myths.

There are two reasons for that. First, I have been through the SHTF, so it is obviously clear to me what are the myths about survival and what are the truths. In other words, it is kinda easy for me to write about it.

The second reason is that at the same time it's hard. It is not hard to write about it, but it is hard to explain to people what it's all about.

The reason for that *is not* because I consider most of the preppers to be idiots. It is about the preconceptions that inexperienced people have about survival or being ready for SHTF.

That preconception is so huge and so deep, it has been plugged in or conditioned into a lot of preppers so hard, over so many years of bombarding from YouTube, blogs, forums, movies, and similar that sometimes it looks simply hopeless to fight.

Where to Look

I remember for the first time seeing and teaching a group of students who considered themselves survivalists and preppers. After few hours of talking with them, my first impression was to tell them, or to yell at them, "You are so f*cking dead when SHTF! On the second day you are dead!!!"

Of course, I did not tell them that, but the point is that their survival mentality and mine were like two completely different worlds.

No, they were not idiots, just regular folks who looked at and checked for the most common information about survival out there available, or the most commercialized, or the coolest.

And no, I do not think that everyone needs to go through years of war in order to become a survivalist. It just takes some common sense and some effort.

It is like they learned everything they knew about survival from the guy on the YouTube channel, who read it from the book, which was written by a guy who heard something from a friend some time ago. So many of the sources they relied on or trusted were dangerously worthless.

Folks, there is much more to learn from, let's say a diary

of a Holocaust survivor, than from the YouTube guy who is testing his new BOB in his backyard. Actually, I would rather have memorized the diary, instead of owning the BOBs that most of the YouTube guys are testing and recommending.

This whole topic is huge, but let's address the more common mistakes I see all the time. Each of them is not a mistake by itself, but if you put these as priorities, it is something that definitely will get you killed when SHTF:

The 'Cool' Factor

Here is a scenario that happened. A student on my survival course has been offered to choose some equipment to complete a survival training task, the amount of equipment to choose from was limited.

He is trying to ensure he has covered all of the 'seven priorities' of Urban Survival. When he gets to the water section there were two items, a camping stove set (The Trangia model), and an old dirty plastic bottle, he could choose one.

He chooses the plastic bottle for the section "water".

I asked him 'can you tell me why did you choose plastic bottle instead of the camping stove set?', his answer was: "I saw on YouTube that plastic bottle can be used for boiling water and making it sterile".

I asked him: "Why did you not choose the camping stove

set, it can do the same thing, much easier, can do even more things, and last much longer etc.?"

He did not have an answer for that, other than his previous one.

Folks, watching something on YouTube (believe it or not) that looks cool, does not necessarily mean it is right or right for every situation.

I believe that YouTube video was about using a plastic bottle in survival when you do not have anything else, but taking it instead of something really useful just because it looks cool or it's a 'good trick'???

This plastic bottle story is just one example. Many other times on various courses I saw very similar things.

The internet is full of good advice about tactics, techniques, and equipment for SHTF. The problem is, at the same time the internet is full of sh*t, so choose carefully where you look to learn something, Check for guys who *credibly* tested something or experienced it, or you test it yourself before real SHTF. I know, it is a big industry and big money out there about let's say "how to survive the end of the world with cool equipment while looking cool" but from my experience, I did not see cool equipment in my time, and the 'cool' people died very early on.

Folks who survived had **stuff that worked and mentality that worked**. 'Coolness' was not important at that time, even if someone had some ideas about looking and being cool, those ideas went with first bullets hissing around their heads.

If you're preparing to have cool equipment (only) and look cool when SHTF, you are doing something wrong. Seriously.

Commodities, Peace of Mind, and Degrees of Knowledge

Again, having a commodity by itself when SHTF, on its own, is not a problem. There is nothing wrong in preparing to be in as much comfort as possible when SHTF.

But a huge number of preppers are preparing *only* for that. And that is wrong.

The simplest example here is the man who is preparing for SHTF by buying a good generator in order to have as much comfort possible when the SHTF, but at the same time he does not know how to start a simple fire.

A generator here is something like an upgrade; knowing how to make a fire is *essential*.

There is nothing wrong with owning a generator, if you also know and have supplies up to the level where a generator fits in.

Or you have a man who has 5 assault rifles, and a lot of 'knowledge' (YouTube again) about tactical movement – but he has NO clue how hard and noisy it is to move through partially destroyed buildings, or he never fired the rifle inside an enclosed space (room, empty corridor) and did not experience the impact of that event on his ears.

Nothing wrong with owning 5 rifles, *if you know everything up to that level.*

Five rifles alone do not mean sh*t.

The Internet is full of advertising that if you do or buy whatever they offer you, you're going to have something like the 'best time of your life when SHTF.'

Of course, it is a lie. Even if you are fully prepared it is not going to be a joyride. It is going to be hard and life-changing.

And by buying solutions, then you are just buying peace of mind, nothing more. Worse still, **you are seriously underestimating the SHTF.**

PLEASE make some common-sense decisions in your preparing. Do not find yourself in a situation where you have 30 spices in your pantry, but you do not have duct tape or an ax.

Start from the basics in every pillar of survival, evenly, then build on that base with logic and sense. Build all pillars up at the same time, don't take 'defense' for example and focus and build that to the highest level while ignoring the six others...

I've written about these before, but just as a brief recap, the seven pillars of urban preparedness are:

1. Fire
2. Water
3. Shelter
4. Food
5. Signaling/Communication
6. Medical/Hygiene
7. Personal Safety

Use the internet to help your preps, but check your sources, and do not believe everything you read or see!!!

I see and read far too many people who are treating prepping like some fun game as opposed to the serious matter it is. Please choose your approach wisely folks.

Survival Notes from Toby:

Lack of context is one of the most frequently seen and repeated mistakes we see in many preppers, both new and very, very experienced. You need to objectively 'confidence-check' your sources. Far too many people take all the information they receive on face value. The Preparedness Industry (and it is an industry) is too big and commercial now to be able to do this.

PART II
PART TWO

Introduction

When I was fortunate enough to spend some time with Selco in Bosnia and Croatia during the spring of 2019, we spent a lot of time swapping tales over a bottle (or three) of homemade rakija. He told me the stories of people he had interviewed in the past and stories of lost friends.

Many of these people had never appeared in his written work but their testimonies were so powerful that I urged him to write them down and share them. I think you will gain a great deal of knowledge from these snippets of their lives during the Balkan War, much as I did.

To protect their privacy, the names and identifying information of those appearing in the following stories have been altered.

Selco's writing is unparalleled. I believe this may be his best collection yet. The stories have been lightly edited for clarity, but I've left Selco's "accent" intact for authenticity.

Grab yourself a drink, sit down, and prepare to be transported to 1990s Bosnia. You'll almost hear the gunfire, the screams, and the explosions in the background as you dig into this book.

To get the most from this book, don't think, "Oh, this could never happen here." Bosnians never imagined it happening there either. Nor did Greeks or Venezuelans or Syrians. We can't predict exactly how bad things will get in a true SHTF event, but we can at least consider the possibilities and learn from the struggles of others. Think about how you can apply this glimpse of humanity to your own preparedness plans.

Thank you for supporting Selco's work.

Daisy

Nov. 27, 2019

Una's Story

Sometimes I am asked a lot of woman-specific questions about my SHTF experience. I decided to interview women because of that. I can talk about my experience, but women live often in the different world of feelings and emotions.

I spoke with the first woman named Una, now 52 (so in her 30s back then) who took care of her family during that time. I recorded the interview and translated it to English.

Una started to describe her situation.

My first and worst concern was what is gonna happen with my kids. I had two toddlers, and I did not have any clue what is gonna happen, or even what is gonna look like when hell broke loose. We did not want to believe it could happen. We heard the sound of big guns miles away and stories of violence, rape, and murder but everything looked so peaceful.

At the beginning, actually right before everything started during my meetings with my friends and colleagues at work, we discussed the deteriorating situation, and pretty soon I found myself faced with an important decision: is it worth to send my kids to some more "secure" region or to some relatives to neighboring country, or keep them with me, and wait to see what happens?"

I never had a question about am I going to leave this

place. I found it normal to stay in my city, with husband, in my house. Looking back now I know it was a big mistake.

If I want to describe my worst feeling through all of that, it was not hunger, danger, fire, cold or anything like that.

It was definitely the feeling of uncertain future, the complete absence of feeling that I control coming events. I was helpless and just like a leaf in a storm. Anything could happen.

Anyway, I chose to keep my kids with me, and I still do not know if it was the right decision. Survival was tough even at places I could have sent them before everything started. I found out after everything was over.

Anyway, they survived, but with some mental trauma like everybody else who survived.

Some of my friends who send their kids through some organization to other countries, had kids getting lost and disappear. In some cases, they found a place somewhere else but the kids lost that connection with their parents. If parents survived, they became strangers with each other.

How did things start to change in your city?

Some very new emotions came up during that time, I was watching how the city was dying slowly, together with the normal behavior of people.

In the beginning, people tried to stay together, I mean in the terms of neighbors helping each other. They had a "normal" way of communication in the beginning. But as more bloody details, murder, rape, and other crime became common, trust faded and was replaced by fear.

Slowly people started to move away from each other and there was just us or them. Groups were not open anymore. No more welcoming newcomers.

I thought of myself as a strong woman before, but that was before being without food and losing normal control of my life. I was a teacher before everything, and of course, I lost my job just like almost everyone. Nothing worked like it was supposed to work. I did not even have the idea to continue to teach my kids at home or try something similar. To just survive took all my energy.

Did you have any idea how you would survive if you had been alone?

I was with my husband and family and I think I would not have survived alone. Not because I'm a weak-spirited woman lacking the will to survive but simply because what I saw and experienced was so different and "out of this world" that I would have not been able to handle it alone.

Being in a family or group makes you part of something. If others depend on you and you have others who go through the same unreal situation it makes you fight harder. I understand those people who gave up and locked themselves in to die.

Did you feel being a woman gave you any advantages or disadvantages?

For me I think it was better because I was a woman. I mean, I was in a way protected from some of the hardest things, like finding food, resources, or fighting. The hardest jobs were done by men, it was a matter of luck for me.

Woman are just more useful for certain kind of job like taking care of kids or wounded or sick people. The women also have more feelings so some things like using violence do not come easy.

Did you realize how bad it would get?

No, definitely not, many times I thought this cannot get worse and then it got worse.

Fighting for survival can reduce people to an animal that we all are. Sometimes it was hard to still see that they or we were human. So much that we think makes us human is removed and then there is something very basic and brutal

left.

It comes as a surprise that people can act without emotions like compassion that make us human. Since that time, I never thought about humans in the way I did before.

How did the close people to you treat you?

I was protected, guarded in a way because I was a woman.

It was not a matter of some kind of gentlemen thing, I believe it was mostly about fact that I do my part of duties, like taking care for kids, preparing food, trying to keep things clean etc.

When I had to shoot, nobody would tell me: you are a woman you can't do that. Everyone in the group had to function and people treat you good if you do.

What was your situation? How many people did you have as support?

I spent that period in a group with 6 men, 3 woman, and 4 kids.

How did that change the way you live today?

I have food in my house for several months, weapons and I am ready to leave everything at the first sign that something similar gonna happen. Everything.

Did anything happen that you handled differently than you assumed you would?

I was thinking a lot about that, and whatever I am gonna say, it could be wrong.

You get into situations that you cannot imagine so there was no way to predict what to do. I saw a hard man break and a weak man be strong. Many people who showed off strength to the outside world before things got really hard were those who broke first. I think they build up a mask to hide their inner weakness.

I broke too but people still relied on me, so I had to do my part. I kept myself together but the whole situation left big scars inside of me.

There were quiet and normal people like you, Selco, who managed to come out of all this stronger and who got used to the situation faster and without much suffering.

Maybe you were born for that I still do not understand people like you.

Were you concerned about hygiene and feminine body issues or would you say the lack of food and water caused this not to be a concern?

How could a lack of water etc. not to be a concern? It was the opposite. But over the time we learned that hygiene is not the most important thing in the world, as dirty as that sounds. Other things occupied my mind, like with what to feed my kids, or how to make any kind of meal from very few things.

What did women do differently to handle the situation, if anything?

I know for myself that a special way of thinking helped me. I just closed myself in my own world, I mean with my thinking and worrying, and it helped me.

When my husband was thinking and worrying about when everything would come to an end, and what are the chances for that, or trying to find some useful information about that, my biggest concern was how to make dinner or to warm the kids.

It was not about "men in the house" thing. It was that he thinks about the big issues and I do not. I am an educated person, but worrying about small, everyday things I think helped me through all of that, without going crazy maybe.

My concern was for example when the kid asked me "can you make a pancake?" how to answer him and make something that only looked like a pancake and tell him something like "those are special pancakes."

Those were the little missions that kept me from completely losing myself as others did.

Did anything at all go the way you would have expected?

Nothing went as expected. Actually, I did not know what to expect. You cannot expect too much when you find yourself in a completely new situation, a deadly situation.

I lived day by day without too much hope or expectation. At some point you stop caring. I survived, my family survived, and that's it.

I do not know what happens next time everything goes to hell again but I'm ready now to accept whatever comes.

I easily could not be here anymore like many people I know. This stays with me for life so I appreciate every day.

Did you have a source of spiritual strength?

I changed all phases, from completely not believing to completely believing and hoping that God will do something. I lost and gained faith many, many times in that period.

But yes, I think my kids and caring for my kids gave me some will and strength to survive and live somehow normally. I think the point of taking care of someone is really important in all this.

Elzi: The Gang Member's Story

I sometimes meet with friends I was with during that time.

Here is how my friend Elzi spent some of his time.

He did not have a choice and joined a gang to fight. It was the only way for him to get some resources and make it through the year.

Most people who joined gangs did it for the reason that they did not have any other way to survive, or they thought that was the easiest way to survive.

Some of them did not have food so they joined, some of them did not have a weapon for protection and they joined, some of them just wanted someone to lead them.

Most of the folks I know who joined did that because they were not prepared. Nobody expected what their life would be like.

It was a trade with the devil, but the trade that had to be done for many to save their families. (Gangs had power and resources, so being in a gang meant having usually more food than others, for example, and of course weapons)

Last time I met Elzi we recorded some things. Here is Elzi's story.

I joined because I did not have a weapon in my house, and no food for me and my family.

Anyway, I had some military experience before, but had never been in real battle before. But I had training and knew weapon and drill.

I joined a group of 8 men. Only 3 of us had a weapon at the beginning. Our city was divided between many armed groups, maybe 7-8 big organized groups, with alliances and hostilities between them. Each of those big groups had many smaller groups, loosely in some kind of alliance more or less. I had to go there because it was the only way to feed the family.

I talk now about first 5 – 6 weeks. I learned a lot more later on.

We "acquired" weapons one night from a smashed vehicle. I guess somebody shot the driver and passenger and car rolled over. In the back there were 6 rifles, still fresh with oil and grease. I guess they were stolen from some military warehouse during the first days of chaos. In a wooden box, we also found 5 mines, on sticks.

This helped us to become a stronger group in our alliance and equip all our members with weapons. When we moved through the city, we learned quickly in those days, **adapt or die***. We saw many people die.*

We always changed location, every day or night a different location. We lived on the move. Enemy groups want to know a bit of the territory before they strike so we did not give them chance to spy out our location. The next night we would be somewhere else. Every night.

When I needed shelter, cover, a place to hide or sleep I always chose the second floor in a house. My group most of the time stayed in no man's land. That land between enemy lines so after a night's stay in one house, maybe the next day we were already in enemy territory.

The front lines were not clear lines, just several rows of houses that were the fighting zone. Our no man's land.

At night, of course, we slept always with the guard. Moving depended on the situation. Because it was a densely populated area, houses were close. Almost without space between two houses.

A lot of time we moved from house to house with a plank of wood (think of something like in pirate movies to enter ships). We just placed that wood on windows of one house and on the balcony or any opening on other neighboring house and walk or crawl to that other house. I became pretty skilled in that very soon. Nobody wants to be on the street in no man's land.

Our place of hiding was chosen based on if it had a safe exit. So actually, in reality whenever I needed a place to hide, I always looked for a safe and fast exit from that place. Without a safe second way out of the place, it was not acceptable, no matter how good looking it was.

Basements were death traps, no matter how well armed and equipped I was. Always higher floors with other exits.

We placed a few traps outside, sometimes with mines and sometimes just with ropes and all kinds of junk so we had some warning when somebody was coming.

Getting captured and taken prisoner was not an option. We had prisoners too and knew what to expect. Nobody is good to the people that tried to kill them. In no man's land taking prisoners was not so common. Better to end the problem directly.

The brutal reality caused many people to go through strong feelings of fear.

A lot of people died because of their fear. Because they ran in panic or fought in panic. Often during the attack there was one point when everyone panicked. When many people ran away the massacre would start.

Run first or run last. Do not run somewhere when everybody runs. Better to run before everyone runs. But when you run when everyone runs enemies shoot in frenzy.

It is a stupid way to die but feelings were often stronger than smartness.

Another good thing in the beginning during the fight was to stay away from the bigger group during the shooting. In the panic folks just shoot at all directions and at every moving target. Adrenaline just gets you crazy.

In many situations, during a fight, it was better to be with one good person than with many. Safer. Quite a few people got shot accidentally by their own people.

In reality, what I did soon, I just chose a position little bit behind my group in a fight. A row of houses behind. Safe for shooting, safe for running away, first or second floor of some house or building.

Anyway, people learned some things quickly. We became creative.

Once we destroyed an armored vehicle with a lot of gas cylinders. We were hidden in drainage ditch during the night, and the next day we waited for the vehicle to pass, blew everything up with one grenade.

Elzi made it through the whole year because he is street smart. While you sometimes need a group to survive always acting like the herd can cost your life.

You've got to make the right choices when it matters, I hope when we share experiences like this, it helps you to get a bit of an idea of what to expect when things get bad.

Small decisions can make a big difference and every detail matters.

Ed's Story

Ed is now 42 years old. At the time of the event he was 20 and unemployed. Now he works as an Explosive Ordinance Disposal operator for private company. The tattoo on his one hand shows a bullet with a heart, and on the other hand there is a tattoo of young woman.

He smiles a lot, and his hands are always moving. His fingers are like he is playing some musical instrument. He is not aware of that.

We are having a conversation in a café. A few tables around us are empty, but the people who enter the cafe choose a place not so close to our table.

During the military basic training (*in ex-Yugoslavia this was mandatory for every healthy man older than 18, lasted 12 months*) I was trained for frontiersman.

We were tough guys, trained by the old bastards that enjoyed crushing our will, old communist army school sergeants.

Besides us, maybe only military police and paratroopers were equally mean guys.

We were taught and trained for fighting, to defend our country, from the capitalists mostly, and Soviets too if needed.

Everyone was potential enemy in that time, they told us. Hungarians, Albanians, Italians... you name it and we were told they hated us.

After the first two months of training I was sent to the Albanian border. And there was something like always an expectation of potential invasion. We all know that they were over there using tanks made from cardboard to try to scare us, and that they barely had enough to eat. But still, we were kinda scared of an escalation.

Occasionally there were problems with illegal border crossings from their side, and incidents with shooting mostly from their side. But nothing serious.

We were kind of eager to shoot, and to go to war. Oh yes, we were young and full of propaganda, I think.

And then one night I saw how death really looks.

While I was with dog, checking my area of responsibility, shots were fired from maybe a kilometer away.

When my shift ended, the guy who relieved me told me that on the other post they shot one "enemy" who had illegally passed the border.

When I came to our guard house there was already an orderly officer, a small Macedonian with a big mustache that gave him a funny look. He was probably thinking that he looked tough.

The guy who made the kill shot was from my "room," one

of the best shooters in basic trainings, holder of one of those badges. He was a "good soldier."

He looked pale, and on his raincoat, there were traces of vomit.

Under the camo was something that looked like body. An officer raised the camo and there was a man maybe sixty-five years old. He looked like someone's father in a dirty jacket.

The bullet had hit him in the head, a bit under the right eye. The back side of his head was gone completely.

And his eye was missing too.

He did not look like the enemy at all. He did not look like someone who was trying to destroy our country.

The officer said to the shooter, "You are good soldier."

His response should be "we serve to the people" but the other guy did not say anything.

What did I feel?

I do not know, not too much, but looking in the faces of the other guys I clearly saw that I was different. That I do not feel too much sorrow for the guy. I did not care. Fuck it.

I was done with basics in few months and came back to my hometown just in time to see that the democracy that brought down the communists had brought down something new.

Everyone wanted to start to live better right away. And some old hates were fueled again.

No, I did not see what was coming. I was not one of those smart guys who left the area before the war started. I was more like hypnotized with all that smell of coming violence.

I was excited.

You know. my grandfather served in World War 2 as a member of 13. SS division. Of course, when partisans won the war and captured him, they brought him to the firing squad as a war criminal.

I never found out what stories about him were truth and what was propaganda. But what I know is that they called him a butcher, and there were stories that he enjoyed killing, no matter whether it was soldiers, civilians or kids. Everyone.

Did my family have problems because that?

Well my father could not have anything like a career. He was always under suspicion as a son of the enemy. And I think he was under some kind of surveillance for years.

Communists never trust.

Personally, I did not have problems from this, but our country was different in the 1950s and the 1980s anyway.

With the first shots fired that started the war, I responded to the call for mobilization, and joined the Army that was anything else than a real army.

In my group of 12 people there was me and two other guys who had some knowledge about weapons. Other folks did not care, or they forgot long ago what they had learned.

There was one man who dressed like he was going to a wedding, not to war. Another was carrying a 40-years-old rifle without bullets, but he was trying to look cool with a big knife on his belt.

He got killed some 20 days after that in an explosion of a mine thrower shell, on the ground there were his boots with feet and beginning of the legs. Everything else end up in the tree branches above our heads or simple evaporated in air, I guess.

Can you believe that I went to the war in a Led Zeppelin t-shirt? I guess I was thinking that I looked cool like that. I do not remember what I thought in those days at all.

It was like a big party, with the possibility of death. Something like that.

My first big meeting with the real enemy was something that looked like black comedy with a very bad outcome.

We were holding a position in woods with a very vague idea of where the enemy should be. It was like "they are there, and we are here" and "there" was somewhere within kilometers of dense forest.

The guys were trying to make some meal over a big fire. Of course, there was nothing like real noise discipline. We all acted like we were hunting deer while drinking.

As one of the youngest in the group I had to pull wood for fire from the forest. While doing that I spot two guys some 200 meters above me in woods, I did not recognize, of course, who they were. I did not even see if they were armed. But what I did notice was that they had complete camo uniforms, and that was pretty rare on our side in the early days of conflict.

I throw away firewood I had gathered and ran to the fire and guys.

I told them, "Guys, I think there is enemy closing in on us, they are there!" And I received big volley of laughter from them.

The leader even said to me, "Kid, this is war. If you are afraid of it, you should stay home. They are kilometers from us, and our scouts would see them long before you."

Later we found out that our watch was a few hundred meters BEHIND us actually instead in front of us.

Some 20 minutes later the guy next to me was trying to check if the meal was ready when hell started.

Do you know the sound when couple of shells are launched, let's say twelve, and before last one is launched the first ones are already starting to explode around you?

Yeah, man. War is terror and confusion, especially before

you realized that you can be killed no matter whether you are you a good man or a bad man. Later it gets easier.

Clearly those two guys were checking us out. We were like sitting ducks for them, sitting ducks without brains.

I do not remember the explosions like separate events, once it started to rain ground and steel around me, it all melted into one big explosion.

I'm not sure how long it lasted, probably not more than minute or two, but it seemed much longer, trust me.

When it stopped, then the screams started.

One guy was walking towards me with his guts in his hands and keeps repeating, "What, what, what, what? "

Some of them just lay down where they get killed.

Small dude, I think he was car mechanic in peace time was trying to scream, but the only noises that came from his mouth were gurgling, and some strange wet noises like you are running in shallow water on the beach. That still echoes in my head sometimes.

He was standing when shelling started. He put his rifle on tree branch, maybe two meters from him. The shrapnel hit his rifle butt, launching small pieces of wood like arrows to his neck.

He died a minute or two later, still trying to scream or say something.

The guys from our medical services showed up but I could not hear a thing. Someone pulled me back to the houses where the rest of the unit was, a few kilometers back. They thought I was wounded too. Luckily the blood on me was someone else's, not mine.

Was I scared?

No, actually not. I was more like surprised at what was happening to the people and how easily they died. It was very fast for me.

Later we figured out more things about how to fight and how to survive.

Also, we learned how to "cover" those feelings of humanity in us, at least I learned it very well.

Did I like it?

At the beginning it was strange. Later I realized that I am strong and powerful.

Actually, later I figured that I like all that.

No, it was not in the moment when I killed my first man, or second or any of them. It was during one of the pretty peaceful events.

We just cleared part of the village from enemy force remains, and while there was still sporadic fighting, we were already were checking houses for looting.

It was nice house; you could see that guys who lived there had been pretty rich.

In small storage room we found cans of meat. Meat was pretty rare in that period.

The house was intact in terms of looting We were first. We did not even worry too much for traps. Yeah, we checked it, but not in detail. We wanted to eat.

There were I think eight of us, dirty, heated from fighting, and we as a joke took plates from the nice closet, plates that probably were used for special guests only.

Then we put meat on plates, and we used forks and knives, for real. One guy I think still had blood and grey pieces of brain on his boot from where he had stepped in some guy's corpse accidentally minutes before that. But there he was, eating like in fancy restaurant.

In that moment I felt that I liked all that. I felt alive and powerful. And I kinda understood why my grandfather was famous.

We smashed the plates against the wall as soon as we were done. One of the men found a 5-liter bottle of homemade alcohol in the basement and we heated ourselves up even more. Soon after that one who got drunk first came out from the house completely naked yelling "Is there any woman in this fucking village? Without women, it sucks!"

There were no women in that village, but in others there were...

That moment passed but that feeling stayed with me even today, I think fear of dying ran away from me in that house, and never came back. Never.

How did I survive fighting?

Hmm, I told you, war is confusion and terror, and pieces of luck maybe.

I will tell you one event.

There were me and another guy, houses that we needed to check were supposed to be cleared from enemy. Another unit had swept the area hours ago, and we were moving pretty freely.

The other guy was carpenter in normal times, a big huge dude. The rifle in his hand looked like a toy. He did not have real friends in unit, but he had a dog with him all the time.

He found that dog months ago in backyard of abandoned house. The dog was chained and almost starved to death there.

He took the dog and carried it for days sharing food with him. After the dog got on his feet they never separated.

As I said we were approaching one of the houses, close to the house there was small corn field. Dog was running around us, maybe 20 meters behind or in front of us, jumping and sniffing everything.

I wanted to check partially destroyed car in front of the house, car was between house and that corn field.

In that moment he grabbed my hand. In that time, I had learned already a lot, so I froze, and looked at him.

He shows me his dog with his eyes.

The dog stood like he was paralyzed, looking at the corn field. He did not move single muscle.

We pointed rifles to the field, and the carpenter shouted, "Drop your weapon, come out, raise hands and we will not kill you."

Seconds later an enemy soldier come out with his hands raised up.

My friend told him, "Yeah, you are a smart guy. You know you do not have a chance. All the while, he was checking his pockets for valuable stuff.

I checked place where that soldier was lying in field, there was rifle, loaded, there where he left it when my friend shouted.

You may understand this story as a story about friendship between man and a dog, loyalty and all that…

I understand it different; you see that guy had us right where he could very easily take us down. But he did not.

Why?

I do not know, probably he was scared to death, or he was not sure that he could shoot us both before we shot him, or he was not sure that we were alone...

Who knows and who cares?

The important thing is that I understood there that life and death are sometimes matter of something that we could not reach.

And if it is your day to die, you will die. If it is not your day, then it is not.

Sometimes you cannot do too much about it.

Oh, I knew that you gonna have questions, OK ask.

Do I believe in God? That is your question?

Fuck I did not expect that.

I do not know man, not sure. I have seen so much weird stuff, so many times that evil wins, that if God exists then he must be lunatic. Yea, if He is there ruling with us then He is one weird dude.

I think I do not care actually.

But I believe that when your time come you cannot do shit.

What did we do with the prisoner?

Yeah, now I expected THAT question, but you see I will not answer you that. Nope. Let us just say that war that I fought was not about honor and compassion. Understand?

What happened when war the ended?

Now when you are reading from books and documentaries you may think that there was something like feeling of celebration or happiness when all ended.

I did not feel anything like that. War for me was an endless game of surviving the fight. It was the same no matter if we lost or won the battle.

You could end up dead in both situations.

My job today is EOD technician. Yeah, I am trying to find the mines that we and other folks dug in during the war.

You see most guys imagine that demining is a job that consists of one big flat field, and what you need is to lay down with knife, crawl around, and check for mines.

Yeah, in the movies maybe.

In reality it is slowly crawling through the dense brambles and thorns, clearing it with small axe before you even have a chance to check it.

Man, 20 years has passed since someone planted a mine there. Do you think that someone carefully went through that area every year with lawnmower in order to keep it tidy for demining?

20 years after man, it is jungle there.

While I am moving through that, I am still feeling strong, you know, if it is my day to die, I will die.

Oh yea, I have more jobs too, you see there are reason why people do not want to sit here in cafe close to our table.

I am still doing that what I learned to do best in war. There is always gonna be a job for people who are willing to take another person's life willingly and without remorse.

War or no war.

Survival Notes from Toby:

The devil is in the detail. Many of us want or even need 'clear' lessons, spelt out for us. Survivor accounts very often do not come 'nicely packaged' like that. It pays to read accounts such as these slowly, thoroughly and sometimes even repeatedly. There are INCREDIBLY hard-won lessons in here:

Lesson 1. Tackling Resource Depletion:

"House was intact in terms of looting, we were first, we did not even care too much for traps, yea we check it, but not in detail. We wanted to eat."

This one sentence encapsulates SO much about the reality of Urban Survival. If finding yourself scavenging for resources, basic necessities such as food, you'll need to be prepared to fight, to kill and to die. You may be well aware of threats in the battle space but time, hunger, desperation and more will demand major risks are taken.

This is multi sided, we can learn from this reality that we want to avoid being in that situation by being prepared as possible, but on the flip side of that if this is the person 'coming to you' to trade for resources you have and you prepared to deal with that level of desperation and risk tolerance?

Resources run out eventually, and in that circumstance these events will not be 'one off' but an intrinsic part of your daily routine, never certain where your next meal or more is coming from... Constantly searching, scavenging and the more you do it the more efficient you become and the more ruthless you will be. THAT is what is showing up to your door (With 11 'friends' maybe?) not a neighbor asking to borrow a cup of sugar...

Lesson 2: Situational Awareness.

"In that moment he grab my hand. In that time I learned already a lot, so I froze, and look at him.

He show me his dog with his eyes.

Dog standed like paralyzed, looking at the corn field, he did not move single muscle.

We pointed rifles to the field, and carpenter shouted" drop weapon, come out, raise hands and we will not kill you"

Seconds later enemy soldier come out with his hands raised up."

The incredible advantages of a dog as a sensory suite aside, the first line is key. Silent communication (grab my hand), reaction to external stimuli ('Reading' dog), in built response (I freezed) Processing the situation and reacting accordingly (Pointed rifles, and interestingly called out instead of indiscriminately shooting, I'll let you think yourself as to the possible reasons why?)

With these details in mind, maybe go back and re-read Ed's account, see what you missed first time…

Sasa's Story

S is 75 years old, retired with a small pension as a civil victim of war (disabled).

At the time of event he was 52-year-old and unemployed. We are having conversation in the backyard of his small house. He lives in little village with his wife, and no kids.

He looks old, but still strong.

The air is full of different smells, some of the smells are strange, but all pleasant. There are different kind of herbs there on the wall where he dries that stuff for different kind of teas and homemade remedies.

We drank some homemade tea and he tells me it is good for everything from back pain to cancer, including problems with potency.

Before the war I was drifter, you know, the kind of man that women would say "stay away from him" to her daughters.

I did not have a real home; I worked a lot of different jobs. Everything from a cook's assistant on big ocean ships to being second helper and picking fruits in Italy during the big season.

I was kind of a dreamer always. I wanted to travel a lot. At the end I saw quite a bit of the world, accomplished nothing, and came back to the country some years before the war started.

You know that ex-state had pretty good social coverage for people like me, so I somehow existed living in one room of distant relatives.

He was heavy drinker, and most of the time I think he was not even aware that I was there, living with him.

Yeah, I drank in that time a lot too, nothing else to do actually.

I even heard that in the neighborhood there was legend about me that I came back from some Africa country after I fought there in some of the wars in the French Foreign Legion.

Remember, in that time being different meant that stories like that are simply "glued" to you.

I did not mind; people would leave me alone most of the time thanks to stories like that.

In reality, the closest to a weapon that I had been up to that time was a knife in the kitchen, I did not even serve ex-Army because I was "badly malnourished "as they said.

Of course, I noticed that a war was coming. I was different a bit maybe, but not an idiot. I guess I did not care.

A few weeks before fights in the city started, my relative sold his house. Actually, I think he lost it playing cards, but the result was the same.

We both left that house in the days when shootings and big confusion had already started.

I remember that the new owner came into the house with a rifle and two drunk girls. The girls were giggling and shrieking like some crows from hell.

As soon as they entered, he started to shoot at the collection of empty bottles on the relative's closet, asking the drunk girls, "Look at this baby, am I the man or what? "

From those beginning days I remember lot of stuff, but sometimes I think it was like I was in some other place. Because whenever I spoke later to the people, they mention confusion and fear in beginning of everything.

But my strongest memory is the feeling of something like a happy madness from the people.

Of course, I remember panic, buses full of kids leaving the town, barricades and checkpoints with armed people, and strange new flags or colors on arms and shoulders.

But I felt that people lost their mind in a way, I saw man playing guitar in the middle of the street, drunk, while 100 meters from him two guys were looting a pharmacy. One of them was drinking baby syrup for fever I guess or antibiotic right in front of the store. I still remember the strong smell of strawberry when he spilled half of that on his shirt.

I guess they both were on drugs, high.

And two hundred meters from them there was a TV crew, with one of the guys from the local authority who was talking into the camera saying that they had it under control, and that everyone need to stay home and follow the orders on TV.

In that time, the electricity was gone already, I think.

I spent that night in an abandoned VW Golf (car), It looked like somebody left it by the road in hurry. All the doors were open, and on the back seat there were a whole bunch of chocolate cookies.

That night, the city started to burn.

I ate cookies, watched fires, and listened to gunshots. Somewhere in the distance, someone put folk music on a speaker, and you could hear how people sang together with the audio and shot guns in time to the chorus.

And in that moment if you closed your eyes you could easily imagine that you are at some big party somewhere, maybe in some village ceremony where they just opened a redecorated church, and all folks are heated from alcohol, so someone just shoots in the air, while folk music is banging, and lambs are turning over the fires.

Happy madness.

People were running all night past me, most of them carrying stuff from looted stores, some with weapons, some with families trying, I guess, to leave the city.

In some time of the night I felt a strong pain in my chest. I woke up to see two guys looking at me – one was poking me with a rifle.

The other guy said, "Leave the idiot. Can't you see he is drunk? "

The poking guy looked angrily at me and asked, "Money? "

I tried to say something, but what came from my mouth was a sound like I was preparing to throw up. Fear simply blocked my vocal cords, I think.

Luckily, they understand that as a proof that I was really completely drunk, and the guy said, "Oh, he is really plastered man."

The guy with the rifle just said, "Fuck" and smashed me in the face with the rifle butt.

You notice that I still have a bent nose. It is a reminder of that night.

But I consider myself lucky. In those days it was simply a matter of will or effort. Is some guy going to shoot me or kill me or give me cigarette?

In the morning, when I left the car, I noticed blood on front seat, a lot of blood. At first, I thought it was from my nose, but then I saw more blood on the wheel, and you know that mark that clearly indicates that somebody who was bleeding seriously was dragged from the car?

Yeah, I saw that too, I did not check who was at the end of those bloody marks.

The next couple of nights or maybe even weeks, I spent days and nights mostly inside ruins, every night in a different place. Once, I spent the night in a looted gas station. I came there late at the night and just crawled inside and slept.

In the morning, when I wanted to go out, I noticed a dead guy who was maybe four meters from the place where I slept.

And what was even worse, shooting started outside close to me and lasted for the whole day, so I was forced to spend like 10 more hours with the dead guy. I covered him with whole bunch of promotional calendars, just so I didn't have to watch him, because somehow, I felt like I was like forced to stare at him. Like I expected at any moment for him to rise and attack me.

Sometimes around that day and night I figured that there was no point in moving during the day, so I started to use night for that.

The first month of everything I was not really aware what was happening. Of course, I knew that war started, but I did not have a clue who was fighting or who was in charge of what.

I ate what I found in empty houses or supermarkets and stores, but it was obvious that stuff was running out. People were starting to empty more and more of that.

Now when I look back on those days it seems funny that I did not try to leave city, but I thought that everything was gonna end soon, and that it was nothing more than one big riot.

Sometime at the end of the first month some kind of provisional government was established, and one day I woke up hearing guy talks over the speaker from some kind of improvised armored car that all men from 16 to 70 need to go and check in to the their headquarters in order to make some kind of contribution for establishing order in the region.

I looked through the broken window and saw about thirty armed men with that car, going slowly through the street. They did not look like any kind of law to me, so I just ignored that call. Luckily, because as I heard later most of those who show up there were imprisoned or killed.

Later the real fighting started, armies and lines of defense, attacks and whatever else.

It was all same to me: a whole bunch of armed people fighting for their causes.

Most of them were fighting just for resources.

The city was slowly starting to be full of desperate civilians who were trying to find food and shelter between endless fights.

One night I met a guy who I knew. During our quick

conversation he told me that now he is something like medic man in one of the units.

I asked him how that was possible because he did not have any clue about medicine. He told me that luckily most of the other folks in the group knew even less about that then he, and that most of the job was to plug holes anyway.

I came home an hour later. My home at that time was the back room of the local newspaper press. The front rooms were burned, but one in the back was still OK.

I sit there and I started to think: "What do I know how to do in exchange for some goods?"

Well, I could not think of too many things, I was a drifter. I know how to tell stories maybe from my journeys, but that would not do too much good in city where people were dying in big numbers.

Then I remember a guy from France. He was a drifter like me, but he also had a pretty good income. He was something like a medicine man. He helped people to heal with herbal recipes.

He would travel a lot and, in every city or place he had his customers. I do not know how much really, he knew about herbs, but I remembered that he lived pretty good from that.

Once he told me that he actually only gave hope and good will to the sick folks. Everything else was in God hands.

I guess he knew a lot about herbs, and then where he could not help or did not know how to help, he gave good words.

Then I looked through my "inventory" in that back room.

There were a few cans of peas, a few pieces of cloth, empty batteries, one flashlight, a small broken radio, and bunch of other useless things.

I was looking for something else, under the pile of rubble I found it. Six or seven packages of spices and teas taken from looted supermarket.

I quickly went through the packages and found a small bag of oregano spice, and there was a package of chamomile tea there.

I remembered again that drifter healer from a long time ago had used hot chamomile tea bags for wounds and rashes. He would simply put tea bags soaked in warm water on the wound and bandage it.

And that was my first idea of what I would do in order to feed myself in those time.

Did I have idea that I was gonna be something like a medicine man, a man who knows a lot about herbal remedies, honey medications, and all this what you see here?

Of course not, my idea was to sneak together with my friend to that group as something like nurse, helper, medic, whatever you could call it, just to have some food and security.

And it worked. My first patient was a man who had a long incision wound on his leg from a knife. I cleaned it and used chamomile tea bags on it.

Of course, most of those guys did not know how little I knew. Luckily that guy had I guess a clean wound and he was strong, so everything went fine.

My next step was to find someone who really know something about herbs, and I found that person one old lady. Her husband had died from a heart attack when armed folks came to their doors asking for gold jewelry. He just dropped dead.

They did not even enter the house after that, they just turned and left, maybe amused how easily that man died from fear and shock.

We exchanged goods, and she gave me some shelter and knowledge. I gave her piece of what I earned.

Oh yea, I learned a lot about things like lavender, garlic, mint, and things about potatoes and garlic.

I learned that sometimes the difference between life and death can simply be whether the guy washed the wound with water or not. Sometimes it was simply whether he had enough will to survive a wound or illness.

Of course, I needed time to learn a few things, and yeah, I had my failures too.

In the beginning of my career as a "man who knows herbs," I treated a woman who had some stomach pain. Later I found out that it was some kind of internal bleeding. They had been pretty important in that time and I could not refuse that.

I could not help her. She died. For a month I was scared to death that her husband was gonna kill me because I could not help her. Luckily, he died, so nothing bad came to me from that.

The old lady with whom I shared a home died after some time. Actually, I am pretty sure that she killed herself. She knew ways to do that easily and painlessly.

That house started to be pretty unsafe for me, so I moved to the empty apartment in ten story building.

In that time most of those buildings were pretty much abandoned and ruined, so I was safe there.

Over time I earned some kind of reputation, and I learned all the time. I looked for older folks who were willing to share their knowledge about natural remedies.

Of course, there was more than half mythology in all that info, but also lot of good information.

After some time, I got the reputation of the man who know the perfect plant for whatever illness and injury there is.

I remember one evening 5 guys came into my home, and then L. entered. I knew him only from stories.

King of the black market, absolute psychopath, but with a very sharp mind.

You know what he needed from me? First, he looked at me and said, "I thought you were gonna be older, man. You look like shit."

I tried to keep my peaceful face there, but obviously I looked very scared because he laughed at me and told me, "Do not worry, man, I need some advice and I will give you whatever you want for that, food, or weapon, or women, no problem."

As I said I had heard stories about him before, I wisely refused to take anything, saying that I'd be glad to help him, expecting nothing for that.

He laughed and said that he liked me, and if my herb worked, he would be my friend.

Of course, it was good to have him as a friend in that time.

And I cannot say what he wanted, some folks from that group who came into my home are still alive, and those folks still pay attention about their image.

It worked then, and I was protected from him.

You know how in hard times legends are built about some people, like "that guy survived in a burning house" or "that guy killed 10 guys alone with knife in one fight?"

Well I guess some kind of legend was built about my herbs, and it worked.

I had food, water, shelter. I even stated to have backup supplies. People gave me gold, batteries, one man gave me signed contract that he was giving me his house forever, of course worthless in that time.

While outside was hell, I was doing pretty good.

And outside it *was* hell

I remember one night I saw a tank, slowly going over the rubble, with few guys on it. One was eating some animal still on a stick (from skewer?). Another guy was waving the flag of a football club. And they had even music loud on that beast.

Happy madness.

I cannot compress all events that I lived through in hour talking with you, but the important thing is that I went through everything almost uninjured at all and I learned a lot.

A few days after peace came, while moving my stuff out from my shelter, part of the wall collapsed on my legs, and my right leg was crushed.

Because of that, I got a small civilian war victim pension.

I married a widow from this village and move into this house, still helping people with natural remedies, and still learning about it.

I am doing actually pretty fine.

Survival Notes from Toby:

"52 year old and unemployed", on the face of it, it would seem 'S' wouldn't stand a chance of surviving serious situation by modern prepper 'standards', yet not only did he survive but even thrived during the conflict.

1. *Adaptive mindset*
2. *Developing skills that were of use in that time (Albeit this approach is a bit of 'a two edged sword')*
3. *Understanding who he was dealing with*
4. *Continuously improving his "skills/reputation"*

One of the most notable quotes however was from the beginning:

"I asked him how is possible because he did not have any clue about medicine, he told me that luckily most of the other folks in group know even less about that then he, and that most of the job is to plug holes anyway."

We can discuss the morals of claiming a skillset you don't truly 'have', but in serious situations merely knowing a little more than others puts you in a potential position of advantage. It's worth thinking on that a little, BUT as highlighted more than once in this interview, failing to 'save' someone in a medic role can cause serious consequences for you individually and more…

Nerko's Story

1. was 39 years old, unemployed, and a heavy drinker. At the time of event he was 17 years old. We were sitting in the city square. He was feeding pigeons by taking small pieces of bread from his sandwich that he was eating. He ate very slow, keeping food very long in the mouth and chewing slowly.

The skin on his hands and fingers looked unhealthy and dirty with a lot of small wounds, dirty and broken fingernails. He was smoking handmade cigar and chewing a sandwich in same time.

While he talked, he very often stopped with the story. It looked more like he was not aware of that than like he was trying to remember something.

I promised him 50 Euros for the story, and he asked me all the time during the story am I going to give him that 50 Euros or we gonna have problems otherwise.

Actually, he is looking like he could not do any harm to anyone, anymore.

I grew up in abandoned kids' home, an orphanage. And we all had something like a game. Some of us who were teenagers imagined that our fathers actually were important people, and some day they were gonna come and recognize us.

Of course, we all knew it was pretend. We did not actually believe in that, but over the time somehow the way we imagined them affected us in a way how we grew up.

My buddy said that his father was magician, and that he travels a lot, and one day he was gonna came from somewhere far away and pick him up.

My imagined father was soldier, an officer, one of the best.

So, you can already imagine that I was into that: army, guns, fighting.

Of course, it did not have too much to do with my reality in that time. I was going to school in order to be plumber.

Yeah, the favorite jobs for kids like us was plumbers, painters, car mechanics...

How was my life there?

I do not know, for me it was only one that I knew. It was not like in the movies. Nobody beat us, and we did not have to get in line for food while someone was standing and watching us with whip.

The people who worked there mostly were really doing their best to make "decent citizens" of us.

But you know, when you come from a place like that it is like you are carrying some kind of metal sign around your neck for your whole life.

People simply expect you to have some kind of problems.

Even if you do not, people are gonna say that you have it. And that's it.

But one thing is definitely true. We all learned from early times that life simply sometimes fuck you over.

A few days before the war started for real, an Italian church organization came to the city offering to the authorities that they were gonna relocate all of us, kids and educators, to the Italy in an effort to save us from war.

Authorities agree, and we all started with packing. Fights had already started but it was still possible to leave the city, especially for a foreign organization.

The day before the convoy left, I watched out the window and saw three guys walking down the street.

Armed, in some kind of uniforms, part military camo and part police uniform and two with berets. One wore a helmet, in jeans with some kind of grey military poncho, and he carried heavy machine gun on his shoulders, with both hands on it.

I do not know what happened, and what I actually thought in that moment, but those guys moved something in me, or woke up is maybe better word.

And I knew I am not gonna go anywhere.

Yea, I was 16 years old, almost seventeen. What the fuck I did know at that age anyway.

In school we had few months before class of the "defense

and protection" (civilian defense) and the teacher pulled from somewhere an ages old gas mask, a first aid bag, a few fake bombs and an old and rusty M-48 rifle. He talked about a socialistic society, how we needed to be ready for everything, covering from nuclear blast and whole bunch of similar rubbish that kids were taught for years and years after the end of ww2.

I stared at the M-48 like it was a laser gun from the movies, not some artifact that stayed locked for years in steel closet in the assembly hall.

Probably if someone tried to shoot from that thing, it would explode in his face.

But I stared at that like it was magic.

Can you imagine then how I stared in those three guys who looked so tough?

My blood boiled, I think.

That night I left that home and never came back. The "son of the magician" also came with me.

I did not have any particular plans, but I knew I wanted to be part of something that was just starting to happen.

Everything looked strange in those days, and events were happening way too fast for us to process them. I saw people who looked like beggars hold speeches in front of e200 people, and how people fanatically followed them, sometimes into death.

The first problems we had happened the next day. We were stopped by a group of people in uniforms. They asked us for papers, IDs.

We did not have anything on us. One of them just smashed my buddy in the face with a baton, just like that, and they kicked him few more times while he was on the ground. And then they just walked away like nothing happened.

The local ambulance worked; it was in chaos but still worked. We got there and saw that they had way more important things to take care of. My friend's busted lips and bruises on his back were nothing important in that moment.

So, we left the place and continued to wander through the city. Fights had already started.

The mobilization of people for fighting was announced, and we went to the place to be recruited.

An older dude was there, sitting on the table in rubber boots that usually people here using while working on agricultural stuff, or if you are a miner.

A big pistol was in the holster around his shoulders. He was a bald-headed guy but with a big mustache. On his forearm there was a tattoo of an anchor, with date "1968" and something. Probably he served as a sailor some 20 years ago, probably in the military. He did not look like a real warrior to me, but hell, he had gun.

He asked us, "What are you two guys doing here?"

We said we wanted to join.

He said, "To join what?"

We did not say anything. He stared at us for a few moments and then said, "OK kids, if you do not walk away from here in next few seconds, I am gonna kick your butts so hard, that you gonna wish that you never been born."

And then a younger guy came from the other door. The older guy stood up, obviously showing him respect.

The younger guy asked him what was going on, and the guy with anchor tattoo said, "They want to join to us, Boss."

Boss looked at us and asked, "How old you are guys?"

We both said in the same time, "19!"

"And what about your families, parents?"

I said, "gone" and my buddy said, "dead."

He smiled with some kind of ugly smile, and said, "OK, you just joined."

And that moment started my career as a soldier. Of course, the word soldier was used then in another meaning than today, a wider meaning.

At first, we were "messengers," but our job did not have

too much to do with carrying messages. It meant that we were too young for anything more important than cleaning stuff, helping older guys, and being something like the unit mascot.

But in war you learn fast, or you die. It's simple like that.

My buddy made a mistake one day. In one of the suburbs, he activated a booby trap and got wounded in his legs. Immediately shelling and firing started on us, and we panicked and ran from there, leaving him lying there.

My last image of him was how he screamed trying to crawl into close house while bullets rained around him.

We came back to the place a couple of hours later, during the dark.

He was not there, and by the marks on ground, we could see that someone dragged him to the close yard and then nothing.

I never saw him again.

For years I was waiting to hear some news about him, that he was captured, imprisoned and released later, or that he fled somewhere or similar.

But nothing.

Yeah, of course he is dead. I do not want to think too much how he died at the end.

Poor guy did not even learn to shoot the proper way. He was too nervous for that.

The man with the anchor on his arm became my mentor. Romeo was his name. He was a pretty decent guy, showing me how things worked in war.

Everything from how take cover, how to kill, to how to cook a potato in a quick way in fire, and how to make that fire to not be visible from far away.

His family was out of the country from a few months before the war, and he never missed the opportunity to point to everyone how he recognized on time that the war was coming so he sent them out.

But on the other hand, he talked to me few times that he lost contact with them, and how he doubts that they will come back to him even when war ended.

And he never explained why he did not leave the area together with them.

I think he had some kind of patriotic duty feeling, like lot of people.

He had habit of taking off his boots at any possible opportunity and soak his feet in bowl of hot water.

So, you could see him sitting in some ruined house, with a blissful expression on his face and his feet in a bowl, while the rest of the guys looked for gold, food, weapons, or anything useful.

Besides how to shoot and kill, I learned also that courage is something that is invented, imagined.

In one of my first gunfights I learned it in some strange way.

We were pretty much surrounded on one street, maybe 20 of us, in two houses. The other side soldiers were advancing the whole day, slowly, but suddenly they attacked us, our position with overwhelming force.

I found myself together with other guys in house without the possibility of retreat.

The tank was slowly moving toward our position shelling us slowly, but with confidence that they had gotten us where they wanted us.

Three from our group jumped through the window just to be immediately massacred with a rain of bullets.

The choice was either to go to the basement and wait there to be buried alive, or to go to the second floor and wait for a miracle.

Guys mostly chose the basement. I chose the second floor with a very vague idea to jump from the window from there. Of course, it was a stupid idea, but in moments like that you choose by some strange logic. I simply did not like idea of being inside the basement without windows.

I think I chose that I'd rather be shot while trying to run than to be buried under the tons of bricks.

Explosions and gunshots were deafening, we shot through the windows and holes in the wall without aiming.

The guy next to me was shot probably by pieces of shell while we were running through the rooms on the second floor.

He sat down on the floor, screaming while manically trying to take his shirt off himself, only to die immediately after he succeed in that from a few big holes in his chest.

Somewhere in that moment, other guys from our unit destroyed the tank in a counterattack, but we still did not know that.

Two of us wanted to jump from the window. The guy next to me spent one whole minute trying to remove curtain from the window in order to jump.

The house was pretty much destroyed, but a curtain on the window was still standing there, with some flowery pattern.

I do not have clue why he simply did not pull the curtain and jump, but in moments like that you just do lot of things without sense, I guess.

He got shot in the head while he was doing that, and he felt down on the floor together with that fucking curtain.

I simply jumped out from the window, without even looking where I was going to land.

Maybe that saved my life. I spent no time in the window.

But I did not do that intentionally, I just wanted to get away from there, even if that meant I was gonna land on steel spikes there.

I landed in mud, up to my knees.

I just stood up and ran.

Some 100 meters from there I met guys from my unit and realized a few things there.

First one of my shoes left in that mud there, I run with my foot in socks, over the broken glass, rubble and everything. I did not even feel that there were several wounds on my leg from that. Second, I realized that I had serious case of diarrhea while doing everything, and I stunk like an animal.

And third, only few of us survived that event from the two houses.

Yeah, I was the target of jokes several weeks because I shit myself, but one day I kicked the butt of one of the guys because of that, and the mocking stopped.

I was learning fast.

After that event, I became something like full member, or real soldier in the unit.

We were transferred to another area of fighting. The land was pretty much flat there without too many hills or natural barriers. Before the war it was nicknamed "pantry of the country" because of the endless fields of corn, wheat, and other food crops.

Pretty soon we nicknamed it shitstorm because of a lot of losses in the unit. People simply could not get used to fighting in the open, where you can get killed from very far distance without knowing what hell is happening.

I was changing fast, my learning about life came in the middle of the war, and I could not learn too many good things, I guess.

Romeo who was something like my mentor became an old boring dude.

He started to annoy me with his life perception, but as I said I was young, very young, and he was old, and become boring to me.

During one of the ceasefires we "camped" in a partially destroyed village, on a small square. We were mostly lying on raincoats, blankets, or simply on the bare ground.

A church was some 50 meters from us. Half of the building was gone, and we could see Jesus inside on the cross, undamaged, so we started to shoot at the statue, even betting in cigarettes who's gonna shoot the statue in the head.

I was born and named as a Catholic, but religion did not mean too much for me.

In the middle of our competition Romeo came, and sat between us, he did not shoot, he just watched us.

I won, I blasted Jesus's head in bits, and won a handful of cigarettes.

Romeo did not say anything, but later when we stay alone, he just said to me, "Kid, you changed a lot, do you know that?"

I said, "Yeah man, thanks."

And he said, "I did not say this to flatter you. You changed for the worse, kid. Wars are happening always, and then they are gone, but once when you change, you are gone, no matter whether it is war, or not."

He was boring to me then in that moment, but years later I understood what he wanted to say.

Once we came in the backyard of an abandoned house, there was cherry tree there, full of fruits, I raise my hands and broke off several branches, sat down, and started to eat.

When he saw me, he asked, "Don't you think that someone gonna need a chance to eat from that tree next year too?"

I laughed at that; the others laughed too. But he watched at me all the time.

Years later I understood that he was witnessing how I was

growing up from a kid to a man, but the wrong kind of person, not good one.

Maybe he saw his own kid in me, and maybe he was trying to help me in that time, but war already took me, and raised me.

My rifle was my best friend. I developed a sense for revealing hidden value inside abandoned houses, I met women, yeah, in different ways, I learned that when I am in doubt I need to shoot. I learned that a knife sometimes is much scarier than a loaded gun and lot of similar stuff.

I felt that war was gonna last forever. I did not know any more of anything else other than that war.

Oh yes, I become one of the best warriors in the unit, and over the time something like the Boss's right hand when it came to some jobs, like organizing smuggling of valuable stuff outside or in, or dealing with prisoners, etc.

Somewhere around that time Romeo gave me one of his last pieces of advice.

He said something like, "Kid, war is gonna end one day, and we all are gonna be ashamed of some of the things that we did, but there's gonna be people whose gonna be blamed for all the bad, even if they did not do it, and you are the perfect candidate for that."

And he was boring to me again.

And then one day he was not boring anymore. He died, got killed. A sniper got him. We sat a whole day under the small hill, pretty far from the front line, and I am not sure why and how but for whole day it was peaceful. We played cards, betting in cigarettes, telling jokes and guessing where next we were gonna go to fight.

Romeo was standing next to one group of the players, watching the game.

A shot was fired, and we did not care too much until we saw that he put hands on his stomach and said, "He shot me!"

Sniper.

We panicked and ran and took cover behind the military truck some 20 meters from there. One more shot was fired when one of us tried to reach Romeo in order to pull him over, but we couldn't.

And then we lay down and waited two hours for night.

He screamed the whole time. That bullet had opened his belly like some scissors, and he held his guts with hands.

Then he went into delirium, calling his kids, and his wife. At the end he quietly spoke with someone or to someone. Then he finally shut up.

Half hour later, at night we approached him. He was dead. We put him in blanket and carried him to the truck.

He was gone.

I saw already the death of many of many folks, lot of guys

who I knew for some time died, got killed, so at that moment I already was numbed.

Yea, I was sorry because him, but that's it, nothing more.

Toby Takeaway:

A conflict will always need foot soldiers. Youth is one of the best and easiest demographics to recruit from. Even with a means of escaping the situation being RIGHT THERE he chose to stay and fight, now all we need to consider is at what cost…?

We are CONSTANTLY teaching the 'don't be there', and 'avoid the conflict' mindset, this interview shows one of the main reasons why…

The Intersection

Through the closed eyes he tried to see things how they use to be a year ago in that exact place.

He ignored the gunshots and explosions. It was not hard. Over a period of the last few months he had learned to do it, to switch off from the outside world for couple of minutes.

Many times, it saved his sanity.

A few times, he almost lost his life because it.

His closed his eye and in his mind he saw the place in front of him how it use to be:

It was an intersection in the center of the city, with roundabout in the middle.

In that roundabout there was piece of land with roses, and as a kid he always asked how thea roses managed to have so red color, like the colors in cartoons.

On one side of the street there was city theater with an old theater pub.

The place was famous because city bohemians liked to drink there and discuss about different stuff, or simply play pool. Entrance for regular folks was not forbidden, but if you were not part of the clique inside, after you entered you would feel not welcomed very soon.

He liked the place a lot because once he spent whole night there when he was 17, with his relative.

The relative was invited for a drink there and they ended up drinking for the whole night in the company of 10 or 12 old actors, professors, together with some "low" folks that made up the strangely bohemian circle of the city.

That night got inprinted in his memory as a mix of feeling:s how people can go high or how low in one night, citing the poems of old poets and crying half hour later as a small kids because someone insulted them over glass of wine.

Right across from the city theater, some 200 meters away, there was college, a medical school.

Hundred-year-old trees made it like tunnel through the front enterance of the college and there was park with benches.

In the middle of that park there was a huge willow, and a bench with one missing board on it.

He had spent many hours on that bench waiting for his girlfriend to finish her classes so they could go to coffee somewhere close and endlessly discuss now seemed like such irrelevant things.

500 meters from college was a big mall. For those times it was actually a *huge* mall. After they had coffee in some coffee house, they would go there and check for music LP

s, or jeans, or just wander around like young people often wander around.

A huge explosion maybe one kilometer away from his position suddenly broke and erased those images from the past. He almost involuntarily jumped from his crouching position into laying down. But he stayed like that for couple of seconds trying to figure out what was it excatly.

The night was cloudy, and clouds covered the moon so there was not too much was new to see.

He heard the distant sound of an airplane and again closed his eyes in the hiding place, and listened.

Airplanes with MREs would come usually around 2 in the morning.

The sound was deep and distant.

During that time he had learned to clearly distinguish different sounds around himself, sounds that only showed up in his life a few months ago.

The sound of an anti-aircraft cannon shooting in his direction from the hills? That sounded like drummer on drugs trying to catch the rhytm.

Then there was the sound of a minethrower mine coming down, hissing and whizzing while you looked at the man next to you and seing in his ridiculously wide open eyes the same horror that he can see in your eyes. It was an expression that said, "This one is coming directly on top of us, it is coming right on our fucking heads!"

The sounds of a tank grinding the rubble while maneuvering through half buried streets somewhere near you, maybe two streets from you is echoing from the walls of apartment buildings, going through the holes in the walls, the sound is surrounding you and mixing with that feeling in your gut that is actually sheer panic. And at the end you do not have a clue where is that tank and in which direction you have to move to run from it.

The sounds of large caliber shells coming from longer distances, you could almost imagine that sound like something big is spiraling around it'self while it is coming (you always think) in your direction.

This night, it was sound of something big, or more precisely it was sound of something mean and fat.

Folks called it "the hog".

The sound of the bomb being dropped from airplane. That sound lasted long, it lasted as it seemed to him for minutes.

The long and high sound of that bomb would make people sometimes act like babies, like wimps.

There is an object with enough explosive to destroy an average house with everything and everybody inside, and there are you, down on the ground waiting.

You listen to the sound if you find yourself somewhere

outside, in pitch darkness, and that sound lasts for quite some time. You at the first moment think "fuck, it it is one bomb and big city."

And then as sound changes its tone and gets louder, it gets into your brain that it is coming to you – to the place where you stand at that moment.

Then you jump under the ruin of a burned van and lie there. Then you jump out thinking that bomb can literally make house to dissapear so there is no sense to be under burned car, then you jump into some hole but the hole is too shallow...

Then you stand on the street in dark, holding maybe a rifle in one hand, you fasten your belt and backpack like there is any sense in that, your feet are wet with some mud and water from the hole you were in few minutes before.

That feeling in your gut that you become familiar with through last couple of months os spreading through rest of your body.

And it is not a completely uncomfortable feeling.

Eventually, you just say, "Fuck it."

The sound of the bomb turns to screaming and then it explodes somewhere far from you.

But sound of big airplanes wtih food drop was different.

First you would hear something, and usually it would turn

out that you were wrong, or that the airplanes were circling high above the area before drops, who knows?

Then you were sure – the sound was deep and powerfull, but it was clear that it came from high attitude.

That sound you could also feel in your gut, a vibration that slowly grows in your stomach, but agood vibration, and often it was mixed with vibration of your stomach being empty.

Depending on your position at that particular moment when you heard the food airplanes, you would immediately try to get better position to get some MREs or other food.

When you tried to run from the shells, bullets and bombs, very often you could not. It was pure luck if it was going to hit you.

And ironically, it was pretty the same with food drops. You wanted to be in a position where the MREs were gonna fall, but again it was pure luck if you were or not.

To those airplanes whole city probably looked slightly bigger than a dot.

It was a dot which had in that moment tens of thousand people hoping that food was gonna fall at their position.

Big things that came down on things that people called "pallets" usually did not produce too many sounds before they went close to ground, but smaller backages that fell apart high above you, like MREs, produced "flapping" sounds.

It was almost like large flock of fast birds were being scared from top of the trees, and they flew fast.

That flapping sound of MREs was a good sound.

In pitch dark you could sometimes, if you were lucky, hear that flapping sound. Then you'd run in that direction hoping that your orientation and understanding of the direction the sound was coming from was good…

…

He concluded that the sound was probably an MRE plane, but it was clearly going away somewhere.

Then he opened his eyes, the clouds cleared away, and he saw clearly the intersection in front of him, and everything else, like many times since war started.

The shock of this sight faded away a long time ago, but the horror in his gut remained because the sight stayed with him.

It looked like something from a nightmare.

Under the light from the moon, shadows of the ruins added to whole picture and he again sensed that feeling in his gut, like someone squeezing it with cold fist.

The theater building was still standing, and strangely looked intact. But it was a false impression, he knew i, because he had searched the building weeks ago. Inside, everything was destroyed or burned. The theater pub looked like someone had held a defense position there for some time, with loads of shells behind improvised barricades made from tables, chairs, bags of dirt and anything that could be found in vicinity.

Under the light of a small flashlight, he found costumes from the theaters, and concluded that the guys who defended the position there were making fun with it, or maybe it was the guys who overwhelmed them.

In one corner of the pub he found a guy who was dead for some time, with gunshot wounds to his head, and pool cues driven through his palms. He searched a bit and concluded that someone had tried to "nail" him onto the plaster wall with pool sticks, before or after shooting him in head.

He did not go back into the theater building again.

...

The clouds cleared away completely and he carefully watched rest of the area.

The college complex that consisted of several interconected buildings was partially destroyed, and the buildings as they collapsed made a completely unrecognizable new shape. As he had discovered a couple of times, it was the perfect place to make an ambush or tp be ambushed because as a building collapsed, or when some floors were destroyed, they practicale made new arhitecture of it, and especially in terms of moving through it.

So it has become a kind of labyrinth.

For example, if you wanted to reach from one side of the complex to the other you had to go to the basement through the window because enterance was buried after shelling. Then you had to move through the corridors, and go through a hole in the ceiling to the second floor because the stairway was destroyed. Then again you went through some classroom window over the rubble to other classroom and so on.

And even that new "map" was changed over the time because constant shelling or fighting inside of it. So you never knew where you could expect a new hole in some wall on the second floor with someone sticking rifle through it wanting to kill you. You felt safe just because you supposed it is safe but you did not memorize that hole because it was not there last time.

It was a mess.

Trees in the park looked like they were sick, completely destroyed by shelling or from being taken down for firewood when it was safe for that.

The whole complex looked dangerous and evil, even from the distance from where he was watching from now.

On one of his visits, he tried to find the bench where he

spent so many hours sitting, and he felt weird when he could not even recognize the area where bench had been.

Everything looked not only destroyed, it looked like a completely different place to him.

The mall was most easier to spot simply because of the fact that it was not there anymore as a building.

It had been turned into a big pile of concrete, rock, plastic, and junk.

He was among the people who had run to loot it after everything started, and he was there when people carried absolutely irrelevant stuff from it, like stereos and TVs.

He himself had carried big sports bag full of kitchen appliances, and that junk was still somewhere in his home, completely useless.

Many times he cursed himself and wondered why he did not take stuff like batteries, knives, tarps or anything similar. He still felt kinda sick when he remembered that store in the mall that held hunting and fishing equipment, stuff like flashlights, knives, and all that.

But he can not recollect anyone who did carry away useful stuff. It was like a big party with free electronic devices and the possibility of a fist fight or a knife fight.

Days later, in the absolutely idiotic logic that occurs often in war, the mall was bombarded with airplanes, and turned to rubble.

Now he was hiding under the remains of a destroyed car watching the intersection and comparing it to the image of that same place in his mind.

He thought the car was a VW Golf that is burned and run over by a tank. Now it had been reduced to half its normal size. It was standing next to a destroyed house and there was enough space between the car and the house for good cover and concealment. He just hoped the wall of the destroyed house was strong enough to withstand the vibrations from explosions.

After months of surviving in the city in the middle of a civil war, he learned that you needed to know a lot of things to survive, and still you need to have lot of luck, because sometimes no matter how good you are with survival skills, simple luck (or absence of luck) made the difference between you being alive or lying somewhere in pieces.

As his grandfather use to say when he took him fishing ages ago about finding the best location, "Good spot or no good spot, we will catch fish if the fish find us, not if we find thr fish."

He believed something similar. You can do all that you can, but a bullet will get you if it is going to get you. If it is written to get you.

Night was reserved for moving through the city because of the emdless fighting and mostly because of sniping. But open places were kept under small calliber fire even during the night, usually on some kind of system. At least, people liked to think there was some kind of system.

The army that sourrounded city kept all "open spaces" under sniper fire during the day from nearby hills and higher buildings. They loved to use AA machine guns on intersections like this.

But during the night, they fired on it in intervals – just in case, firing blind, knowing that people move down during the night a lot, and knowing that there are chances that they are gonna hit someone.

The point was to understand in what intervals they will shoot, and hoping that it is not going to be time when you run through that open space.

There were hundreds of spaces like that through the city, and over time people learned, or thought that they learned. when and how they need to move through the open spaces, when the snipers were going to shoot, which caliber they'd use, and similar.

Rumors spread wildly about those places and "correct" informations about safe passage through them. Over time, of course many legends were bron, so people used to talk about places where you can walk slowly but if you run you'll get shot, or you need to go not in groups or vice versa or the first one needed to run then the rest of the folks needed to wait 5 minutes then run together.

It was like a lottery, and there was people who thought they knew the winning number that would save your life.

Most of that was nonsense, but sometimes you simply just have to believe.

From the moment when he arrived at his cover next to the intersection there was no fire from the AA gun fired, so he started to curse himself why he did not run through it 15 minutes ago because every moment longer he laid under VW there were more chances there would be firing at the moment when he start to run through that intersection. But he could not help it.

He had a feeling the guys on the hill are drinking beers, and as soon as he crawled out fromw under the car some of them were gonna say to his buddies "ok lets employ this beast and give those suckers some" and old russian type AA gonna start to spit death on intersection with him in the middle of it.

And now again, even without closing his eyes he saw his neighbor smiling while lacing his boots, making jokes about how he lost extra weight with this "war diet" of eating boiled grass when they were preparing to go and trade for alcohol. 30 minutes later he was dead on an intersection smaller then this one and less dangerous. He even had system how to cross it. "We'll run together."

High caliber bullets ripped through his right leg in seconds, and the only thing that was holding it tied to his body was piece of his pants.

His neighbor's only luck was the fact that he was probably dead before he realized he had been shot. The same burst of bullets continued up his body over his chest and head.

He truly believed that his neighbour was dead before he realized he was shot.

He thought later about that event many times, and it was not about death and the ugly face of that. He'd seen a lot of that before and after that event.

It was the fact that his neighbour ended up dead in a moment and he stayed alive, even they rab one next to the other.

Many times he went over and over that event, trying to figure out how he survived and his neighbor ended up dead. But he never had a clue. Everything happened in a second, and he survived.

"You will catch fish if the fish finds you."

"There is bullet with your name on it, and you cannot hide from it when time has come."

…

He was brought back to the present when he heard someone singinsg an old traditional, drinking song somewhere in distance. Through the window of silence between explosions he could clearly feel how the singer had invested emotions in singing i. The song lasted for a couple of seconds and then it was melted back into gunshots and explosions.

Probably someone killed that singer in this crazy new world, he thought.

The voice reminded him of a small bottle of rakija in his backpack. He took it out and took a few sips.

The strong drink immediately brought tears to his eyes, and fire in his belly, but he did feel sharper.

Now he wanted a cigarette, but he knew it was foolish to smoke here in dark.

He moved his head more outside of the cover and started to scan the area of and around the intersection, planning where exactly he will run through it.

He did not know yet if he was going to run all the way or crawl or what.

The difference was in question: was the intersection being observed from someone else? And what was the intention of the possible observers?

From his position under the light of moon he tried to see details.

Lanes leading to the intersection were blocked by destroyed cars. One lane was more or less clear (close to his position) because some heavy military machinery had cleared away abandoned and destroyed cars to get through.

In between the cars, there were visible all kinds of junk, and a couple of bodies here and there.

No movement at all.

He finally made plan to slowly crawl to one rolled over truck with sign that said "Pepsi" still visible on it. He would pause there and then probably run from there to the nearest ruined house on the other side.

The truck was destroyed in a way that the front part where the driver and passenger seats use to be was splattered in a ridiculously way, and the back part where a load would have been hauled was partialy burned.

As a result truck looked like toy truck that he used to play with when he was kid.

It was interesting as a child to take that toy apart and watch the result.

He started to crawl slowly and carefully, holding his rifle by the belt, at the point where belt meet the rifle body, trying to carry it on his forearm.

Half way to the truck he cursed himself brcause he forget to fasten tightly his backpack on his back. He tried to understand what kind of picture he was giving up to someone if they were watching him: a man who crawled down in an old front line, between abandoned positions, and scattered bodies in different stage of decay.

A man who while crawling had funny looking backpack on his back, a backpack that ridiculously went from one end of his back to other, because the idiot forgot to fasten it.

In some situations, you simply lose the feeling of time passing. If someone had asked him later how much time he needed to crawl through that area he would not have known.

But he reached the Pepsi truck, and silently pushed his back against the wood of the cargo part.

In his ears he heard buzzing, and after a short moment of panic – "what is? this" he realized that he simply lost his breath.

It happened more often in the last month or so, and also as he heard, it happened to a lot of people: shortness of breath, blurred vision, loss of strength.

The current way of living, and mostly way of eating – what all of them ate for weeks meant that the body could not function in a good way, especially after moments of intense physical activities.

Being on a diet of homemade grass pancakes did not give you enough energy.

Meat was matter of having enough luck to catch an MRE, or trade something important for it.

40-year-old cookies in big tin cans, powdered milk, cans of meat with suspiciously missing information on what kind of meat was in it, and similar stuff was occasionaly available through the black market.

But even those items were not enough for the amounts of physical and mental shocks that were an everyday occurence.

Before the war and chaos he weighed 95 kilos. Now he roughly estimated that he was around 70.

He looked at the cargo part of the truck, on one part it was still visible "refreshing non alcoh..." and then couple of bullets holes, and rest was burned and destroyed.

Immediatelly he felt the taste of cold Pepsi on his tongue, and with one part of the brain he enjoyed it, with the other part he hated it, because moments like that were as if he was high on drugs, not present in the moment. And moments were dangerous.

Those moments were very needed in these hard times, otherwise you could lose your mind if you stared too much at the hard reality. But staring at memories too much also could pull you away from reality at an important moment.

He was sitting there, with his back next to truck, clouds were flying above his head, and moonlight ocassionally would shine an eerie light on everything. Then when clouds again covered it, everything went back to a game of shadows – a game of guessing what is what.

He concetrated all of his attention, trying to see if there was anybody across the lanes of the streets in the place where he should be safe after he reached it.

It was safe there because it was part of a street where rows of ruined houses gave perfect cover and concealment, both from firing from hills, and shelling too. It offered places for cover at almost every step.

And for him, it felt psycologically safe, because after crossing the intersection and entering the street with the ruined houses he know he was close to safety of his home.

So he carefully monitored the area.

The choice was actually very simple, and all came down to the decision of whether he was going to be very fast or very slow.

Many times in this war, making right choice between those two things had saved his life.

The real problem here was that many times, it was only by pure luck.

He could crawl very slowly and use ruined cars and other junk like safe points where he was gonna take stops and rest and reass the situation. Or he could forget everything about stopping and reassesing and just run as fast as possible across the lanes into the safety.

Both choices theirs own pros and cons, and success was based on many different combinations of events.

For example were the guys on hills gonna shoot at the intersection right in the moment when he began to crawl? Or is there somebody around the intersection with bad intentions? Is someone following him?e

He reached with his hand, and pressed his backpack to feel the 4 MREs inside. For the moment he asked himself again, is all this worth the those MREs that he got through trade 45 minutes before?

But he already knew answer. He had risked his life many times for food, water, weapons, or whatever. It was the way of living, the new way of living and you needed take risks. What else you could do? Lay down and die?

He force himself to stop the philosophical discussion in his head, and observe the intersection one more time.

Somwhere pretty close, a gunfight started, but to him it did not mean much. It was not connected to his decisions and his intersection crossing.

He decided.

He checked his backpack and rifle one more time, stood up and started to run, trying to be as close to the ground as possible but at the same time running as fast as possible.

Like many times before, his whole life condensed in those couple of seconds of running across the lanes. It was like he put all his past and future into running, and running was all that was left to do.

After the last lane, he jumped over something that in dark looked like an old trash bin, and quickly climbed over the small fence, then he lay down in the shallow ditch.

He had survived again..

Nothing happened. It was still the same background sounds of shelling and shooting in the distance. He pressed again his backpack, to feel those MREs, and continue way to his home.

He survived one more time.

Survival Notes from Toby:

There is a fascination, bordering on obsession, with 'barter and trade' within the Preppersphere. This story gives us a glimpse into the reality of the true 'price' of disaster dealing. The trade itself is a tiny piece of the overall puzzle, with all the pieces having their own risks and hazards...

Survival with a Guitar

He lived alone, had a job as salesman, did not have any knowledge about shooting, military or anything connected to survival or similar things.

His knowledge was more about singing and playing the guitar. He was not famous, but pretty known with his group, playing at local weddings or local festivals.

He missed a few chances to get out at the beginning of everything. Some his relatives from America called him a few days prior everything starting and offered him money and help to get out. But he just thought this mess was a temporary thing.

Even when people started to get killed on a daily basis, he still thought it was going to stop very soon.

But it didn't.

They came for him in the middle of the night, like many others. At that time, they were just doing a sweep. That means a gang searches a street or several houses in an area, in order to mobilize you to fight for them, or in other cases to kill you or imprison you (robbing is included of course).

He was not material for a fighter. He looked more like a shy girl than a grown-up man, passing out even at the mention of blood. So, they just imprisoned him together with bunch of other people.

Many years later he told me that hardest thing for him was not to suffer some occasional beatings and the lack of food or water. The worst thing was the feeling of desperation and sometimes the feeling that it all was only a dream. A bad dream, like a nightmare. His psychological suffering was bigger than his physical suffering.

On one occasion he mentioned to those who imprisoned him that he is good with guitar playing. From that day, he become something like their member, he played for them while they drank and beat and tortured other folks.

It was hard for him to focus while other people suffered, but he played encouraging songs that made some men beat others in frenzy. Men adapt and get used to their surroundings.

He told me that he was not in that time either a prisoner or their member. He was something like their clown, a man who amused them, playing and singing songs on demand, not sure if one of them was going to shoot him in head because of a bad song, or give him a gold chain for a good song.

But the point is that he was under some kind of protection. He was valuable because there were few sources of entertainment.

Other imprisoned folks hated him and were scared of him at the same time because he was more popular than they were. After a few months he took chance with some foreign news reporter's crew and ran away, carrying a big camera and wearing a blue helmet and blue body armor through numerous check points.

I lost contact with him for years, then I found him on some discussion about war and music on the web. He is working as a room cleaner, in a country far away. I started some discussion with him about prepping and found out that he is still does not know anything about fighting, shooting, or survival.

But he told me that he is playing the guitar every day, alone in his room, so I guess he is now much better with that.

I think about him sometimes, trying to figure out if he is a good or bad man. Just a man making the best out of his situation, probably.

We were all grey and did what we had to do. Sometimes ugly things. But keep in mind simple skills give you extra value that might save your life.

Laura's Story

"Laura" was 42 years old at the time of the event, a clerk at the local bank, two kids in school, and her husband was a driver for the city bus services.

She is now 64 and the house where we are having this conversation is small and wet. On the floor there are several pots, probably used for catching rain from roof leaks. She looks like she is sick, smoking homemade cigarettes. The smell is awful.

She looks like she has given up, like she is going to kill herself right after our conversation.

She told me her story of the war.

Do you remember the period of hyperinflation when you could buy with credit and when that check came to payment it would be worth maybe 10% of the original value, some few months before killing and chaos started?

Inflation was like a toy for some folks.

Now when I remember that I feel like an idiot because I did not realize that everything was going to shit when something like that is possible.

Women from bank, my colleagues, were bragging how they bought extra stuff that way with almost no money, I was proud because I did not do that.

You know, my father was one of the first who organized an uprising against the Germans here in the big war, a real Communist. He even went as a volunteer in Spanish civil war there, fought against Franco.

He told me a story that once he met Marshall Tito in war, at some Communist conference. It was deep in the Bosnian woods in the winter of 1943, while they were encircled by Italians and Germans.

He told me that he was not like a man, he was an idea, he was the state. The movement that you just need to follow because he knows best.

I was raised to believe in the state, in the communist system, in the ideals of the state for workers and peasants.

When the war started in Croatia, I, just like most of us, believed that somehow someone will recognize that we are all same people, Socialists and Communists, and that we just needed to stick together, and everything would be fine.

But I did not know that the Western world did not want us to have Yugoslavia. We were simply too strong for them. They wanted us to hate each other, and to pull out that old hatred between Yugoslav nations.

And then one day my husband came home earlier from work. He looked badly shaken.

He told me that his coworker was absent from work for two weeks, officially he was ill, with pneumonia.

Rumors were that he was volunteering as a fighter in Croatia. Some people believed and some did not believe.

But when he came back to work, he had golden necklaces around his neck, golden rings, and big smile on his face.

Some folks said that he was bragging around that there in Croatia if you are willing to fight there were a lot of things to plunder, money and gold, and he whispered with sick smile that if you have the will and if you wanted there were lot of "available" women, too.

Husband said that guy was always bit weird when it came to women and alcohol, but after he returned from that "weekend fighting" for money, he always had a sick smile on his face, like he had seen that you can get money, gold, and women in much easier ways than standing all day long in a decades-old bus and selling tickets to angry workers and confused school kids.

My husband never was a brave man. He was good man, but he liked to pull back from situations where people used fists or knives.

You could say that he was coward in some way.

After few stories he heard from that colleague, the fear installed in him for real and forever. Anyway, that forever did not last too long.

Shit moved from Croatia to our town pretty soon. One morning I realized that my coworkers who were other nationalities were missing from work.

And I realized too, that their workplaces were empty more or less. While I was talking about how we should stick together in the spirit of socialism, they were organizing how to get the hell out of town.

I still believed in life together between people of different nationalities.

And then one morning my husband came earlier from his job. He told me that people in uniforms came and confiscated the buses in the name of the "Cause" and the state. Nobody said what cause or state, but he saw that they had blood in their eyes, and nobody was willing to ask too many questions.

They told the workers that they need to go home and follow the orders of the local "crisis government."

In that time there were already several of those crisis governments, each with their own agendas, militias, and orders. People still tried to understand which of those government represented the state.

What they did not understand was that the state was already gone. There were wars between those people too.

My husband finally beat his fear and went to the local criminals to buy a rifle. He gave almost half the money that we had saved for new car for that thing.

When he came home with the rifle, he was even more afraid.

He did not talk too much, but I understood that he was more afraid to use that rifle than to be without it.

He was a weak man. He could not help it.

Somewhere around that day when he bought the rifle, we sent our kids to my sister, some 200 km from our place.

It was the first and probably last time when my husband's fear was used to make a good decision. I did not want to be separated from my kids, but he just kept on telling me, "Laura, you do not know what is happening, and what are people saying outside. The kids need to go away from here.

They left town in one of the last of the Red Cross organized convoys. Their small faces were confused behind the glass. While I was waving them at the local market where the transport was organized, my husband was in our backyard trying to kill beer bottles with bullets from his rifle.

Our neighbor was trying to teach him how to operate the rifle. Rumors in town were that this neighbor had some violent history. Some even said that he was in the French Foreign Legion.

My husband was a cook during the basic training in army, and he forgot even the basic stuff that he learned in the army.

After we got word from the Red Cross that our kids got to their destination in good order, we were kind of more relaxed, but silence moved into the house.

For days we listened to the radio on our car battery. Electricity, water, and all other services were gone. We still were trying to figure who was fighting, who was defending who was liberating, and who was representing the law in our city.

And then one night we awakened to strong kicks at the door.

"Police!" they shouted. "Open the door, now! "

My husband shouted at me, "Where is the rifle?"

I did not know of course, and I still believe that he simply forgot where he put it. He was completely lost in fear.

Anyway, he opened the door. They told him that they were newly organized police and that they trying to organize law in the city.

Of course, he believed them. They had uniforms, helmets, weapon, and authority. He simply was that kind of man. He wanted to trust.

He even remembered where he left his rifle when they asked him. And then they told him that he needed to go with them to the police station and fill out some simple paperwork because that rifle, nothing more.

I never saw him again.

I still remember how he was very calmly putting his jacket on while he was having a conversation with those guys. He had trust on his face. He was happy there was someone finally who he could trust, who would tell him what to do.

What else does a law-abiding citizen need? Fuck!

I never saw him again.

But I saw those people again the very next night.

They did not knock or yell this time. One of them simply crushed the doorknob with his boot.

When they entered house one of them punched me in the face right away, and he said to me just one word. "Gold?"

He kicked me with his boot few more times before the meaning of that word finally got through my brain and then he kicked me few more times before I caught my breath and strength to tell him where my gold necklaces and rings were.

You are asking me did they do anything more to me? You mean did they rape me?

Yeah, they did. Two of them raped me while the two other guys were collecting interesting stuff in my house.

I still do not remember if the other two guys raped me, or if they did not.

After the second one somehow, I kinda left my body. It was like I was floating next to the ceiling while he was on me.

I remember the words "Let's just kill this bitch."

Much later I realized that those words were spoken about me.

Did I want to be killed after that?

No, actually not. In that moment I felt only physical pain, but I still had the will to live. I did not want to die. Not yet.

I survived that, just like hundreds of other women in that time.

I do not remember how I lived the next month or two.

I mean I remember everything in a way: black market, famine, diseases, endless killings, side switching, rumors about peace and everything else.

But from the moment when those guys left my house, everything was blurred. I simply pushed on and on.

I learned how to treat wounded in one of the local militias, I found a man who protected me, not because he loved me or because he was a good man. It was because I was a woman.

I remember endless wounded guys screaming and in pain.

And then one day peace came, I was hearing from all sides that peace has come, and finally everything was gonna be fine.

And that was moment when I broke.

I was an old woman. My husband was dead, but actually

officially he was still missing. I could not even get a pension from state because officially he was not dead. He was not founded in one of the thousand improvised graves.

He was probably killed immediately after he was taken from our house, maybe 500 meters from our house. Turned to dust or just pile of bones somewhere in someone abandoned well, or on the bottom of the river.

Where are my kids?

One is in America. She is some kind of small boss in a local fast food restaurant. Whenever I speak to her on phone, I understand her less. Each time she uses more English then our language, and each time I am happier.

Why?

I want from her to forget this country, this language. I want from her to forget me, to never come back here, I do not want her to be one day outside her body while some guy is on top of her and another searching her home for gold in the name of state.

My other kid?

Well, he is some kind of musician. Lives in Italy. I think he is homosexual.

What are my feelings about that?

I do not care, as long as he does not come back here. I do not want him to be taken from the house in the middle of the night in the name of the cause, in some future "Balkan conflict."

Sometimes I have a dream that he might be on the other side in some future war here. What if he was one of the guys who searched for gold and valuables after he killed a woman's husband?

And next morning when I wake from that dream, I even more want from him to hate everything that is here, country people, system, even me.

Just as long as he does not come back.

What do I do for living?

I do what I learned in that time. I care for sick folks. I have a few older people that I take care of. I wash them, clean them, take care for this disease, and similar.

It is enough for cigarettes and beer and that food that I eat.

I'll be fine.

Do I trust in living together with harmony between different people?

Hmmm, I do not care for that. I do not give a shit.

Survival Notes from Toby:

This is a story for all those that are insistent that they'll:

A) Shelter in place (Bug In)

and

B) State (and believe) they can and will fight to defend their homes from ALL intruders.

1st she had to send her children away. Just take a moment to let that truly sink in

Then they were 'behind the curve' in defensive preparations, and their attempts to improve that situation (Buying an 'illegal' weapon of sorts) was a major contributory factor to justify the 'disappearance' of her husband'.

Left alone she was then exceptionally vulnerable, not only to theft, but for sexual assaults as well.

'Protection' of sorts was eventually found, and here she reveals the true price of these things...

The nation state she SO believed in at the time, she is ashamed of now, to the point she is 'glad' her children have no plans to return to their country of birth. This is a genuinely difficult part of survival and aftermath, the undermining of those DEEPLY held beliefs.

Baron's Story

During the period of my SHTF time, I met all kind of folks in all kind of situations. Bad people, desperate ones, lost ones, confused ones, dead ones.

After some time, I had this idea that I knew all kind of human characters, or even that I was some kind of "expert" when it came to knowing human nature in bad times.

Of course, I was wrong.

During one night looking for resources, my neighbor got caught by one of the enemy groups. He simply stumbled in the middle of dark into their hands, however stupid that sounds.

After they disarmed him and give him few casual kicks in the kidneys, they took him to their captain. The captain was a big dude, dressed in a brand-new uniform, with rank markings and beret on his head. He was completely in contrast with his soldiers who, in short, looked and smelled like animals.

The neighbor said that the man looked and smelled nice, and always had a smile on, but when he heard that his folks call him Baron, he froze. Baron and his unit were something like mercenaries, fighting for anyone and against everyone, as needed.

They were quite well-known for a few things: they had a private prison, their headquarters was something like a mix between Roman and crazy seventies parties, with lots of women, violence, drugs, and alcohol. But the thing they were most famous for was that they beat and killed for fun.

That night, Baron asked my neighbor a few questions, then started to beat him even before he answered it. My neighbor said that he stopped with the beating only after the few punches because he saw blood splashed on his uniform.

He looked disgusted with that blood on his uniform and went to clean it with water. My neighbor lost one tooth in that few minutes.

Baron's soldiers kicked my neighbor a few more times and then threw him in something that was before the war a tiny weather observation post. Nobody came to check him all day. He spent the day losing and gaining consciousness. He awakened in the middle of the night because of strong noises, similar to shots, but not really shots. Then he realized that something was hitting that container where he was locked.

Through the small hole, he sees soldiers running everywhere around, and laughing and screaming like they are having fun. Then he realized that Baron's camp found itself in the way of airdrops, and MREs were literally raining all around.

Maybe one hour later one of the soldiers unlocks the door,

came in carrying hands full of MREs, asking him: "Are you hungry?"

My neighbor did not answer anything. Guy repeated the question. My neighbor said "Yes." The guy kicked him in the stomach and asked again, "Are you hungry?" My neighbor said, "No".

The guy said, "F*ck it, man, so much food is all around and you are not in the mood" and left the room. My neighbor lost account of time. He remembered that they gave him a bottle of water to drink but no food.

And then their leader Baron came in. He carried a steel bar in his hand and had a smile on face.

My neighbor said that it was clear that this time he was gonna beat him to death with that bar and he tried to make some kind of peace with himself and world.

Baron started to ask questions about his family, kids, where he lived, and similar stuff. My neighbor started to talk in a panic about everything and he mentioned my name.

Baron stopped and asked him again about my full name and how do I look. My neighbor tells him that we are neighbors and kinda friends.

He looks for a few moments at him and then called two of his guys and ordered them to help him to get on his feet. They put some big bag on his shoulders, very heavy for his state. Two of the guys helped him out of their camp. When they released him, Baron told him, "Say hello to him."

The neighbor walked some 200 meters like in a dream, expecting to get shot in the back as a part of the usual game. He said he tried to remember any kind of prayer, anything, but his head was blank. Then... nothing happened. When he was safe, he checked a bag and realized it was full of MREs. Small fortune. His weapon was there too, without bullets.

He also realized that during that 200 meters he peed in his pants. He said later it was because the hits in his kidneys and I said yes, but we both knew that those 200 meters were longest 200 meters in his life.

Later when we met each other and when he told me that Baron sends greetings to me and because that greeting my neighbors life was spared, I was surprised because I knew that man from the bad stories, but I never met him.

Anyway, we split the bag of MREs, sure that it was some kind of misunderstanding about that greetings.

Years later, after all was finished and a lot of things forgotten, I read the small news in the newspaper. That famous Baron was shot to death in an overseas country during a bank robbery. He was living there for years under the false name. His picture was there and his real name too.

I realized that we went together to elementary school, play football together, listen to the same music. Once we fall in love with the same girl. I was something like his older brother or protector because he was always kinda weak or scared of conflict.

We were friends. He was a shy kid and I cannot remember that he ever got involved in any kind of fight. He could not stand the blood. We lost contact after elementary school.

I had mixed feelings when I read that news and realized that infamous Baron from the war and my shy school friend were the same person. He turned out to be a bad man, but again he spares one life maybe in memory of that school playground or Iron Maiden LPs. Weird.

Life has very strange paths, and some very strange ways to show you that somehow everything is connected.

When SHTF you'll see that a man who has power and force is making decisions over life and death and it is kind of a tempting and addictive thing.

Do not get caught in the thinking and acting that you are invincible or can play God just because there is no more law out there and you have a gun. Sooner or later you are gonna realize that you are vulnerable and that there are meaner people than you. You will learn you get what you give.

Stick with your family or group and try to survive. To survive you want to minimize your risks and playing those evil "games" is not worth it.

Goran's Story - Part 1

In his dream he was suffocating in cold pitch darkness. Mud and soil entered his mouth and nose, and he was trying to remove it by his fingers. But as soon as he removed it, new mud entered and he kept on and on to fight for air.

There was no light, not even smallest trace, and he was not sure what was the reason for that earth in his eyes. Was he was buried alive?

He kept suffocating in darkness, but death was not coming. As things usually go in dreams or nightmares, everything was in slow motion, prolonging his terror...

Then he woke up, because someone shook him hard by his shoulders.

He opened his eyes and saw a guy above him, still shaking up his shoulders saying, "Wake up Goran, you were dreaming."

He was not sure where he was or what was happening for a couple of seconds, then he realized and remembered everything: the war, the cold, the fights.

The guy who woke him up returned to his small fire, mumbling, "Coffee is ready too."

They were positioned in an abandoned agriculture

machines factory. His squad was in backup for the last 24 hours, resting in the middle of two front line shifts.

The front line was some 500 meters away, and now the factory was their place of safe haven close to hell.

The guy next to fire pored boiled water over the "coffee" mixture in an empty meat can, stirred it carefully with a bayonet, and handed it to Goran.

"Here it is, no sugar, since we live healthy since this war started."

The joke was old. Sugar was rare, and that drink was not coffee anyway. It was a mixture of ground barley with the addition of maybe a tiny trace of real coffee.

Over the last couple of months people had tested different substitutes for coffee, and among the afwul combinations, the least awful was this barley mixture. It almost tasted like coffee if you added a tiny pinch of coffee and enough imagination.

It did mess with blood pressure, but...

Goran checked his stuff around him, his rifle and backpack. He took the old sleeping bag and move closer to fire.

The guy who made him coffee was known as the Farmer, and nobody in the unit called him different. At the beginning of the war he had fled from his village to the town, while enemy units torched everything and killed everyone.

He moved to some abandoned house in the city and joined one of the army units.

Most of the conversations with him eventually ended up in discussions about the animals and land that he left in his village, and how he missed that.

The rest of the squad was around fire mostly, some of them sleeping, others staring into flames.

From the front line there was sporadic shooting here and there, and something that they called "testing," which was just making sure each side was letting the other side know that they are there and ready, so there was no use of trying something.

In other words it was ordinary day, or night, to be more precise.

In front of them 500 meters far was the front line. Some 4 kilometers behind them was city, and if you climb to the roofs of the factory you could see it.

If it was daytime (and if you were stupid enough to climb the roof during the daylight) all you could see was dust and smoke in the valley where the city was, and a few of the highest buildings.

During the night you could see fires that were constantly burning here and there. They started with explosions after shelling.

It had been more then 10 months since war started.

There was a period of complete chaos. Initially there was also constant hope that everything will be solved somehow. That hope was gone.

In terms of fighting, more or less the lines had been established, and you now had some kind of clue who is who and where is who, but in terms of hope in quick solutions also kinda "lines" had been established, and everybody knew that this was going to last.

Hope was substituted with thoughts about how to find enough food for you and your family, how to stay warm during the harsh winter, thoughts about whether the city was going to fall into enemy hands.

Hopes about eletricity, water, or any other service coming back soon had gone away too. Esndless peace conference between leaders that were held in European cities did not bring any positive things.

People joked about "is this 23rd or 24th peace agreement signed succesfully?" that nobody cared about following.

Where to find cooking oil or shoes for example were the foremost thoughts.

"Anything new?" Goran asked Farmer.

"Nope, while you were dreaming nice dreams, we listened to the evening news on the radio, and they said our glorious fight gonna last maybe 10 years, but we will prevail."

"Well, I hoped for something more useful and logical, something about UN convoys or similar."

"No, nothing like that," Farmer said. "But whenever they mention our glorious defense, something bad is coming, and I have a gut feeling we are going to be fucked."

After a couple of months of war, the goods distribution inside the city were dependent mostly on UN convoys bringing (and guarding) goods on their way to the city. Even with that most of the people suffered malnutrition.

The black market was reserved for people with enough resources for it, and yes, you could find exclusive and good stuff if you have the means to buy it and the right connections.

But UN convoys were mainly a way to bring goods to distribution centers, and to take out badly wounded civilians.

Convoys were rare and usually not announced. The food that was brought inside the city was officialy taken to "distribution centers" controlled by goverment forces, but in reality, even that food was delivered to people in power first, then the army, and at last to civilians, if there was anything left for them.

Even UN officers had to pay a "percentage" of goods to armies sourrounding the area before they broke the circle, sometimes those officers sold goods to people who offered more.

Nothing was for sure.

A shell exploded somewhere in the factory complex, probably a mortar shell, since the factory was positioned beneath hill. On top of the hill were lines of defense.

Soldiers around the fire "shrunk" their shoulders. Some of the sleepers woke up. Farmer continued to stir something on the fire.

Numbness, Goran thought, it is numbness in us.

After months of shelling, shooting and fighting a lot of the people became numb to all that. The other reason was that they adopted a philosophy of "It will be what it has to be and you'll die anyway when your moment comes."

Nobody threw himself down on the floor. The explosion was pretty far from them, and they could hear the rain of not dangerous shrapnells on the tin roof.

One of the new guy woke up and asked, "What was that?"

"War," Farmer said. "Relax kid, it is far from us, stay cool, we have couple of hours more to stay here then we are going back to the city and some other poor bastards will replace us."

A few hours later they slowly walked back to the city.

The way back led them through a small industrial zone that was stripped completely down of anything useful, and all that was left was the big steel skeletons of buildings and machinery that was too heavy to drag.

They passed the industrial zone and entered into something that was similar to suburbs, an area that was neither city nor village.

There were rows of houses similar in designs, with small roads full of intersections. Most of the houses had backyards that were used before the war as small gardens for vegetables, a lot of homeowners had chickens then.

Now it was destroyed completely, since a couple of months ago the line of separation between armies led directly through that suburb.

Goran still remembered the chaos of fighting there, people being unwilling to leave their homes, shooting through windows of some house at a truck with at couple of enemy soldiers on it, while the truck was moving fast through the junk-filled streets.

He remembers moment when he replaced the magazine in his rifle and he spotted a photo on the wall in the bedroom where he was standing.

That photo was probably 50-60 years old, showing a couple of people, husband and wife for sure, in traditional clothes, photo was heavily edited in a photography shop, so the faces of grandma and grandpa (in their young age, maybe even their wedding photo) looked almost like they were made of plastic.

It was the kind of photo that almost every house had here, a photo of parents or grandparents when they were young, taken in 1920s or 1930. Sometimes it was 2nd World War photos.

Those kind of photos would be usually made from small old photographs, usually damaged from th years, enlarged and edited in shops to repair damage. They were almost always placed in bedrooms.

In other houses, other rooms, while he was hiding there, or simply making defensive position he could see photos from WW2, Grandpa standing with German machine gun that he took probably from a dead German. Some of those photos had handwritten letters saying where photo was taken, after what fight.

Some had added typewriter text, saying that "Comrade has been reckognized from High Communist Command for his brave fight against the German occupying force."

Pieces of history in destroyed houses.

He often asked himself if those guys fighting in WW2 felt like he is feeling fighting today: poor, miserable, frightened, or it was really "glorious?"

Anyway, the frontline moved back to the hills outside of the suburbs, and stood there. But people did not come back to their homes, simply because they were too destroyed and not safe to stay in. They all moved to the city.

Now the whole place was something like a buffer zone

between the city and front lines, and often under shelling and sniper fire.

Writings on a wall written with paint spray said "Watch SNIPER" in dangerous spots, and blankets were thrown on some openings next to the spots where you needed to run, because of danger from snipers. Those blankets were full of holes.

On a small driveway in front of one of the houses a piano still stood, where a few soldiers dragged it few months ago. Goran was passing by there then as a replacement unit, and a few soldiers stand next to it, while one played it.

The guy who played it obviously knew what he was doing. He played some theme from the Tom and Jerry cartoon. His helmet was on ground next to his feet, and his rifle was on the piano cover.

Next to the piano, 3-4 soldiers stood, trying to "catch" the rhythm and clapping their hands.

Goran approached them, asking for cigarette. The guy who played the piano showed with his finger in his mouth and lifted his eybrows asking.

Goran refused, then another guy offered him pack of cigarette from pack that was made in local cigarette factory, from old pre-war stashes.

Due to the lack of eletricity, cigarettes were packaged in

junk paper of any kind, usually from books, newspapers, or similar.

This pack was packaged in something that looked like an elementary school chemistry book.

The brand of tobbaco was quickly renamed by replacing few letters from the original name, so folks call it "Death".

In that moment Goran understood complete and absolute absurdity of the scene, while smoking Death cigarettes, listening to the "Tom and Jerry" theme, and moving his rifle onto his back in order to light the cigarette.

Explosions in the city added to the rhythm of the song, the smell marijuana teasted him.

But the moment passed, and he just felt how hungry, dirty, and numbed he was.

Now while moving back to the city, he saw piano again, destroyed by weather, and bullets fired from bored guys passing there.

After the buffer zone, they reached the city, guarded by "last defense" barricades, anti-tank traps, and positions with soldiers manning them.

Goran and his comrades simply called them "faggots".

There was a clear distinction between "grunts" who manned the toutside perimeter lines, and the units that took care of the inside of the city and the positions there.

In its core, that distinction was about whether you had the connections or money or power not to be forced to go out on the frontline. So for Goran and folks who did not have any of that they were "faggots".

Faggots checked them, and they entered the city.

By the rules, they should go to the brigade headquarters, positioned in ex-city bank basements, for rescheduling, debriefing and similar. But nobody cared too much about it, as long as the brigade managed to gather enough folks to man the frontline through a high death toll, desertions and similar.

It was not unusual for those days that military police (faggots) chased soldiers through the city in order to have enough people on the lines. Small wars happened in the city because of that.

The city was a mixture of chaos and hopelesness.

Since the electricity went away people rediscovered fire as their old friend, and the city was literally choking in smoke. Smoke from people using fires everywhere for heat and cooking, and smoke from fires that were started because of enemy shelling.

Shelling was constant, and after some time it simply moved to the back of people's conciousness, like constant wind, or rain, or maybe mosqituos.

It was like you are doing whatever you are doing and wind is blowing. What are you gonna do? It is weather!

You still have to live, make food, look for water, make love.

Wind that might kill you at any moment, yes, but you still have your every day jobs to finish.

There were directions from where shelling came or from where snipers perched, and you just adjusted your life to it.

The main roads were more or less cleared, so that military or emergency vehicles could pass. Traffic was almost nonexistent due to lack of fuel. But yes, you could see military vehicles or emergency vehicles driving fast here or there through the streets without their lights on because of possible snipers.

People walked fast and you could say with kinda clear intentions. Most of the folks wore some kind of uniforms. Most of the folks were mobilised in some kind of "defense section" but it was a very vague and broad term. You could be mechanic in brigade headquaters, holding weapons, or frontline grunt, or nurse in local what's left of the hospital.

Or you could be a local nobody, connected to the black market, giving a percentage to the high ranking folks, and living outside of all the rules, as a ghost.

You all were under martial law and under the orders of the war council.

Basically military police by law could come into your house and take everything they saw fit for the war effort.

His fellows stopped by an illegal liquor store, that was used in the same time like a pub. Actually it was in the back of a destroyed vegetable and fruit shop. In two small rooms the owner sold liquor and marijuana. You could sit there drink and smoke, and there was guitar on one table so who ever knew how to play could use it.

20 days ago someone threw a hand grenade inside and a couple of guys were wounded. It was most probably competition, places like that were everywhere. Some offered heavy drugs, others offered women, and it was matter of who had the more powerful protector from authority. This was based on larger percentage of bribe usually.

He continued to walk and entered a part of city where communistic architecture were very visible in a form of huge building blocks, with large parking areas, and playgrounds.

Apartments buildings were built in 70s, and they offered a "working man's paradise" in buildings that looked like match boxes produced in the Soviet Union. But now as Goran realized, everything looked like paradise compared to the new reality.

In a parking lot, most of the cars were not usable. Some were burned, others were stripped down of anything useful. It was a junkyard.

He looked up to the apartment buildings, and everything was in darkness, he paid more attention and stared into the building then he started to notice candlelights here and there, but very faint, since most of the folks put blankets or similar over the windows due to the constant and neverending threat of sniper fire.

A Ford slowly passed by him, manuvering through the junk between the parking lot and building, and he reckognized 4 guys from the "special police" unit inside. They did not pay too much attention toa him, just regular glimpse at his uniform and red stripe on his shoulder-unit marking, and the rifle on his back.

The Ford moved away, and disappeared into the labyrinth of junk, destroyed cars, and passages between apartment buildings.

They belonged to the unit who supposedly looked for enemy activities inside the city, spies, snipers and similar. In reality they did more stealing and kidnapping people for ransom.

The word was that they owned a private prison, where they held kidnapped people until they got ransom. It was a place with alcohol, good food, music, and even electricity through gasoline-powered generators.

He look a couple of moments at the place between two apartment buildings where they disappeared. In the sky there were the first traces of dusk, and his apartment building stood in front of him.

A couple of steps more up to the stairs, and he knocked on the apartment building outside door. Through the dirty glass and bars on it, he saw the faint glow of gas light.

A man from inside looked through the glass on him using gas lamp light, and then opened the door after unlocking it.

The old man from the 4th floor closed the door and locked it, when he moved in.

A small table, a big notepad, and a glass with tea were on table. The old man put back the lamp on the table and asked him, "How was it, anything new?"

Goran sat on the end of table, lighting a cigarette and offering one to the man.

"They shoot at us, we shoot back at them, lines are where they were 10 days ago, nothing new... so it is your shift?"

Grandpa took cigarette, and for the moment Goran think he is going to eat it, based on how he looked at it, then he put it in mouth, and lit it on the gas lamp.

He took couple of moments, took two long puffs, held it in lungs while he watched in tip of the cigarette. Then he carefully put the cigarette down, by carefully removing the burning part with his fingers. He fixed the tip so tobacco would not spill out. He put what was left from it in his pocket and said, "thanks, man. this is gonna last me for some time. You know sometimes I fantasize about volunteering to go to the frontline only because of the cigarettes you got because that."

"Leave it, Grandpa. With your age you could not reach it at all."

"You never know, kid. You know, I was a tough man back in my days, now please sign in here."

Grandpa pushed a notepad to Goran and gave him a pen with "best pizza in town" printed on it.

Goran signed his name, and time of entrance into the apartment building.

When the war started, in order to make some kind of order in the city, the government made something like civilian guards in every larger appartment building. Usually it meant older homeowners from the buildings sat inside where the entrance was in 8 hours shifts. They had the duty of checking who was entering the building and when, by signing them in on a notepad.

Police often checked those notebooks for suspicious people moving around the city.

Same folks have the duty of checking for anything suspicious, taking care of basements as shelters during heavy bombings, taking care that stairways were clear for walking (since elevators were out of function) and similar things.

On paper it was not a bad idea, but in reality folks with weapon could easily raid couple of apartments before any help would come, if any would come at all.

Goran put his backpack on, and started walking up the stairs to his 11th floor apartment.

"Watch for rubble on the 3rd and 7th floors!" Grandpa

yelled at him when he climbed to the 1st floor. "We had direct hits 2 days ago."

Goran took a couple of minutes on the 1st floor, letting his eyes get used to the darkness. When he started to notice faint light through the hall windows, he continued to climb the stairs.

...

He slept for almost the whole day.

In his dreams, again he was choking with earth, under tons of mud, in pitch darkness, the ground was shaking from detonations, moving around him.

Now when he woke up he was not sure if it had been in his dream or if the city had been shelled again. He had taken one of the last sedatives before he went to bed.

It was time to look for new magic pills.

He went to the window, partially blocked with a closet and completely covered with a blanket. He removed the blanket and the city still was there choked by the fog.

He looked down and realized that his boots were still on his feet. For couple of seconds he whether it was gonna make any difference, then he stood up removed his boots and clothes, lit a small oil lamp, and went to bathroom.

He used about 2 liters of water for his "bath" then washed his socks.

When he left the bathroom he checked his stash of firewood on the balcony. He took a few pieces, sat down next to his small stove, and started the fire.

Again in his thoughts, Goran thanked the socialistic planning and building of appartment buildings for including chimney system in buildings that were gonna have central heating, just in case.

And again, the smell of oil lamp reminded him of donuts. Warm, beautiful, fresh jelly donuts.

Instead of fantasing about donuts for some time, rolling the joint seemed like good idea, so he did that, inhaling the smoke deep and started to think about his life.

He was 26. He had barely started to live when the war started. He'd had a couple of relationships, a few different jobs as a car mechanic, a few dreams and plans.

Then the war started.

The girl that he had in that time left the city in refugee conwoy, while that still was possible. In the first few months after that received a couple of messages from her through the Red Cross organisation, that took messagess in and out through UN conwoys.

Then there was nothing, so he guessed that thing was history.

No close relatives, no brothers or sisters. His parents died before the war.

Since he did not have any close relatives he was surprised when he got message through his buddy from unit, few days ago that his second cousin is in the hospital, wounded, while her parents got killed in shelling.

For the past few days he was thinking whether he was going to ignore the messages or check who was there in hospital, whether it was his relative or it was a mistake.

The joint was finished, his decision was made.

He opened can of meat, ate it without enjoying, checked if it was dark enough outside and started to get ready.

For few moments he thought about carrying his rifle and pistol, or pistol only, but by the rules he was not suppose to walk through the city with a rifle unless he was going to positions, or back to headquarters. Not too many folks paid attention to it, so Goran put his military jacket on with unit markings, civilian pants, checked is tape still holding on two magazines taped together on his rifle after moisture and mud on the frontline. He took the pistol and extra magazine under the dirty but pretty pillow with words "welcome home" on it, and left the apartment.

...

It was freezing outside, and suddenly he remembered his grandfather's words. "War is hell, but war in winter is fucking hell."

On hills positioned 10-15 kilometers from him there were flashes of orange light every few seconds. A few times the flashes joined together making something like a weird new dawn over the hills.

Low clouds were visible on that place, because of the light, and for a moment it reminded him of a New Year celebration in his chilhood, with firecrackers and rockets firing while freezing air chapped your cheeks.

The whole thing looked amazingly beautiful, if you forgot fact that people were fighting and dying there. Signal rockets being fired, and explosions making people fly like puppets in the air, landing down with body parts missing.

He did not feel sorry for the folks there fighting. His only emotion in that moment was a bit of happines because they are there, and he is here.

One more quick check of his backpack belts, rifle on his shoulders, and he started his trip to the hospital.

Goran's Story - Part 2

The city had its own life during the night time, and you could feel it. Actually you *needed* to feel it in order not to get yourself in trouble.

The government's main objectives were to hold the lines where they were, outside on the hills and mountains. All stories about victories and similar were pure propaganda since even holding the status quo was barely possible, and most of the people had constant feeling everything would be overrun soon.

Frontlines were not complete and clear line everywhere, so in some parts, the enemy army was actually in the city, holding a couple of building blocks stretching maybe 2-3 kilometers. So while walking through the city you should know in any moment where are you otherwise in some moment, a sniper might get you from some apartment building that you forgot about.

The absence of food, water and almost non-existent city services caused something like a new philosophy of living, which in essence meant that people were constantly on the run for something.

Food, water, fuel for heating or cooking, medicines… everything actually was in short supply so you had to get out and find the ways to obtain it.

You could get in in several ways, but for lot of folks, those items were to hard or impossible to get.

As a result, the shortages of everything were everywhere in city. Night was time when you tried to find things through trade on the black market, or through many other less nice ways.

You could see beggars on the street who literally did not have enough strength to find food, trade, or steal it. It was common that these people were a professor maybe or a clerk, whose world collapsed a couple of months ago when he realised his retirement check waws not coming, his savings were worth one-tenth of the value, he had food in house for 3 days when war started, and his wife died from pneumonia because he did not have the connections or goods to buy antibiotics.

Or you could see people dragging firewood through the streets on improvised carts made from baby strollers, or simply carryng it on their backs.

Here andd there, from back alleys you could hear gunshots or screams, or both, probably as a result of goods being obtained in other ways.

The city was alive and fuctioning, but on a completely different level, and under a completely different set of rules.

After 15 minutes of walking, Goran spotted a police car parked in front of the partially destroyed house. One guy was waiting next to the car, and two guys were dragging a man with blood on his face, probably from a rifle butt.

As Goran closed in on them, he casually let the rifle slide from his arm to his hand, without changing the rhythm or pace of his walk.

The guy who stood next to the car spotted him, and also changed his stance. He already had his rifle in hands.

The car was an old Caddy, a type of car used before the war for the delivering of goods like bread, or milk. It had two seats in the front and a big white boxed space in back, now changed to a small space with two benches for people.

On the white box made with duct tape, there was writing that said "police"

Now they were few meters away, and guy had spotted military jacket on Goran and the unit mark, and with flat voice told him, "Pass on, he is a military deserter, fugitive."e

Goran said nothing, just passed them. He felt their looks on his back, and after few minutes he put the rifle back on his arm.

He did not recognize the police unit, but there were many in the city, literally every stronger armed group, if they had enough manpower could offer their services to the government as a police, or some kind of police. Swome were loyal, others were less so. Some were trying to maintain order in the city, while others were more about the black market. You could say that the government tried to maintain some order in that mess, but you could also say that some people from the government used those groups for taking percentages, personal protection, influence on the black market, or anything similar.

There were a lot of cases of small wars between groups, or between them and army units.

The main beef between them usually was in fact that some were on duty to be grunts on the frontline, while othera were "policing" the city, (and doing lot of other things.)

He reached the place that before the war was the main city promenade, a pedestrian street with cafes and restaraunts on one side, next to the walking zone.

He used to know every caff there, every bartender, every chair...he spent hours and days there, sitting with friends, watching girls pass by. The world then was beautiful, the future was unknown but bright.

Now that place was in the dark, and the future was still unknow but it was dark too.

And it was a place where snipers could got you. or higher caliber fire from the enemy.

At the beginning of the street, there used to be cafe called Papilon, and if you watched carefully you could still see a painted butterfly above the cafe doors.

Now the doors were missing, and it looked like something pretty strong and armored had smashed through it.

He entered the cafe, took a few minutes to check if there was anybody inside, then slowly started to move through it, to reach the back of the cafe where here twas huge hole in the wall leading to the backyard of a neighboring cafe.

Moving through that street was slow, and by walking through the ruins, and back yards of those places he reached the other area that was an apartment building block in two hours.

In thos moments, through the constant background noise of random detonation pretty far away, Goran heard familiar hissing sound. He ran to the closest available cover, and it was that moment that the cover was big pile of rubble, which once was a small corner shop, selling tobacco and newspapers.

Right at the moment when he jumped next to the some 30 centimeters remains of wall shells started to explode.

The first shell exploded and the ground vibrated and his ears started to ring. He estimated the distance around 200 meters from where he was, based on sound and rain of soil, concrete and pieces of metal, and he thought in panic, "Is it one, or are several more to come? Is it getting closer or going away from here?" And he wondered what he could do about it.

The answer came in the form of more explosions, and he concluded there was a high chance of being blown to pieces. It was Howitzers, probably, based on how he bounced from the tground after each detonation, and there were probably about 6-8 more to come.

The last few explosions all kinda melted into one big blastthe , and he got urge to use his fingernails to dig under the damaged asphalt and hide. But he was reasonable enough to know there was nothing he could do.

When the shelling stopped, he realized something heavy was laying on him and using his hands was not enough to get free. In a moment of panic that he was gonna finally be buried alive he painfully, slowly changed his position, so that his legs could be used to lift whatever was lying on him.

Finally he made it. A big piece of thin metal wall from the tobacco shop was laying down next to him, and he was free.

Suddeny he again appreciated the fact that life is beautiful and there is sense in living, and thanked God for his luck.

His ears were ringing, and there was a kind of chemical taste in his mouth that forced him to throw up on same thin metal.

After regaining his breath, Goran felt a sharp pain in forearm, checked it and felt the wound. As his arm regained movement, and he checked wound more thoroughly, there were no exit wound, just an irregular incision, pretty deep.

While having vertigo and ears ringing, he was looking around for his backpack, then felt like an idiot when he realised it was still on his back.

He searched it and found a small bottle of rakija, still intact. He poured some of it on his wound and drank few sips.

He covered the wound with a military-issued trauma bandage that was opened and not sterile, but it was better then nothing.

There were nobody around, at least he did not spot anyone. In the distance there was the sound of some engine, probably a tank or armored car. Somewhere closer the dog was barking, and somewhere else, pretty far in the city he heard a similar barrage of shelling.

The city still was there, surviving at night, and he was there, still alive, now laying on his back, trying to calm down, and regain his hearing and his balance so he could move on.

While lying on his back he saw it had started to snow, then again felt like an idiot when realised it was not snow, it was pieces of dust, ash, and burned tiny particles, leftovers after the shelling.

He smiled for first time after some time, feeling happy that he was alive.

...

20 minutes later, he was entering an apartment building

complex that was before war something like the pride of the city. In that time, they were pretty new buildings, and built in a way that tried to stop with tradition of building appartments just to fill as many people as possible in it.

This complex was built in a way that many apartments had their own garages, and even small yards with flowers for those who lived on ground levels. It had small parks with fountains.

It was the first step in building complexes that were sustainable in a way that they have sport terrains, shops, parks, places for young and old. It had areas where the youngest played on the green grass in parks while the oldest read newspapers on benches.

It was the pride of socialistic architecture, often portrayed on post cards with "Greetings from the city of...". Very few relised it was pride of a *dying* socialistic society.

It was very nice place for living before the tbegining of the war put that complex in the bloodiest weeks of urban fighting in the erea.

For days and weeks, armies and militias butchered between themselves over that part of the city with luck that changed from day to day, often in a matter of hours.

Goran was there with his unit. To him now it seemed like it had happened decades ago, not a few months ago.

He and his comrades fought from building to building, from apartment to apartment, tanks were rolling between buildings. While they were running through rooms they prayed the barrel of the tank was not moving in their direction. While moving and jumping they stumbled over children's toys, or pans in kitchens. The buildings in those days regained new internal architecture, with holes in walls or ceilings, with the enemy jumping at you from an elevator, or shooting on your own unit members because you could not figure in that chaos who is who.

Once in midle of that chaos they broke into an apartment to find 3 enemy soldiers eating dinner on a refrigerator that had tumbled down, and the homeowners were lying next to them, shot in the head.

Prisoners were taken rarely.

You could in those days find people, civilians who refused to move from that area, and stood there while people fought around them, ooften taking position in their apartment while they were in the other room.

After weeks of that chaos, the enemy finally moved away from the area, retreated. But it was no cause for celebration. They moved away only to start a couple of days later with shelling and bombarding area so heavily that right now looked like once when war ende (if this thing was ever going to end. Goran thought) the only good thing to do is to level down what is left, and rebuild it from scratch.

In that part of the city you sensed that everything was dead, destroyed to the point of no repair. Even explosions and gunshots from other parts of the city or frontlines when you were there seemed somehow dead, muffled.

It was a dead zone.

Goran was there, in that part when it was destroyed like this, and he knew it pretty well, but every time after when he walked through it, he felt an eerie feeling on his neck, and inside his guts.

Someone who is superstitious would maybe say those were the spirits of people who were killed there in large numbers, and often in a very painful death. Many of them were still there under the ruins. But Goran knew it was about the absence of life, or the absence of activities, that it was simply a dead zone. Dead people, dead buildings, dead park with dead swing, dead destroyed fountain. They killed that part of the city, and he killed it too.

...

He put aside his memories and feelings about the place. He knew it was a bad thing to go deep into feelings, especially when you were out moving, and he had job to do at that place on the way to the hospital.

He reached the spot where a destroyed tank had been standing for months, and chose it to check for activities.

The place was dead yes, but that did not mean that people didn't still come there for their own reasons. Even some old tenants got back into their apartments, partially or completely destroyed, simply because they did not have anywhere else to go.

That place was famous for selling and buying drugs. Anything could be found there if you knew people and had some resources for buying.

In that dead area, there were a couple of groups who used it as a selling place, and one (and not the only) reason for that is because whole area was completely inaccesible with cars, trucks, or anything similar simply because of the huge amounts of ruins, junk, and destroyed vehicles in the way around and through the complex.

So basically if you knew that complex very well, you could move fast, very fast and not noticably through the labyrinth of ruins both out and inside the buildings. If you were coming from outside, you moved slow.

Groups simply used it as a place for their operations of selling and smuggling, and they knew the area very well.

Goran stood behind a destroyed tank for a couple of minutes, trying to observe the building with 5 separate entrances.t

Then he spotted the entrance and sign that he was looking for. On each building entrance, right above it, there was place for flag poles, 3 places. It was used for flags on the biggest state or federal holidays, and flags on that occasion that were displayed there were federal flag, state flag and party flag.

It was usual that every goverment building or apartment buildings have those "holders" for flags.

On the building that he was looking for, there was a toilet seat hanging from the holder.

Goran took his backpack, and carefully hid it under the tank, using the destroyed Caterpillar as a additional hideout.

It was not a perfect place, but it would serve his purpose.

Then he carefully checked his rifle and pistol, and started to walk toward the building entrance. He tried to look like man who was not hiding. He walked like a man with intention.

When he approached the doors, he thought for a few seconds and lit his small flashlight. As much as he hated to use it, he wanted to look like man who was not sneaking, like a man who had no bad intentions.

In the hall of the building he used the light to check it, and spot the opened door from elevator. On the walls there were holes from the bullets and different markings painted with paint spray.

He just stood there with the flashlight on, trying to look casual.

"Do not move," he heard on his right side above his head. He froze.

"What the fuck you are looking for here?" the voice asked.

"I am here to see Seb," Goran said, careful not to make any move.

"Why?"

"I want to buy stuff, I bought from him before, several times."

"Where?"

"He used second building from this one the last two times, 1st entrance, in the basement."

There was silence for couple of seconds, and then the guy said "OK, do not move before I tell you so, and do not point that flashlight in my direction."

Goran heard the guy standing up from whatever cover he had up there.

"Now, sit down. Put flashlight on floor, pointed toward you. In front of you, take out slowly the magazine from your rifle, put it in your pocket, check rifle and put it back on your shoulders."

After he did that, he heard the guy coming down on stairs.

"Get up, take your flashlight, and turn it off."

Now the guy was next to him, lighting his own flashlight.

All that he could see was that guy had balaclava type of cap on his head and PAP rifle pointed in his direction.

"Yeah, I know you, the guy from the 2nd brigade right? Seb is here, follow me."

The guy move on through the corridor without using flashlight, and Goran followed his steps. A few times he lit the corridor with his flaslight, going over obstacles carefully and pointing to Goran where exactly he needed to step, probably avoiding preset traps.

They started to go down into something that looked like a utility space with water pumps, or central heating pumps.

Then another guy stepped in from the dark and whispered a few words to the first guy, and lit oil lamp, quickly look at the Goran, and raise give sign to first guy, first guy said to Goran „see you man, on the way back somebody will escort you, we do not want you to blow the building by stepping on something"

Under the light of oil lamp Goran now saw that first guy was almost a kid, probably 16-17 years old, wearing jeans, sneakers, and a green combat vest over a black jacket. In the back of the vest in pockets, there were a few rifle grenades.

The second guy was an older dude, and Goran knew him from previous meetings. The older guy was chewing something, carrying an oil lamp in one hand and a shotgun in other. He smelled like he was soaked in rakija.

Finally the guy moved a double blanket from some doorframe and they entered the room.

Seb was sitting on a chair that looked like they took it from some excutive office, and he stood up when he saw Goran.

"Goran, my man how are you?"

Seb was around 30 years old, but he looked probably 10 years older. He hugged Goran, and then sat in a wooden chair. Seb went back to his comfortable chair. Between them was table which was actually plywood on car wheels.

In the room there were 2 more guys, one was sitting on the floor, on a sleeping bag, and reading something that looked like a partially burned women's magazine. On the front page Goran read the words "discover your inner self." The guy reading had a beard and a black bandana on his head, he too had a combat vest and a rifle on his legs.

The other guy was sitting on piece of concrete wall, looking at Goran. On his sleeve there was a patch that said "MotorHead – Ace of Spades" and in his hands he held a pistol, playing with it, putting a magazine inside and out. The rifle on the wall about meter from him was also his probably.

By the look in his eyes Goran concluded he was on something, something heavier then marijuana.

Rakija-soaked guy left the room as soon as Goran sat in the chair.

He looked at Seb and remembers how he has looked some 10 years ago.

Seb was one of the best football players in region. He was young when he became famous, and pretty rich. Goran together with the other teenagers would watch how he trained, and often Seb took those kids and trained with them, teaching them to play football. Those memories were some of Goran's favourite ones.

But Seb was just another kid from neighbourhood, so probably he did not know what to do with all that sudden fame and money. So he made usual the mistakes and started to spend it on drugs.

After short period of time his playing days were done and it was big news when the police arrested him because of a big stash of drugs.

A socialistic society did not look well on failed idols, so he finished in prison as a poor man. When he got out he was a nobody, but he still kept his charm, and folks loved him.

When the war started, propaganda portrayed him as a famous guy in the army, then again he disappeared and re-emerged as a player for guys who owned part of the black market.

Goran kept a connection with him here and there. He was a shadow of the old Seb. Drugs did not help him.

"So, what's going on? I did not see you for some time, did your pills went away?" asked Seb with his smile, that was only shadow of his old charm. "How much of those you are taking man? Those stuff will kill you eventually, it will take away your sharpness."

Goran was looking at him, and thinking about amount of drugs that gone through that man.

"It is OK. I'm just taking it to push days when I am home."

Seb was looking at him, and suddenly he looked very old, and sick.

"Listen kid, I like you, and I have known you since you were real kid. You are welcome to come here. As your friend I can tell you it is bad, but as a salesman I have to ask you what do you have to offer?"

Goran reached inside his jacket pocket and put on table two golden rings.

Seb took them to carefully look at it, then said "hey!" to the guy who was reading a magazine, throwing the rings to him.

Magazine guy took rings, put them on his fingers, then took off from fingers, reached into his backpack and took out a pair of glasses.

He looked carefully at the rings for 10-15 seconds, then stood up, put rings back on the table, and nodded to Seb.

Seb took away the rings in his hand, and said to Goran "OK, we can do bussiness. I can give you two packs of sedatives, one for each ring."

Goran was pretty satisfied, but he said, "No way man, 200 kilometers from here for the value of those rings, I can get 20 packs, or even 30."

"Yes, you can. Actually 200 kilometers from here you can get even 40 packs, but here is the thing, 200 kilometers from here you would not need it. 200 kilometers from here there are working pharmacies, people have jobs, and kids are going to schools.

200 kilometers from here there is no war, but here it is war, and there is only me, and guys similar to me. And you know what? I have people coming every aday with their gold, selling it to me for a can of food, or antibiotics. Gold is not valuable in this city, and you know it. This is not the first time we are dealing with this."

Of course Goran knew all that, he was actually out of all his valuable possessions because of it, but still he wanted something more.

"Give me something more, something," he said to Seb.

While looking at the rings, Seb was smiling and looking at the guy who still played with pistol and magazine and said to him, "Look at him, I knew him when he was kid, and now he think he is a big shot. What do you think about it huh?"

Pistol guy did not change his face expression for even a second, saying nothing.

"OK, I can give you some painkillers too, but that's it, man."

Goran realized it was all he was going to get, nothing more, and agreed.

Seb again said "hey" to the guy who read the magazine,

and the guy stood up and left the room to find the pills in the stash that was somewhere close but not in the same room.

"Do you need something for that?" he asked Goran, pointing to his torn sleve, and traces of blood. "It looks fresh to me."

"No it is ok, it is a minor incision, nothing big."

They chatted for minute or two, and then the guy brought back the pills.

Sedatives were in packaged boxes. Goran opened each one, checked seals on each blister pack and checked expiration dates. The painkillers were just one blister of 10 tablets. All looked genuine and not tampered with.

There were many type of scams with every kind of good that was circulating in the city, and you simply never knew. Everything had to be checked, even though Goran knew Seb from before and did several deals with him.

It was time to move on. He shook hands with Seb, but the other two guys did not have any intention of saying goodbye.

Seb acompanied him through the corridors, out of the building, and once when they were out in dark he asked him, "Is that jewelery yours, those rings and necklaces that you traded with me last couple of months?"

Goran could not see his face expression in dark, and he was not sure what was the point of question.

"Well they are mine, at least they were before I handed them to you. Why?"

Seb look back to check where his guard man stood in dark, then he put his hand around Goran shoulders.

"Listen man, if you come to me several times during the last few months, bringing the same stuff, or similar stuff that tells me few things. You have big stash of that at your home, or you like many other soldiers take that stuff from dead folks on the frontlines, comrades or enemy. Now, since I know you from before, I do not think you are participating in pillaging during the fights. I might be wrong, but I think I am not. So, you are bringing your own stuff from home, right?"

Goran look at him, trying to see his face. "Yes, actually it is my parents' stuff."

Seb tapped him on back "Good! So I was right, but here is my point. If you have bigger amounts of something you are becoming interesting to us. Maybe one day it will be interesting to visit you and take all that from you, right?"

He started to feel uncomfortable, and it looked like Seb felt it, so he quickly added.

"I think you did not understood me kid. I know you, I am not going to pay the visit to you, so no worries there. But I am in organisation that is not the army. Every one of those guys inside can decide to take that chance, to get that stuff, or to get that stuff and by that to take my position in this group. Above me in the chain there are people who would appreciate that. So here is my thought. Do not come here for some time. Use other dealers, or if you come here do not bring gold. Bring something else. Understand?"

"I do."

Seb shook his hand, "So, see you then. and good luck"

Goran was looking at him while he slowly walked back to the building asking himself what kind of man that guy is.

Goran's Story - Part 3

The hospital was close, 30 minutes walking, and nothing more serious then a cold wind happened.

It was in part of the city where the system was still kinda "stiched" together.

Before the war, the hospital complex consisted of a couple of separate buildings, with clinics, parking lots, a helicopter pad, and similar.

Now the main building was heavily damaged from shelling, and not used at all.

Underground passages, that connected different buildings of the hospital complex, together with additional hallways and rooms were now used for patients.

Goran remembered that before the war in that space was a laboratory, and under the other building were food-preparing spaces.

Some of the buildings were still in use, but in completely changed roles. So if you were coming in hospital for the first time, it was a strange place.

You entered inside the complex, into the place that was used before for laundry services, mechanics, and similar.

Now the small doors were bigger, and the entrance served

its purpose because it was in a spot where it was pretty well covered from 3 sides with other buildings.

He was walking to the entrance, through a small parking lot, and the sound of a generator could be heard somewhere.

Parking was under a small light on wall, and lots of people were there.

One military "Pinz" truck was parked in front of the entrance, and people were carrying wounded people from it.

On the back of the truck, a soldier stood up and yelled at the folks who carried out the wounded people. He had a flashlight in his hand and under its light Goran saw that the floor of the truck was covered in blood.

Hospital staff together with soldiers and civilians carried away the wounded from truck to the hallway of hospital. The people who swere wounded screamed, some cried, others were not concious.

One guy sat next to the truck, holding his thigh, pressing the trauma bandage hard, while blood was pouring through it. Next to the hospital entrance there were 3 bodies, left there probably because they were obviously dead.

Goran entered the hallway, and one soldier stood there, smoking cigarette, with traces of blood on his shirt.

"Comrade, where are these wounded coming from?" he asked them.

The guy looked at him, with an angry face, and Goran felt he wanted to tell him to fuck off, but then he saw unit marking on Goran's shirt, and the rifle on his back. H looked at his own cigarette and said to him, "They (the enemy) surprised us, many casulties, we pick up those from field hospital, and then on our way to here we picked up a few civilians, mortar round wounded, on the site there are probably 12 dead."

The hallway quickly filled with the wounded, and it was pure chaos. Doctors and nurses ran in between them, trying to figure who could be helped.

The hospital smelled like death, slow dying and death.

Down the corridor there were two military police guys standing. Goran aproached them, and saw that behind them were the doors to the what was before the orthopedic ward.

"I need to see a wounded relative."

The two guys watched him. They had neat uniforms. One had an AK, and the other had shotgun. They tried to look dangerous, but Goran was sure they had not spent time on the frontline.

"Civilian or soldier?" the older one asked.

"Civilian," he answered.

"We need to see your papers, and you[ll have to leave your weapon here with us."

Goran showed them the papers, with details about to which unit he belongs, and he gave them his rifle and pistol.

They were not to detailed in checking him, his papers were legit. They just quickly checked his backpack and stored his weapons in a steel closet behind a small desk next to them.

They kept his papers for the duration of his stay, and explained to him that he needed to go down to the basement, and look for additional information from the nurse there.

He went through the door, and here it was bit more calm. He could still hear distant explosions, but mostly he heard the sound of the generator.

He went down the stairs. Above his head ceiling leaking water, and on the floor there were pieces of plaster.

Another door and he was in basement.

The lights on the ceiling were very faint, and flickerring all the time, so all looked kinda desperate and depressing, not to mention the constant bad smell.

A woman was sitting on a chair and cutting a big piece of gauze, making somethings like small handkerchiefs from it. She raised head and asked him what he wanted

Only then he spotted on side of the corridor something that looked like piles of dirty laundry. He saw but he processed it 2 seconds later.

Bodies, maybe 10-12 bodies, wrapped in sheets.

It was eerie for him, not because of the bodies, he guessed. He had seen many bodies in this war. Also he had made some living people into the bodies, so that was not problem.

He felt the power of the moment, flickering lights, bodies in sheets, traces of blood on the sheets...

He could spot the shapes of the bodies under the sheets, where blood was on the sheets, he saw one person's head shape at the place where the blood went through, or another body looked like it had legs only to the knees, and then there was big bloodstain.

For the moment he asked himself who were they? Civilians? Soldiers? Kids?

He looked back to the lady, and realized she was asking him a question.

"I want to see my relative. She was wounded a few days ago."

The lady looked like she had not slept the whole last week, and she definetly was not in the mood.

"Listen soldier, do you have any idea how many wounded people are brought here in last few days? Does that person have any name and what kind of wounds, do you know any of that?"

He told her a name, she grabbed a book from the box next to her feet and checked it for minute.

"OK, go to the second door on the right, then ask for Dr Z."

Something exploded pretty close and the lights started to flicker even more, so he froze for a second, looking at lady.

"Do not worry. The generator is dying for months, but it still works."

He moved on.

Another corridor was full of junk of every kind. Most of it, as he could understand it, was partially burned stuff from parts of the hospital that were destroyed, probably taken down for anything that could be salvaged.

He opened another door and he was in something that looked like bomb shelter improvised hospital.

The lights were stronger, and rows of beds were behind improvised shades. On the floor there were many cables, and one nurse was pushing a cart with some instruments covered with gauze.

He stops her and asked for Dr. Z.

Finally, after another corridor, he found the doors, without name on them but with signs that someone broke into them some time ago. The handle was replaced, and the wood parts were damaged.

He knocked on it...no answer. He knocked on it again with more force, and someone from inside said, "Go away, dammit, I am not on for two more hours!"

Now Goran used his fist, a bit angry.

The guy opened a door. Behind him was a room was full of smoke, with an oil lamp on table.

He was around 50 years old, with messed up hair and blanket around his shoulders. Obviously, he had been sleeping.

"Yes?" he asked Goran.

"I am here to talk about one of the patients/" Goran told the name of the girl. "She was wounded in the shelling and her parents were killed."

"Your relative?"

Goran thought for a few seconds what to say. "Yes, she is my relative."

The doctor looked for a few seconds like he was gonna tell him to go away, or something in that way, but then he just said, "OK, step inside."

Goran entered the room and sat down on the old couch while doctor was putting on his shirt and white coat.

"Sit here, smoke one, have a drink, or something. I am gonna go get the logbook."

The doctor left the room, and Goran lit a cigarette.

It was hot in the room. Goran stood up and checked the radiator. It was hot, the hospital still had a central heating system that worked on coal, and only parts of the buildings were still heated both because of a lack of coal reserves and also in some parts the system was destroyed.

He checked the doctor's table. There was mess on it. Papers, empty glasses of rakija, empty packs of cigarettes, patient's info...

There was a small bottle of whiskey, at least the label stated it was whiskey.

He opened it, smelled it...yes it was whiskey.

He found a relatively clean glass and poured some in.

The doctor opened the door, walked in and sat on other side of table, putting the book on it that said "log" written with marker.

"I see you found the whiskey. Good, pour one for me too."

The doctor stood up, searched in a cabinet filled with books and logs, where he found an old emergency lamp, used usually to show the exit door when the electricity went away, and turned it on.

Under the white neon light Goran realized how old and tired Doc was, and probably how much he drank.

"This room is not on generator, but we luckily can charge batteries in the hospital."

He sat down again, and started to check the book, while mumbling something.

It was warm in the room, and the whiskey added more warmth, so Goran had almost fallen asleep while sitting there when Doc said:

"Found it! Shelling close to market, a man and woman killed probably right there, at least they were dead when they got them to hospital, multiple wounds, a female child, around 6 years old, on arrival conscious, protruding wound on left thigh, broken femur, and couple of incisions on head, in shock."

"Do you have data about the parents, names, ages, and similar?"

The doctor looked at him for few seconds, then checked book again. "Yes, based on the IDs they had on them" and he told Goran the names, address, and ages.

Goran went in his mind through all possibilities and finally realized what he already kinda knew. The girl was not his relative, they only shared same second name.

Doctor looked at him, and asked, "What is going on? You do not know these folks, right?"

"No, it is a mistake. They were not my relatives, the girl either."

The doctor searched through the empty packs of cigarettes, starting to mumble and curse, then stood up and again searched in the cabinet, where he found a pack with cigarettes inside. He lit it on the lamp, sat down again, and loudly closed logbook.

"OK, it happens. Actually, it happens all the time, people looking for their missing relatives after shelling, or simply for persons who did not come home. And people not recognizing their family members in hospital simply because they are injured so bad that they do not look any more like that person. I have seen all combinations of that here."

"Has anyone looked for that girl here before me?" Goran asked.

"Nope, you are the first one, but that also happens, especially with kids."

"So, she is without any relatives looking for her? She is alone?"

The doctor poured another whiskey. Two detonations somewhere outside rumbled "Yes, she is alone."

Goran felt strange, still without a clear intention or plan. He asked, "OK, what is her condition, and what is going to happen next with her?"

"Well," the doctor scratched his cheek. "How simple you want me to be here?"

"As simple as possible" Goran said, already kinda knowing that the answer was not going to be good.

"Then I will be very simple and short. Not good. At the beginning, all the wounds looked pretty clean and let us say minor considering what we are seeing here. But... not good now. She is slowly sinking; our prognosis is that her kidneys may be failing to work"

"Why?" Goran asked.

The doctor suddenly had anger on his face. "Why? You are asking me why? Did you see what kind of hospital this is? We are running on good will, UN medicines, and alcohol. Everything is falling apart. We are piling bodies. We are having promises that the electricity will be returned to the hospital area by some UN peace talks, and until then we are using ages old generators – "

"OK, man, stop, I know the story, I have been around, you know?"

The doctor glimpsed over at Goran's unit marking and said "Yea. Fuck it, I know man. Sorry, it is just hard when you want to do something that you spent years to learn, but you simply canno.t"

"Leave that, Doc. Is she going to live or not?"

The doctor again for a moment had anger on his face, but then that disappeared, and he said "I don't know man. If this continues to go like it has with her, then no, probably she is not gonna make it."

"What about the UN convoys out of the city, for the wounded and similar?"

The doctor smiled sadly, "We would need a 10-kilometers long convoy to take out from the city everyone who needs to leave. The injured, the sick, the orphans. They are doing that, but at this rate it is simply an impossible mission. The next convoy as they told us is in a few days, but she is not on the list."

"Why she is not on the list?" Goran asked.

Doc took another cigarette and said, almost whispered, "Well man, if you have been around, then you know how that goes...the board of doctors make the lists and suggestions of who needs to leave city with the convoy. A UN officer checks that and approves it, but you need to push connections to be on the list. I have seen perfectly well and healthy people leaving the city in UN convoys for injured kids, but they had money, connections...power."

Goran looked at him. Yes, he knew how that worked. There are cannon fodder and there are others.

"Can I see her?"

"Well if you are not relative you should not, but if you insist."

"Yes, I insist," Goran said.

The girl was laying there, unconscious, and Goran thought that she was too small for a 6-years-old girl but taking in consideration her state he thought it was normal probably.

He did not feel too much looking at the small girl with a tube in her nose.

The room was full of mostly injured kids, and after seeing huge amounts of death during fights he thought he know all faces of death, but here it was different.

As he already expected, he did not know the girl.

But in that moment, he made a decision. He felt like he had found reasons for everything.

"Doc?"

"Yes" doctor said, with his hands in the pockets of his white coat.

"I do recognize her. She is my relative and she is going out in next convoy."

…

It was snowing.

Goran was lying down in shallow hole, behind a big pine tree, and when he looked up to tree branches it was so calm and beautiful, with snowflakes falling down slowly, it was perfectly silent.

But it lasted only for a moment, he look down to tree

and saw on it scars from bullets, and in the same time somewhere far he heard few gunshots and long burst from machine gun.

He was back to reality.

He and 50 other people from his unit were lying down in woods, for last 2 hours, he was wet, and very nervous.

The plan was to take the enemy positioned some 200 meters from there, and they were to wait for the first signs of dawn for the attack.

The enemy position was actually just a ruined house, fortified with sandbags, and trenches in front of it.

Nothing spectacular, hundreds of similar positions were everywhere around the city, just a dug in position on perfect place that overlooked their movement in and out of the city, and one or two scoped machine guns.

They were lying down in woods waiting for the first signs of dawn, and for the sounds of hand grenade explosions that couple of bravest (or craziest) guys were going to throw in trenches, if they could to sneak up to that point.

His clothes were wet, but just like always before a fight, he did not feel cold. He felt he was burning, and he wanted to start already, to finish already, otherwise he felt he gonna burn up and lose his mind.

He had thoughts that it seemed like in the last couple of months they were taking and losing similar positions like this, and nothing changed.

At the moment when he finished with that thought, several strong explosions shook him, and in the same moment he heard shots, machine gun fire, screams and through all that someone was yelling "Go, go, go!!!"

He stood up and started to run up to the hill. It was still dark in woods, but the shadows already were there, like glimpses of daylight.

Bullets were hissing around him. He just kept running, trying to keep his head down and avoid trees. The guy next to him made a gurgling sound when a bullet hit him. Goran kept running.

Suddenly he found himself out of the woods, on more steep terain. In front of him there were wooden planks holding soil, as a defense position, all that covered with logs, soil and planks. On his left side, guys from his unit had already jumped into the trench, two meters from him there was man from his unit, they jumped on logs together in same moment. On the other side was trench, and suddenly guy in enemy uniform show up holding something in his hand.

Goran and his comrade fired together, and guy fell down immediatelly, then something heavy hit him in the head and everything turned to black.

...

He was swimming through the mud, and it was dark. He tried to scream, when he opened his mouth mud entered his mouth and he began to cough in panic.

Then he hears people smiling and spearking.

"I told you that your rakija would wake him up."

He opened his eyes, and Farmer again was above him, holding his rakija flask.

"How bad it is"? Goran asked.

Farmer said, "How bad is what? A log hit you in the head after the explosion. You'll be fine, no wounds. That helmet works, huh? Now on your feet, man. we are done here."

Goran sat down, feeling very naseous. He prepared to throw up, but the feeling lasted for couple of seconds only.

He checked his head. There was nothing broken and no wounds, but it was gonna hurt.

The guys around him were checking position for anything useful, quite in hurry, expecting enemy shelling soon.

Two enemy soldiers were sitting on ground with hands behind their heads, one of Gorans comrades was searching their pockets, when he found pack of Winston cigarettes.He said "Wow, nice! Thanks, man."

He slowly stood up, checked his rifle, and went down to the trench.

The guy that he had killed lay down on his back. In his right hand he was holding a military canteen, Goran took it and smelled it. Coffee. So guy who he killed in the middle of the attack was carrying a canteen with hot coffee in his hands.

His rifle was still on his back.

Probably the attack came while he was making coffee.

Ridiculous... and sad. Guy looked very young, younger then Goran, probably just a new conscript who had not even learned what is what on the frontline.

"Maybe one day I agonna end up like this," Goran thought. "Surprised and dead, and nothing gonna change because of it."

It was nice day. The air was clean, snow was falling, gunshots were heard somewhere far away/ If you closed your eyes and ignored smell of gunpowder and well-oiled machine guns it almost sounded like someone was chopping a tree in the woods, and you are in nice forest cabin somewhere for the weekend.

One day later, the enemy took back that position.

Through the window of his apartment, the city looked bit cleaner, but Goran knew it was because of the fresh snow, and soon it was gonna turn to dirty mud. After that he hoped that new and more serious snow would cover that mud.

It was cold, and and he was working for last 6 hours in order to move his small wood stove from the old place closer to balcony door.

While he was on frontline, couple of shells hit his building, destroying some of the chimney oppenings on top of the building, as a result of that chimney trough the whole building simply did not worked, at least not for apatments abouve and beneath his, including his.

He finally managed to put stove close to the balcony door, and install smoke pipes trough the hole in door that he made, and put it on balcony concrete fence.

Now he started a fire and watched how the smoke went through the pipe over his balcony, checking how heated his door was.

It looks like it will work for some time.

It would be better to make hole in wall and put smoke pipe trough it, but it would needed more work, and he needed fire as soon as possible.

Temperature in apartment without heating from fire was pretty much close to outside temperature. Nylon tarps on windows and blankets could not really substitute for the glass that went missing a long time ago, from the time of the first shelling and explosions.

Now when fire brought back in his apartment bit feeling of real home, he stood up, and look out to the city again.

The city was living its own life, on and on, and he philosophicaly thought like many times in last couple of months that city will be here no matter what shit happens.

Many times before in history, people lived and died here,

armies conquered it, and lost it, people were killed, hanged by the lamp poles sometimes, or get shot from firing squads in prison yards...

But it kept to live.

Then he opened cabinet in his living room, and through the mess there, reached for shoe box, took it and sat down next to the stove.

The box was full of documents and photographies.

He took few of photos out randomly, and looked at them.

In one photo he was around 6 years old, probably the same age as the girl in the hospital. In it, he was wearing a funny costume of Donald Duck, sitting on his father shoulders.

In the background of the photo there were a whole bunch of the kids, and a funny looking Santa. It was a New Year celebration and his father took him there to receive "a present from Santa for good behavior" Goran look closer at the photo trying to see if he recognisede or remembered any other kids in the picture, but nothing.

He took another photo. It was a celebration of socialistic "young pioneers" in his elementary school. He was 10-11 years old. He was standing there together with 25-30 other kids, with mouths open, singing something, probably an anthem.

He checked to see how many names of his old friends and classmates he could still remember. Not too many. Some of them moved before the end of elementary school, some ran from the country at the beginning of the war, some got killed... for most of them he did not have a clue where they were.

One of them, he met 8 months ago, in the middle of street fighting. Actually when he met him. his old classmate was dead already. Goran and his squad were moving carefully through the destroyed neighbourhood, because a sniper there was active from one of the old apartment building, killing a few soldiers that day, and a couple of civilians the day before.

Finally they got news the sniper was dealt with, eliminated. The guys from the other squad located him, broke into the apartment he was shooting from, and threw him off the building.

When Goran and his squad approached the sniper laying dead in the parking lot, next to the burned "Yugo" car, he recognized his old classmate.

After elementary school he saw him from time to time, but they were not really friends.

Goran was watching him laying there all messed up, wondering what made him shoot at civilians. Was he was told that we are monsters? His neighbors? Old friends?

It was confusing.

Goran put back the photographs box into the cabinet, leaving out the photo wih his father

He took that photo and placed it on the book shelf.

Then he lay down, preparing in his mind to do thing that he had decided to do several days ago.

...

Again it was night, and again he was walking out of his neighborhood.

Under his boots snow made the sound that he loved since he was a kid.

Again, folks here and there dragged things. Now couple of them used sleds to drag canisters with water.

Some grandpa in front of the one apartment building with a "Ushanka" hat on his head, scraped snow with small toy shovel, and loaded it in a red wash bowl, for melting at home probably.

Suddenly he stopped. Something was wrong.

His insticts were screaming to him that something was wrong, then he realized what exactly: it was silence.

No gunshots in or out of the city, no exlosions. He could still hear that grandpa scraping snow.

It was beautiful and horrible in the same time, just when Goran started to thinka about some ceasefire that he slept through, he heard gunshots far away. It sounded almost like a dog barking in the woods. Then he heard a few distant detonations, then the whole background noise of war was there again.

That moment of absolute peace lasted for couple of seconds maybe, but to him it was louder then any explosion that he had heard in the last several months.

The city simple went back into its everyday, or every night, usual wartime living.

While Gtrandpa finally filled the washbowl and started to carry it, Goran was thinking how it was going to look one day when this war stopped. Is silence going to be really so loud and unusual?

What he is going to do with himself in that silence?

Is he going to be able to live a "normal" life?

The prospect of living again a normal life without a rifle in his hand or arm made him smile silently in the night, with dark sarcasam.

…

His destination this evening was a high school complex not so far from his apartment. He knew that place before the war pretty well because he used to hang out there with his friends who went there to school.

At the beginning of the war, that school was used as the headquarters for one of the units, and unit HQ remained there for whole time.

Basically the unit was described and named like special police unit, and used in street fighting, both on the front and as a counterinsurrgent unit, countersnipers unit and what not.

The unit was under goverment chain comand, like all units. The point is that some of those units were loosely under that chain.

This unit was very, very loosely under the goverment chain command.

In the early days of war, in chaos, groups like that emerged everywhere, somewhere even starting like small neighbourhood group that wanted to defend city. Elswhere it was groups that emerged from ex-soldiers or similar.

This unit started as a group of pre-war criminals who basically put themselves under the rule and command of the goverment, and defense of the city.

It grew pretty far and quick. The fact was that they were tough and good soldiers. The other fact was that they were not fighting by rules, and they pretty much ruled in their part of town, often not choosing who they going to terrorize.

Six months ago Goran's unit fought together with the guys from that unit against the enemy, and he talked with their leader, who was quite an interesting figure. He knew him before the war, as he had repaired his car a few times.

After the sucessful fight ended, their leader let him know if Goran ever wants to join them he knows where to find them.

Now, he is going there, to find him.

The school was partially destroyed, but still in a usable state. The big square yard that was used before the war for sport manifestation, and in summer time for musical concerts of local musician now looked weird to him, because three armored cars were standing there, and people in uniforms were working on them.

Guards stopped him at the entrance to the yard, and as he explained to them that he wanted to see "the Boss" for personal reasons, they checked his papers. Then one of them escorted him to the building entrance.

A generator was working somewhere inside building.

At the building entrance, two guys briefly questioned him, and again, he explained he wanted to see Boss because they know each other from before. They searched him, took his weapons, and one of them took him to the room, that obviously before was chemistry classroom.

He sat there with couple of guys from the unit.

They were checking their equipment, and cleaning weapons, and smoking marijuana. Goran lit a cigarette still thinking about his decision, when a guy opened the door and called him.

They walked down the corridor to the square hallway, then

to another corridor, where two armed unit members were standing guard.

Then they entered a room that looked like before had been a library or something similar. It was a large room with a lot of wooden shelves on the walls and maybe 8 formerly nice tables, now pretty ruined.

On the shelves there was a lot of different equipment and weapons, as well as different kinds of uniforms and boots, combat vests and similar. In one corner on the floor Goran saw boxes with RPGs. Next to that there were piles of bullet proof vests.

On one table there were 2 boxes marked with UN, and one of the guys was taking stuff from it saying what it was, while other was writing the inventory into a book.

From the other part of the room, a man aproached him saying, "Goran, I did not see you for some time!"

The Boss was in his late 40s now, a big man and very dangerous.

Before the war he was a small time criminal, car theft, smuggling stuff from Italy. He had his crew and they were pretty successful, and locally famous.

Just as he and his crew started to grow rapidly by jumping into the drug business and more serious theft and crime the war started. They continued to grow, but now as a "special police" unit.

"Come over here man, we will have drink!" he told Goran,

leading him to the part of the room behind the cabinets. As they passed next to the guys who were taking stuff out of the UN boxes he said to them, "Watch it man, if you break again something in there I'll break your fucking neck."

He said that with smile, but the guys working on the UN boxes did not smile.

Behind cabinets there was small table. He sat there and Goran sat on other chair. Boss reached into the cabinet shelf and put the vodka bottle and two glasses on the table saying, "Courtesy of our UN friends."

Then he took a Marlboro pack out of his pocket, offered one cigarette to Goran, telling him, "Remind me to give you few packs before you leave."

Goran light Malboro and enjoyed for few seconds...

Boss looked at him smiled, and said, "Quite different stuff from usual grunt poison huh?"

"Yes," Goran said. "Quite different."

"OK, so how can i help you man? I doubt you came here to say hello to me, so you need something, drugs, medicines, weapons..what excatly?...Or you want me to kill someone?"

Boss laughed after saying that, but Goran know it was a legit question, and killing someone would not be out of question if needed.

He enjoyed the real cigarette for couple of more seconds then said to Boss:

"I want to get someone out of the city."

Boss looked at him through the smoke of the cigarette.

"Hmmm, you kinda surprised me. I thought you wanted to get rid of someone or something similar… OK, let's see. It is doable, but expensive. There are few ways, depending if the person is a civilian or a soldier, or if he or she is going to be wanted and similar."

"It is a kid, a little girl, and she is wounded in the hospital," said Goran.

Boss took another sip of vodka and hought for a couple of seconds, then said, "It is doable again, but it is now very, *very* expensive."

Goran was not saying the word, he simply waited there, knowing exactly what is the only thing that he had to offer.

"Listen, Goran, we are long way from that car repair shop where you worked, and me pushing drugs…this is a new time, and in this new time new people emerge, people like me. I own the things in this city, I own the people in this city, and I do plan to own more of the city and more of the people. I could not do that if I am not sharp. Everybody needs to pay, with something, so… what do you have to offer for that ticket out of the city? And you know only way out for her is with the UN convoy, with mobile medical care?"

"I can offer myself."

"What?" Boss said.

"I'll join you, I'lll join your unit."

Boss looked at him, a bit surprised.

"What make you think that is worth a ticket out of the town? And what makes you think I need new fighters?"

Now Goran smiled. "You pay your fighters with stuff like gold, drugs, medicines, or simply by fear, fear of you, and you do need new fighters all the time. You want to grow, especially if the new fighters are not drug addicts."

Boss was silent, and now he was not smiling. "I think, kid, that you know too much."

"I will be in your unit and in life debt to you, if you take that kid out of the city," finally Goran said.

"Do you know what life debt means? Do you know that I will own you practically? Now please be careful here and think more about it. You are smart enough to know what kind of unit I have here."

"Yes, I know," Goran said "And I thought about it a lot."

Boss was silent now. Goran was silent too. He had said it, and now he felt relieved. He felt like his emotions were gone. He was flat.

"It is a deal," finally Boss said. "The kid is going out with next convoy and you are staying here. Consider all work about transfer from the unit done. I'll take care of it. You are a member of my group now"

...

Three days later, Goran was standing with Doctor Z in the hospital parking lot. Patients were transfered from the hospital to UN cars, and then driven to a meeting point in front of the goverment building where armored UN vehicles would make convoy and go out of the city.

An Italian humanitarian church organization had prepared for their stay in ana Italian hospital.

The UN workers were carrying wounded and sick kids together with the hospital staff.

Goran and Doctor Z were silent. The doc did not comment on the paperwork and "ticket" out for the girl, but he saw Goran in a different uniform, and he was not a fool. He understood.

"Wait!" Goran said to the hospital staff when he saw his "relative" is being carried out of hospital, then he approached the stretcher and girl, who still was unconcious. He reached into his combat vest pocket, took out the photo of him and his father at that long ago New Year's celebration, looked at it for a few seconds, folded it, and put it under the girl's back.

They put the girl in car and drove away.

Goran and doc stood there, somewhere gunshots were fired, and few explosions.

It was a regular day in a wartime city.

***

The girl survived, grew up, and became a good person. She still lives in Italy. Goran disappeared during the fighting half a year after the girl went out of the town.

The girl was looking for him after the war, but the country had many mass graves everywhere. Officially, Goran was never located in any of those. Probably he will never be found.

Some of his unit members were put on trialfor war crimes. Some became heroes.

I like to think that he is out there somewhere, under a different name, living somewhere like Spain or Canada.

Toby Takeaway:

Goran's story gives us a much needed insight into the 'grind' of a long term Urban Survival scenario. I am hoping these articles, these stories and this book, will make many readers see a clearer 'reality' of what they need to be preparing for.

While Selco and I wish no-one to go through troublesome times, if you find yourself in them, don't say we didn't let you knw how it was REALLY going to be...

About the Author

Selco survived the Balkan war of the 90s in a city under siege, without electricity, running water, or food distribution.

In his online works, he gives an inside view of the reality of survival under the harshest conditions. He reviews what works and what doesn't, tells you the hard lessons he learned, and shares how he prepares today.

He never stopped learning about survival and preparedness since the war. Regardless what happens, chances are you will never experience extreme situations like Selco did. But you have the chance to learn from him and how he faced death for months.

Real survival is not romantic or idealistic. It is brutal, hard and unfair. Let Selco take you into that world. Read more of Selco's articles here:

https://www.theorganicprepper.com/category/preppers/selco/

And take advantage of a deep and profound insight into his knowledge and advice by signing up for the outstanding and unrivaled online course. More details here:

https://learn.theorganicprepper.com/cartflows_step/what-you-must-know-when-the-shtf/

Made in the USA
Columbia, SC
09 March 2022